INDUSTRY IN TROUBLE

*The Federal Government
and the
New England Fisheries*

Margaret E. Dewar

INDUSTRY IN TROUBLE

*The Federal Government
and the
New England Fisheries*

Temple University Press

Philadelphia

Temple University Press
© 1983 by Temple University. All rights reserved
Published 1983
Printed in the United States of America

Library of Congress Cataloging in Publication Data

Dewar, Margaret, 1948–
   Industry in trouble.

   Includes bibliographical references and index.
   1. Fishery management—New England.   2. Fisheries—
New England.   3. Fishery policy—New England.
4. Fishery policy—United States.   I. Title.
SH221.5.N4D48   1982   338.3′72′0974   82-10748
ISBN 0-87722-284-3

To my mother and father,
Janet and Wilfred Dewar

Contents

Figures

Preface

*I*N NEW ENGLAND one has to be aware of the fishing industry. Scarcely a week passes without an article or two in the newspaper or a report on radio or television. Sometimes these are news bulletins, but just as often they are features. During spring 1977, the bombardment of stories seemed particularly intense, and they caught my attention. The 200-mile extension of fishery jurisdiction, effective March 1, 1977, promised to revitalize the industry, the articles said, if only the State Department followed through in getting foreigners off the fishing grounds.

The argument did not sound right. Why should excluding foreign fishermen suddenly make the fishing industry prosper and grow? More reasonably, either the industry had fundamental problems that the 200-mile limit would not solve, or fishermen and boat owners were already doing well and their prosperity would continue. What was the rationale for such government involvement, I wondered, and what effect was the government effort having? I decided to look into these questions.

As I began to attend the many meetings on fishery problems, mostly concerned with implementing the 200-mile limit, and began to read through shelves of congressional hearings and to track down a fraction of the hundreds of federal and state documents on the industry, I found that the 200-mile limit was just the latest of many efforts to aid the New England fisheries. Few people either in the industry or outside seemed to know the full range of the industry's history since the hardships began after World War II. Those who were still alive of the leaders from the industry's efforts to get government help during the 1950s and 1960s were not centrally involved in implementation of the new law. New leaders were absorbed in current problems and not particularly interested in old issues. Most scholars studying the industry were aware of earlier programs, but no one had written about their results.

Furthermore, understanding of the current status of the fisheries seemed limited. Public officials and industry representatives argued that other public investment to spur the industry's growth should accompany the extension of fishery jurisdiction to 200 miles. Maine, Massachusetts, and Rhode Island sponsored studies of what the state governments could do to help. Public agencies in Boston, Gloucester, New Bedford, Portland, and numerous small towns planned construction or rehabilitation of port facilities for fishing and applied for millions of dollars of federal funding. Yet, as several planners told me, although fishing was an important source of employment for their communities, they had a hard time getting an idea of how the fishing industry would grow or what government should be doing.

I proceeded to look at the story of the federal government's efforts to help the New England fishing industry. As the study emerged, however, I realized that it has implications beyond the fishing industry. The fisheries' experience offers a case study of government efforts to turn around the fortunes of a troubled industry. As troubles in the auto and steel industries have attracted national attention, understanding what happens when government tries to help seems particularly important. Any new public efforts to help troubled industries may be more effective if they can avoid errors of the past.

As the analysis in this book suggests, the fishing industry's problems and the government efforts to solve them did touch all these issues. However, the problems of the industry and the reasons for the failure of public efforts to help were far more complicated than I expected when I began the study.

In the process of researching and writing this book, I relied on a great deal of assistance from other people. Several groups gave me financial support. The National Science Foundation awarded me a three-year predoctoral fellowship. The Joint Center for Urban Studies of the Massachusetts Institute of Technology and Harvard University gave me a fellowship and a peaceful office. Dr. Arthur Solomon, director of the Joint Center, made it possible for me to continue to work there even when my fellowship ended. The Gorton Corporation in Gloucester, Massachusetts, gave a grant to me as the Gorton Fellow for the Study of the New England Fisheries. James Ackert, whose career spans the period this book discusses, served as my tie with the Gorton Corporation. A biography of Jim Ackert would tell many of the same stories and address many of the same issues as this book, so our conversations were particularly valuable to me. Woods Hole Oceanographic Institution named me a predoctoral fellow in Marine Policy and Ocean Management, with funds from the National Marine Fisheries Service (NMFS) making the fellowship possible. I am especially indebted to Woods Hole Oceanographic

Institution's Dr. Leah Smith who worked to arrange the fellowship and to Dr. Bradford Brown and James Kirkley at NMFS for backing my efforts to find support. The National Science Foundation also gave me a National Needs Postdoctoral Fellowship, and Woods Hole Oceanographic Institution also awarded me a postdoctoral fellowship in Marine Policy and Ocean Management. These awards allowed me to do additional research that greatly enriched the work I had done as a graduate student. Finally, the Hubert H. Humphrey Institute of Public Affairs at the University of Minnesota provided me with funds for the final stages of writing and revising through a research project on industrial policy.

Several people helped me considerably in my search for information on the fishing industry. Robert Dewar worked as my research assistant to track down the hundreds of government documents which address fishery problems. Ralph Mayo at the Northeast Fisheries Center did computer work for me on the National Marine Fisheries Service data files. Jasmine Isobe, at that time a member of the staff of Congressman Daniel Akaka of Hawaii, helped me gather information from the House Committee on Merchant Marine and Fisheries as well as from other congressional offices and administrative agencies. Meta Cushing of the Gloucester Economic Resources Center and the Gloucester Fishermen's Wives Association provided me with access to the files of the Gloucester Fisheries Commission and, through conversations over two years, gave me a better understanding of the Gloucester fishing industry than I could have acquired by myself. Meta and Mary Lord, a graduate student in Urban Studies and Planning at the Massachusetts Institute of Technology, interviewed large numbers of Gloucester and Chatham fishermen to provide me with important data. Others too numerous to name—fishermen, fishermen's wives, and fish dealers from every New England port; the members and staff of the New England Fishery Management Council; and others concerned with the fishing industry as journalists, researchers, government representatives, or planners—taught me a large share of what I know about the industry and its present problems through our conversations and through their testimony at meetings on fishery management.

A number of people helped in production of the manuscript. Many typed and retyped large parts of it. They included Irene Goodsell, Angelina Ferreira, Ann Goodwin, Martha Bertrand, Sharon Lakin, and Louise Straus. Patricia McCobb drafted the map and graphs.

Finally, several people read and responded to my work. Their comments were enormously helpful in clarifying my thinking and direction. They included Bennett Harrison, Lawrence Susskind, Leah Smith, Janet

Dewar, James Ackert, Susan Peterson, Herbert Mohring, and Simon Fass. Most important, Robert M. Fogelson offered steady encouragement; he read and criticized chapters at every stage of their development.

INDUSTRY IN TROUBLE

*The Federal Government
and the
New England Fisheries*

1 *An Industry in Trouble*

O<small>N</small> JUNE 10, 1974, the "Sharon and Noreen," a fishing trawler from New Bedford, Massachusetts, traveled up the Potomac River to Washington, D.C., in the culmination of the "Sail on Washington." She carried fishing industry spokesmen and state elected officials to a House of Representatives committee hearing on bills to extend United States fishery jurisdiction to 200 miles from the coast. The Sail on Washington had started nearly a week before in Kennebunkport, Maine. The boats stopped to gather supporters at fishing ports along the coast on the way to Washington—at Rye, New Hampshire; Gloucester and New Bedford, Massachusetts; Point Judith, Rhode Island; Atlantic City and Cape May, New Jersey; and Quantico, Virginia. The speeches and sendoffs were particularly effusive in New England where "Save the American Fisheries," the group that organized the Sail, had been founded and drew its strength. In Gloucester, Massachusetts, Governor Francis W. Sargent told the crowd that "at stake in this Sail on Washington is America's oldest industry." After ceremonies in New Bedford, vessels from farther up the coast and a flotilla of smaller fishing boats, tugs, workboats, and sportfishing boats escorted the "Sharon and Noreen," the vessel chosen to go all the way to Washington, out of the harbor.[1]

In Washington, the spokesmen from New England voiced concerns about the industry and the fish resources. Maine state Representative Elmont S. Tyndale, co-chairman of Save the American Fisheries, warned that if the overfishing of foreign vessels were allowed to continue, "Our fishing industry will be destroyed." Rhode Island state Senator William O'Neill stated that the fishing industry in Rhode Island "is threatened with extinction." Harvey Mickelson, representing seafood dealers in New Bedford, declared that "this particular moment . . . is our last chance to prevent a national disaster." Gaspar J. Lafata from the

3

Gloucester City Council predicted, "If something isn't done soon we will probably be back here for a new first, asking for federal grants for historical restoration . . . so our future generations and tourists can see how fresh fish were caught." Walter Curtis, a vessel owner from Gloucester, held up a small carving of a haddock skeleton, the symbol for the Sail. "I brought with me here a symbol that shows the haddock fisheries of New England," he said. "That bloody well is all that's left. There's nothing left of the haddock fisheries of New England. It's been desecrated, it's been ruined, it's gone."[2]

In this hearing and others leading to passage of the 200-mile limit legislation, fishermen, boat owners, processors, industry spokesmen, and elected officials talked about the problems of the New England fishing industry mainly since the early 1960s. They emphasized that foreign fishing fleets caused the difficulties when they came to the Georges Bank fishing grounds at that time. Through the 1950s and 1960s, however, fishery groups had come to Congress many times with other stories of troubles and with other explanations for their difficulties.

Those who testified were right in thinking the industry had problems. If they had looked as far back as 1950, they would have seen long-term decline relieved only by occasional, brief increases in landings. In 1950 New England fishermen landed well over 940 million pounds of fish. In 1960 they brought in 783 million pounds. The value of the fish went down as well, from $39.3 million in 1950 to $33.7 million in 1960. While the value of the fishermen's product declined nearly 17 percent, the gross national product grew by almost 80 percent.[3]

As weight and value of landings fell, the New England fishing fleet shrank and the number of fishermen declined. In 1950, 865 boats displacing over five tons fished out of New England ports; by 1960 about 740 vessels remained. In 1950 nearly 6,000 fishermen worked on these vessels. In 1960 about 4,300 men fished from them.[4]

The picture was just as bad for the years after 1960, which fishermen and others described for the congressmen at the end of the Sail on Washington. By 1973, the year before the Sail, landings of fish were down to 445 million pounds, although that low figure was an increase from the 412 million pounds in 1972. The value of the catch was up from 1960's $33.7 million to $52 million in 1973, an increase in value of about 54 percent, but that increase had not kept up with inflation and growth in the rest of the economy. The gross national product had increased more than two and one half times in the same years, so that the industry was comparatively worse off than it had been in 1960. The number of boats over five tons which brought fish to New England ports was down to about 690 with 3,000 fishermen by 1973.[5]

Industry decline also affected some of the processors and wholesalers who handled the fish. Unlike the pattern in the fishing sector, changes in the number of processing and wholesaling firms and in processing employment were uneven. From 1950 to 1960, the number of firms increased slightly as employment in processing declined; from 1960 to 1973, the number of firms fell while employment increased by a few hundred workers. Changes in the volume and value of processed fish became more favorable. Production and revenues increased considerably after 1950, and growth after 1960 was even more marked. The value of all processed fish more than doubled between 1960 and 1973 while the value of fresh and frozen fish nearly quadrupled in much faster growth than the rest of the economy experienced.[6]

These trends reflected changes in the character of the processing industry. Some processors and wholesalers expanded their production with imported fish. Some introduced a new frozen product, fish sticks, which captured a large share of the market. Others, especially those who continued to depend exclusively on fresh fish landings from New England boats, decreased in number. Except for this last group of processors and dealers, problems in the fishing industry concentrated in the harvesting sector.

For New Englanders outside the industry and for congressmen who listened to fishing industry spokesmen talk about the problems during the 1970s, it was easy to believe that the decline of the industry was due to the foreign fleets' devastation of the fishing grounds. After all, unlike blacksmithing or carriage-making, fishing was certainly not obsolete. And in contrast to the textile and shoe industries, fishing still seemed to have strong locational advantages in New England. Fishermen could reach some of the richest fishing grounds in the world in less than twelve hours' travel from the major ports of Boston, Gloucester, and New Bedford, Massachusetts, and of Portland and Rockland, Maine. Fishermen from those ports fished Georges Bank and many shallow areas in the Gulf of Maine (Fig. 1.1). Some traveled as far as Browns Bank near Nova Scotia, and many had once worked regularly on the other rich grounds near Canada such as the Grand Bank. Thousands of other fishermen made their livings in the fertile shallow waters close to the New England shore.

Partly because the fisheries' problems looked curable, listeners sympathized with the industry's concerns. The pleas touched listeners for other reasons, too. The loss of fishing-related jobs was miniscule com-

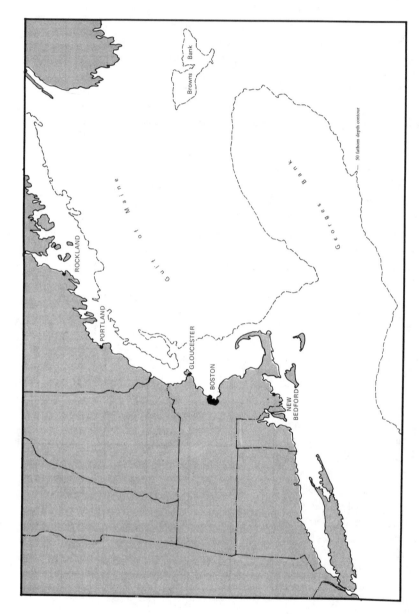

Figure 1.1 New England's Principal Fishing Ports and Fishing Grounds

pared to unemployment connected with the decline of the shoe and textile industries, but the loss of jobs and income mattered a great deal in the coastal communities most dependent on the fisheries. Fishing also mattered to many people because it had been part of the region's culture and economy for so long. The fishery had provided subsistence since the first colonial settlements. As early as the 1660s, the Boston and Gloucester industries supplied salt cod to Europe. Sailing vessels from Gloucester and Maine had established strong fisheries for salt cod and halibut on Georges Bank by the mid-1800s; and fishermen from Gloucester, Boston, and Maine occasionally ventured that far for haddock. A "sacred cod" has hung over the speaker's desk in the Massachusetts legislature since 1784 as a symbol of the importance of the fish to the state. The salt fishery flourished until the 1930s when the new technology of refrigeration, quick-freezing, and filleting made possible the growth of frozen and fresh fish markets. By that time steam-powered vessels had replaced the schooners, and diesel engines were gradually superceding steam.[7] As industry spokesmen campaigned for the extension of fishery jurisdiction to 200 miles, they often mentioned the hundreds of years of the industry's history, the hardships fishermen had endured, and the adventuresome, colorful work on the offshore grounds, no doubt calling up for their listeners the vivid stories of Rudyard Kipling's *Captains Courageous* and Herman Melville's *Moby Dick*.

Solving the industry's troubles might not have seemed so straightforward to those who listened to the industry's arguments in 1974 had they known about the long history of federal government attempts to solve the fishery problems. Extension of fishery jurisdiction to 200 miles was the latest of many proposals for dealing with the difficulties. From the end of World War II through the early 1970s, industry efforts to get help had resulted in shelves of committee hearings and congressional statements, more than a dozen major pieces of legislation, and the expenditure of many millions of dollars. The diagnoses of the reasons for the industry's difficulties and the programs designed to cure the problems had changed over the years, so that by 1974 the reasons cited for the problems of the 1950s and 1960s seemed nearly forgotten. The programs for which the industry had lobbied and which government had put in place in those years had failed to turn the industry's fortunes around. Furthermore, as the 200-mile limit went into effect in 1977, nearly three years after the Sail on Washington, the industry and those in government realized that getting the foreigners off the fishing grounds would not solve all the industry's problems. Planning for the rebuilding of the fish resource, which was required by the new legislation, was proving remarkably difficult.

This book looks at the fishing industry's campaigns to get help from the federal government since World War II. These efforts were often successful with the result that a large number of programs were aimed at helping the fisheries. This account analyzes the industry's problems and the accomplishments of the programs and tries to explain the failure of government efforts to assure the industry's prosperity.

The troubles of the fisheries continue to affect the welfare of many workers and communities. Fishing-related activities could easily have provided between 15 and 20 percent of a coastal town's jobs in the late 1970s.[8] Certainly this many jobs were linked to fishing in the early 1980s. Analysis of the various largely unsuccessful efforts to preserve those jobs and to solve the fishery's problems in the past can inform new efforts and even point to ways government should not intervene.

The problems of the fisheries and the results of government efforts to solve the difficulties hold much broader policy interest, however. The New England fishing industry's efforts and the responses they have received are not unique. Many industries have turned to government for help when they are in trouble. Specifically, business lobbyists have traditionally sought higher tariffs on competing imports; in the 1960s and 1970s they also looked for and often received government loans, subsidies, contracts, and regulatory protection. By the late 1970s the auto and steel industries were appealing for massive government assistance to prevent further contraction or even bankruptcy. Agriculture, shoes, textiles, apparel, shipping, the merchant marine, and others sought and received aid for many years. The political pressures from workers, managers, and distressed communities to stop the decline of troubled industry are so strong that government will probably continue to try to solve those problems, although the types of aid will change as ideas evolve about the appropriate ways to intervene.

The tradition of government help for troubled industry and the prospect of continued aid raise many issues that the story of the fisheries can address. In most cases, as with the fisheries, government assistance has not lifted industries out of their difficulties. The range of possible explanations for this poor record include: the nature of problems was not clear; solutions did not address the problems appropriately; no one seriously intended the programs to help; or efforts ran into implementation problems. Beyond explanations for what happened when government intervened to solve the problems of troubled industry are issues of appropriate policy direction. The fisheries experience suggests some ways that government help could be more effective and raises some questions about when government should step in. The analysis of the story is at the intersection of questions in politics, economics, and public policy regarding government intervention in industry affairs and the proper role of the public sector in the private economy.

The chapters that follow explore these issues in two major periods of fishery problems since World War II. A look at the structure of the New England fishing industry shows that the problems were concentrated in one sector, the offshore groundfish industry. During the 1950s and 1960s the industry pushed for government aid and received a range of programs under one set of assumptions about the nature of their problems. For many reasons those programs did not work. The industry and policymakers redefined the character of the industry's problems in the late 1960s as the foreign fleets worked on the offshore grounds and later as the United States set up a fishery management program. The new efforts also ran into serious difficulties. The reasons for the failure of government efforts to solve the fishing industry problems suggest how much difficulty government is likely to have in trying to improve the health of any troubled industry.

2 Structure and Problems of the Fisheries

As WORLD WAR II ENDED, New England fishermen, boat owners, dealers, and processors hailed an era of prosperity. The fishing industry "is destined to enjoy a steadily increasing demand for its products, as a result of the public becoming better acquainted with the fine qualities of fish and shellfish," proclaimed an industry journal. The demand for quick-frozen fish will not only "take up present productive capacity . . . but will provide an outlet for still larger catches in the future," a reporter stated in a reflection of industry views. "In fact, it is possible that with the great expansion of the frozen food business, fish consumption could be increased to two or three times its present level."[1]

Government officials fed the optimism by predicting that new technology would expand the market. Fish would be marketed farther inland, a Department of Agriculture report concluded. "Quick freezing will revolutionize the marketing of fish," said Charles E. Jackson, assistant deputy coordinator of fisheries for the federal government. "Fishing vessels will dress, freeze, and package fish at sea, arriving in port with a high quality product ready to market. Air transportation will carry ocean fish and shellfish to interior communities within a few hours' time."[2]

Vessel owners showed their optimism by making enormous investments in boats. Despite wartime shortages, from 1940 through 1944 boatbuilders supplied 238 new vessels more than forty feet long to the New England fleet. One hundred twenty-eight of them entered the fishery in 1944 alone. Owners converted ten more vessels from other uses. Although the government never returned 78 boats taken for war use, 141 more vessels over forty feet long fished out of New England ports in 1944 than in 1940, a substantial increase over the approximately 540 boats operating in 1941.[3]

Only occasionally did industry spokesmen hedge their predictions. Some feared that when postwar prices for lobsters declined, lobstermen would lose money unless innovation lowered costs and made year-round

11

lobstering possible. Others warned that without industry attention to product quality, postwar demand could fall. In May 1945 when the House Ways and Means Committee held hearings on a bill to reduce tariffs 50 percent, the government's area coordinator for fisheries predicted that Iceland, Greenland, and other north Atlantic countries would undersell New England producers and "drastically affect the fishing industries." "It is urgent," he said, "that some plan be developed and adopted which will provide for sharing our markets with our neighbors to the extent consistent with the maintenance of operations in our own industry but not beyond."[4]

Prosperity during World War II inspired the postwar optimism about industry prospects, but the fifteen years preceding the war's end had also included some of the worst times the fisheries had known. The Depression had given fishermen no cause for optimism. In 1931 landings of fish in New England ports fell to 540 million pounds, nearly 200 million pounds less than in 1930; and the value of the catch declined from $27 million to $20 million. By 1933 fishermen landed only 500 million pounds of fish, and the revenue they received declined to $13 million. A crewman on a groundfish vessel earned only about $600 in 1933. A worker on a mackerel seiner reported about $300 in wages in New England fisheries, although he probably doubled that amount by fishing in the South during the winter. All other fishermen paid on a share basis earned about $680. This meant that fishermen who had jobs earned much less than full-time employees in most other industries, which in 1933 paid workers in manufacturing an average of more than $1000 and wholesale and retail employees nearly $1200. Only farmers and domestic workers received less than fishermen.[5]

These statistics reflected great hardship in the fishing industry. In 1931 and 1932 Atlantic Coast Fisheries, one of the largest boat operators in the region, kept its trawlers tied up for most of the summer, the best season for fishing, because revenues could not cover trip expenses. Observers were shocked by the severe poverty of fishermen in Maine, living in shanties with their listless families.[6]

Gloucestermen described their plight during the early 1930s. "It has been impossible for the [boat] owners to pay the material men, not to speak of the seller of the engine, or the builder of the boat," representatives of the Gloucester Chamber of Commerce stated. "The danger . . . is that creditors of the material men will push so hard for payment, that the material men in turn will try to realize money on numerous of their bills against the fishing vessels. This means . . . the offering of the vessels for sale at public auction. . . . there will be a chaotic condition in the industry." In the first "sail on Washington," in April 1933 the Gloucester vessel "Gertrude L. Thebaud" carried New England industry representatives to Washington, D. C.. They presented boats' records to President Roosevelt and Congress which showed that income from fishing did not cover operating expenses even when wages and fixed costs were excluded. In 1934 some Gloucester vessel owners tied up their boats because they could not afford to go out. Others fished without insurance and used worn, unsafe gear in order to cut costs.[7]

By the late thirties larger boats that could fish far offshore did better. Gloucester trawlers served new demand in the Midwest for redfish, marketed as frozen fillets of "ocean perch." Gloucester redfish landings jumped from zero in the early 1930s to seventeen million pounds in 1937. In Boston, new vessels using diesel engines powerful enough to drag otter trawl nets along the bottom brought in profitable trips. At the same time, older, steam-powered vessels harvesting fish caught on hooks on long lines laid out across the ocean floor still operated with very low profits. Fishermen could earn several times more money on the newer boats, which still meant wages were low, but not notably out of line. Forty-four percent of the fishermen who lived in Boston earned more than $1000 in 1939; slightly more than one quarter of them earned more than $1400. Service workers and laborers in manufacturing and in construction now did not do as well, although firemen, policemen, and operatives in manufacturing did better. Unemployment in the fisheries was still high. In Boston more than 200 out of 960 fishermen looked for work.[8]

Dealers were also recovering by the late 1930s. Stores on the Boston Fish Pier remained in demand, and the Boston Fish Market Corporation which rented pier buildings to dealers increased its surplus account between 1931 and 1939. New Bedford opened a freezer for fish freezing in 1937, and the following year processors introduced flounder filleting. With the help of the new methods and new technology, the New Bedford industry expanded for the first time since the decline of whaling in the nineteenth century.[9]

The improvement in these groups' fortunes paled as incomes increased throughout the fishing industry during World War II. Incomes rose with changes in the conditions influencing supply and demand. As the United States joined the war, several developments cut back the harvesting capacity of the New England fleet. The Navy appropriated many of the largest boats for use as minesweepers and patrols. By the end of 1942, the New England fisheries had lost 107 vessels over forty feet long to the Navy from a 1941 total of about 540 vessels. German submarines made fishing dangerous on the offshore banks for the boats that remained; they sank three Boston trawlers within the first year of the war. Material shortages interfered with the activity of other boats. At the beginning of 1943 many Gloucester owners tied up their vessels because they could not get new engines. Shortages were most acute in equipment and in vessels; but in addition, vessel owners occasionally had trouble finding crew in part because the government prevented Italian fishermen in Gloucester from working if they did not apply for citizenship.[10]

At the same time that harvesting fish became more difficult, demand for fish increased. The Army and the Lend Lease program purchased practically all canned fish. Civilians who could not obtain meat bought more fish. This increased demand for the catch of the smaller number of boats guaranteed higher prices and incomes.

Despite the cuts in harvesting capacity, New England landings increased from 626 million pounds in 1940 to 714 million pounds in 1944. The value of the fish rose even faster. Revenue from landings more than doubled from 1940 to 1943 as the price of fish at the dock went up. Haddock and large cod sold for about 4 cents per pound in Gloucester, Boston, and Portland in 1940, while in 1943 dealers paid nearly 10 cents per pound. The price of yellowtail flounder rose from nearly 2 to 7 cents per pound; and the redfish price increased from 1.5 to 4 cents. New species in demand for food brought in additional income. Maine fishermen had always used mussels as bait but now found they could sell them. Mainers had processed alewives for fertilizer and feed for hogs and chickens but could now earn more by canning them for human consumption.[11]

Incomes in the fishing industry shot up. "Captain Courageous has hit the jackpot," one reporter proclaimed. Many Gloucester skippers purportedly made $20,000 in 1942, and crewmen could earn $6,000. One captain seining for mackerel made almost $10,000 in five months, and his fourteen crew members each earned nearly $4,300.[12]

More complete accounts of fishermen's earnings supported these stories of great prosperity in the industry. Fishermen on medium draggers, between 50 and 150 gross tons, fishing out of Gloucester, Portland, and Boston in 1941 earned nearly $2,300; in 1942 fishermen earned almost $4,000 and in 1943 close to $6,200. The crew on smaller draggers, less than fifty tons, which fished nearer shore and could not work in bad weather, earned less—about $1,800 in 1941 and over $2,800 in 1942 and 1943. Late in 1944 men working on large trawlers and on draggers could earn as much as $16,000 per year compared to a prewar high of about $2,500 per year. Fishermen on the small boats of the inshore fleet could earn $6,000 per year in 1944 compared to a high of $1,200 before the war.[13]

Dealers prospered, too. In Gloucester about one half of the twenty dealers in business in 1949 had started operations during the war. Five of the firms operating between 1942 and 1946 more than doubled their combined retained earnings in that time. In New Bedford more than twice as many dealers operated in mid-1944 as in mid-1943. Dealer margins set by the Office of Price Administration were 150 percent over the prewar level. In Boston seventeen dealers increased their combined retained earnings from $935,000 in 1941 to $2,200,000 in early 1947.[14]

As the war ended, the fishing industry expected continued prosperity, not a return to the troubles of the Depression. By 1950, however, falling revenues had shattered their hopes. Although everyone did not share in the difficulties, the offshore groundfishery, source of nearly 40 percent of the weight and nearly 60 percent of the value of New England landings, did so badly that the decline dominated all industry statistics and perceptions of the industry's condition.[15] Indeed, the offshore groundfishery, the vessels and fishermen who fished for cod, haddock, and redfish and the dealers who bought their catch, faced deeper, more prolonged difficulties during the 1950s and 1960s than during the Depression. Discussion of the character of the New England fisheries and the experience of different sectors in the twenty years after World War II shows how some parts of the industry fulfilled the early postwar expectations while the offshore groundfish industry did not.

CHARACTER OF THE INSHORE FISHERIES

The New England fishery is extremely diverse. All groups harvest fish or shellfish, but no other generalization applies.[16] Understanding the differences among segments of the industry is crucial to looking at the source of decline in the fisheries. The most important division in the New England fishery for the purposes of this study is between the inshore and the offshore industries, which differ along virtually every socioeconomic dimension. Their financial positions diverged after World War II.[17]

The inshore fishery[18] is composed of boats which are not seaworthy enough (usually because they are too small) to fish the offshore banks except occasionally during the best summer weather. Fishermen say that generally these are boats which displace less than sixty gross tons. Technological change did not alter this size limit after World War II, but improved navigational aids and depth-sounding equipment increased the number of fishing days and enabled some boats to travel farther from shore.

Immediately after World War II the number of inshore boats increased until around 1950 when the number began to decline. In 1946 about 12,500 inshore fishing boats, almost all extremely small, worked in New England. Nearly 12,000 were less than five tons, and more than 5,000 of these did not even have motors. By 1950 the numbers had increased: about 13,800 inshore boats fished from New England ports, but only 600 were larger than five tons. During the 1950s and 1960s the number of inshore boats declined. By 1960 the numbers were close to 1946 levels—about 12,500 inshore boats, about 475 larger than five tons, fished in New England. In 1965, 420 inshore boats between five and sixty tons and about 10,800 smaller ones landed fish in New England.[19]

Regions of the coast shared unequally in fishing activity. Maine and Massachusetts waters supported the largest group of inshore boats. Of the New England inshore boats more than 50 percent fished from Maine and 30 percent from Massachusetts in 1950. Rhode Island also had a large number of boats but far fewer than Maine or Massachusetts at slightly over 10 percent of the total. Even fewer inshore boats worked in Connecticut and in New Hampshire. As the total number of boats declined, the number in Massachusetts climbed to about one third of the total, and Connecticut's share declined.[20]

The number of fishermen who worked inshore probably also declined after 1950. In 1946 about 10,000 inshore fishermen made nearly all their income in fishing and another 9,000 earned less than half their income by fishing. In 1950 nearly 11,000 fishermen earned most of their income inshore, and more than 8,500 worked part-time earning less than half their income in fishing. By 1960 only slightly over 9,000 fishermen depended on fishing for nearly all their earnings. By 1965 about 7,000 fishermen earned most of their income fishing, and about 10,000 worked more casually.[21]

Many of the part-timers who figured so importantly in the statistics held other jobs and probably did not call themselves fishermen. Large numbers of them fished on weekends and during vacations to make extra money and for recreation. The discussion that follows focuses on the group who depend heavily on fishing for their livelihood.

The size of the boat makes every difference in fishing. The smallest inshore fishing boats, the majority, rarely work more than a few miles from land. Boats at the other end of the inshore range, those closer to sixty tons, may go one hundred miles offshore in good weather. Usually these larger boats and slightly smaller ones make longer trips when weather is good but fish closer to shore or do not go out at all in winter. The style of fishing imposed by the character of the boats determines the markets the fishermen serve, the skills a successful fisherman must have, the location of ports, and the possibility of owning a boat.

Because the boats make short trips, the fish they land have usually been out of the water less than a day. Even when properly gutted and iced, fish deteriorate rapidly. Local dealers truck much of the inshore catch to New York and to Boston for distribution as fresh fish; or, less often, fishermen and dealers peddle the catch in restaurants and stores in their communities.[22]

Because their boats are small, inshore fishermen cannot fish in bad weather and cannot follow the fish migrating farther offshore and along the coast through the year. Chatham fishermen explain, for instance, that they switch from longlining to quahogging (raking for hard clams) when dogfish migrate inshore in spring and fall and eat the bait and the hooked cod off the longlines. In Maine, fishermen begin to harvest cod in late March as the winter weather moderates and the fish move closer to the coast. Fish migrations and changes in the seasons impose an annual cycle of movement among fisheries.

Because fish behavior and weather conditions so sharply constrain their work, inshore fishermen need to be able to move quickly and without too much expense from one fishery to another. Catching different kinds of fish and shellfish frequently requires changes in gear. Inshore fishermen use otter trawls or line trawls to catch cod, haddock, and flounder; but they need otter trawls with finer net mesh to catch whiting, dredges to harvest scallops, seines to capture herring, and traps to bring in lobsters. Therefore, inshore fishermen need boats designed to handle different kinds of work and to adapt to a variety of types of gear.

Decisions about shifting the direction of fishing effort are based not only on weather and on fish migration, but also on market prices. Fishermen in Point Judith, Rhode Island, explained that they fished for cod and haddock when the price of scup, butterfish, or other species fell. They claimed this flexibility kept them in business as a small-volume fishery. These kinds of changes do not necessarily make annual cycles as do responses to fish migration and weather. A fisherman on Cape Cod described how he geared up for scalloping in some years, "handlining" (using long lines with hooks) haddock in others. A Maine fisherman worked a fish trap for a while, then invested in seines for herring fishing, and then moved into lobstering over several years. Such changes involve continual evaluation of market conditions and speculation about future prices. According to a Martha's Vineyard fisherman, "It's a little like playing horses."[23]

Decisions to look for different kinds of fish always take account of weather, availability of fish, and price; but work preferences also figure significantly. Scallop prices have to be very good to make scalloping worth the unpleasant culling and shucking involved, one fisherman explained. A Maine fisherman's description of his decisions showed how all these factors contributed: "You quit shrimping because the shrimp disappear, usually around the tenth of April. And then you've got your choice: you can either go dragging for fish, or you can go spring lobstering, which is a short season. Now, I could keep dragging all summer if I wanted to, but I prefer to go lobstering then, because there's more money in it, and besides after you've been dragging all winter, you kind of welcome a change."[24]

Skills in understanding the movements of the fish, in estimating the price fish will bring, and in deciding when to move to another fishery have major influence on an inshore fisherman's financial success. Also extremely important is his knowledge of the fishing grounds. He needs to know the location of different types of bottom and of rocks and wrecks in order to drag a net successfully or to lay traps. He also has to know exactly where fish are likely to be by knowing the patterns of fish behavior. This knowledge has become less important with the introduction of fishfinders, loran,[25] and fathometers; but large numbers of small boats did not have these instruments even by the mid-1960s.

By acquiring these skills, inshore fishermen may improve their incomes, but other factors impinge as well. The character of the market in the ports where the fishermen land their catch influences fishing revenues. Because the boats are small and make short trips, one or two dealers can handle the volume of fish landings, and small-scale dock facilities can accommodate the boats. Fishermen sell their fish in a large number of small ports which meet these requirements: Chatham, Provincetown, Menemsha, and Scituate, Massachusetts; Point Judith, Rhode Island; Stonington, Connecticut; and a number of others, as well as in the large ports of Boston, Gloucester, and New Bedford, Massachusetts; and Portland and Rockland, Maine. Fishermen land lobsters and shellfish in most rural communities along the coast. Almost without exception, the fishermen in small ports have decided to start cooperatives because the one or two dealers profit by holding fish prices down. Where coops have survived, most fishermen believe they are paid higher prices for the catch than other dealers would pay.[26]

Small boats require little capital investment, although older fishermen point out that the cost of a boat rose considerably in the decades after World War II. Fishermen can get started with little more than a skiff. Large numbers of small boats carry no crew besides the captain-owner, although on the larger inshore boats up to three crewmen may join him. Because inshore boats cost relatively little and take small crews, many fishermen own their boats, therefore controlling their own work, which is usually particularly attractive to them. Almost all who stay in fishing own several boats during their lives.[27]

Inshore fishermen respond to fish migration, market and weather conditions, and preferences for different kinds of work in deciding which fish to catch, but the flexibility this implies should not be exaggerated. Fishermen's locations along the coast limit the types of fisheries they can enter. Water temperatures, currents, and the character of the ocean bottom influence which species of fish and shellfish survive and their abundance.[28]

Many inshore fishermen have a particular commitment to certain kinds of fishing work. For instance, even though a Maine fisherman harvested groundfish or shrimp for much of the year, he called himself a lobsterman. When they cannot fish for the species they prefer, other fishermen build traps, mend nets, or overhaul their boats. A few others take onshore jobs instead of moving to new fisheries for part of the year, although other employment is hard to find in coastal communities because the major sources of jobs—tourism, fish processing, and housing construction, for example—hire most people in the same seasons when fishing is best.[29]

TRENDS IN THE INSHORE FISHERIES: 1945–1965

Because most fishermen are limited to certain fisheries due to geography and because many prefer some fisheries to others, they could not remain untouched by biological and economic changes in the inshore fisheries between 1945 and 1965. Major sectors of the inshore industry fared very differently after World War II, some sectors justifying the post-war optimism while others did not.

For example, fishermen who trapped herring for the sardine industry lived along the Maine coast where small herring run inshore from April through October. Over 1,100 fishermen working weirs and stop seines caught 90 percent of the herring in Maine in 1950. The catch of Maine herring fluctuated considerably in quantity and in value after World War II, from 92 million pounds valued at $1.2 million in 1945 to 185 million pounds worth $1.3 million in 1950 to 60 million pounds which brought less than $1 million in 1951. Between 1952 and 1960 the catch varied from 100 million pounds to 171 million pounds. In 1961 the herring failed to show up in the inshore grounds, and the effects were "disastrous," according to James Warren, who has worked in the sardine industry since World War II. Landings fell to 54 million pounds worth about $1 million. Even though the catch increased to close to old levels for the next two years, the herring industry did not recover. As of 1965 about 690 fishermen landed only 70 million pounds of herring worth a little over $1 million.[30]

Fishermen in Maine and in Massachusetts depended heavily on lobsters, too, from the postwar years through the mid-1960s. Lobsters usually appear in most abundance inshore at about the same time as herring, from April or May through October or November; but residents of offshore islands have had a profitable winter lobster fishery, too. The catch of lobsters increased after World War II from about 18 million pounds in Maine valued at $7 million to a high of 24 million pounds worth $11 million in 1960, and declined to about 19 million pounds worth $14 million by 1965. The catch of lobsters for all New England rose from 23 million pounds in 1946 to more than 29 million pounds valued at more than $13 million in 1960 to somewhat over 28 million pounds worth almost $21 million in 1965.

Between 1945 and 1965 the number of lobstermen and the number of lobster traps increased tremendously. Lobstering attracted large numbers of fishermen who earned most of their income in other ways, and the introduction of hydraulic winches made it possible for one lobsterman to haul hundreds more traps. In 1945 nearly 4,200 lobstermen handled almost 356,000 traps. By 1960 almost 6,600 lobstermen hauled nearly 710,000 traps. In 1965 the number of fishermen had declined slightly to 5,800, about 2,700 earning less than one half of their income in fishing, but they used nearly 790,000 traps.

The increase in number of traps fished as catches stabilized or declined reflected the depletion of the lobster stock. Even before the 1950s Maine and Massachusetts introduced rules about the size of lobsters which could be sold and prohibited sale of egg-bearing lobsters to try to conserve the resource. Concern about the condition of the lobster stock and debates about appropriate conservation measures occupied the state fishery agencies.[31]

Maine inshore fishermen not only harvested the largest share of lobsters but also dominated shrimping in the postwar years. In 1945 Maine fishermen caught virtually all shrimp landed in New England. The shrimp season, from the end of January to mid-April, coincided with the poorest fishing times for lobsters and herring, so many of the shrimp fishermen came from those fisheries. End

In 1945 fishermen landed more shrimp than ever before. About thirty shrimp boats harvested 580,000 pounds worth $29 million. This peak came after six years of market development and of growth in processing capacity which allowed fishermen to sell the shrimp. In 1946, however, the shrimp harvest fell to 162,000 pounds, and the fishery was virtually defunct by 1949 when fishermen landed only 9,700 pounds and only twelve boats fished intermittently for shrimp.

In the 1960s when shrimp reappeared in large numbers, the shrimp fishery developed again, growing much larger than it had in the late 1940s. By 1964 shrimpers harvested 925,000 pounds of shrimp, as Maine Department of Sea and Shore Fisheries officials worked again with processors and fishermen to assure processing capacity and consumer demand. The wild fluctuations in the fishery seemed due to ecology as much as to economics. Biologists suggested that shrimp were particularly sensitive to temperature, so that slight warming of the water killed them in large numbers.[32]

Inshore fishermen from southern Maine and from Massachusetts, primarily Gloucester, fished for whiting (or silver hake), which was valued for food and for industrial purposes such as fertilizer, animal food, and fish protein concentrate. Whiting congregated inshore from May through November with the best catches between the first of June and mid-October. Until the 1940s fishermen considered whiting a nuisance fish to be discarded at sea; but as methods of handling, processing, and distribution improved, consumers in the South and Midwest ate more whiting. Landings rose from 78 million pounds worth almost $2 million in 1945 to a high of 126 million pounds valued at $2.2 million in 1957. Gloucester fishermen brought in more than 60 percent of that total; by 1961 thirty-five small otter trawlers—draggers—as well as some medium trawlers fished for whiting from Gloucester. In 1957, 1959, and 1960 whiting brought in more income than any other food fish landed in Gloucester. In Provincetown, too, whiting became the leading species. In Portland, Maine, small otter trawlers made whiting the second most important fish landed. By 1965, however, the whiting catch was down to 75 million pounds valued slightly under $2 million.

As landings declined, fishermen argued over which boats could work the inshore grounds. In 1961 the Maine legislature passed laws that excluded larger trawlers from waters off Portland. Smaller Gloucester boats could not make profits in such long trips so the Maine fishermen gained control of the Maine coast whiting fishery.[33]

When whiting stocks were less abundant, when their prices fell, or when they were farther offshore, the draggers joined fixed gear fishermen—line trawlers and gillnetters—in harvesting flounder and groundfish such as cod and haddock. On Cape Cod and the south shore of Massachusetts, inshore fishermen also sought groundfish and flounder. In 1965, inshore fishermen brought in almost 20 million pounds of cod and haddock valued at $1.7 million. These landings made up close to 12 percent of the total New England catch of cod and haddock.[34]

Cape Cod fishermen also depended on sea scallops from grounds south and east of the Cape. Demand improved through the early 1960s so catches at first increased and then decreased as the resource became depleted. In 1965 inshore fishermen caught 2 million pounds of sea scallops worth over $8 million, 18 percent of the total New England scallop harvest.[35]

Cape Cod fishermen also brought in many other species of fish that migrated to southern New England waters in summer, such as scup, butterfish, and fluke, and still others, such as tilefish that lived in New England waters year round. Rhode Island and Connecticut inshore fishermen depended on these species as well. Most of these fish were more attractive in the New York market than in New England.[36]

Inshore fishermen from Gloucester, New Bedford, and especially Point Judith relied on low-value industrial or "trash" fish for substantial parts of their income from May through September or October. In Gloucester whiting contributed to the industrial fishery. Point Judith developed the strongest New England industrial fishery after 1950 under the leadership of the fishermen's cooperative. By 1957 industrial fish amounted to 90 percent of the weight of Point Judith landings and declined slightly in importance after that.[37]

Fishermen from Cape Cod, the Massachusetts islands, and Rhode Island relied on shellfish for an important share of their incomes. In fall or spring when bad weather prevented longliners, lobstermen, and others from taking their boats to sea, the fishermen raked or dredged for shellfish in bays and ponds. A few fishermen quahogged full time. During the cape, or bay, scallop season, beginning in October or November, many fishermen turned to scalloping for a few weeks because the prices were so high.

The shellfish landings declined with depletion and pollution of the beds. In 1950 the Massachusetts and Rhode Island landings of quahogs (hard clams), soft-shelled clams, bay scallops, and oysters amounted to about 8.6 million pounds. By 1965 the catch had declined to about 4.8

million pounds. Quahogs made up the bulk of the harvest, nearly 50 percent in 1950 and more than 60 percent in 1965.[38]

As this discussion shows, although inshore fishermen moved among fisheries during each year and from year to year, their options were not completely open. Fishermen in Maine could not earn a living from quahogging; Rhode Island fishermen could not choose to catch herring for the sardine industry. Environmental conditions determined which fish and shellfish lived along different sections of the coast, and fishermen depended on the species in their region. The major trends in the inshore industry reveal that the fisheries for different stocks fared quite differently between 1945 and 1965. Some, most notably lobstering, expanded; others, for example herring, contracted; and others such as shrimp and whiting expanded and then contracted. Therefore, fishermen had to change the direction of their fishing to maintain their incomes.

THE FORTUNES OF INSHORE FISHERMEN, 1945–1965

Because fishermen could move among the fisheries in their region to keep their earnings from falling, the trends for species do not show what happened to the incomes of inshore fishermen. Besides moving among species, many may have chosen to leave fishing at least temporarily and therefore prevented more decline in the incomes of those who remained.

For whatever reason, inshore fishermen were comfortable financially following World War II. Fishermen's wages were "about the level of a semi-skilled worker" after 1950, said Dan Arnold, a fisherman and director of the Massachusetts Inshore Draggermen's Association. They earned about $7,000 per year in 1960, he remembered. A group of high-income boats in Point Judith paid a crew share well over $9,000 in 1964, while a group of low-income boats provided a crew share just over $6,000. Fishermen could have supplemented these wages by shellfishing or by working in jobs outside fishing when the boats could not go out. These earnings compared very favorably with the average wage of a full-time manufacturing worker in 1964, about $6,200.[39]

Other evidence fills out the picture of an industry that did not face particular hardship. Throughout the 1950s and 1960s, Arnold said, fishermen sought "sites" or jobs, and captains easily found crew. Point Judith fishermen maintained "a steady and prosperous fishery during the 1950s and 1960s," said Jacob Dykstra, president of the Point Judith Fishermen's Cooperative Association. In Chatham, Massachusetts, on Cape Cod, only the fish trap companies faced prolonged hard times, with most of the traps on the Cape going out of business before the mid-1960s. Chatham fishermen who started fishing between 1930 and 1960 do not speak of difficult times after the Depression ended.[40]

Another sign that inshore fishermen were not badly off is that they did not organize politically to get government aid. Lack of political action does not necessarily mean that no problem exists, but inshore fishermen had plenty of opportunities to describe problems and did not do so. Nearly every year spokesmen from the offshore groundfish industry testified before congressional committees about fishermen's problems. The sardine packers appealed for aid when the herring fishery declined, but the herring fishermen did not. Inshore fishermen could easily have joined either group. Furthermore, among inshore fishermen organizations already existed that could act on their behalf. Lobstermen's associations worked to influence lobster regulations in Maine and Massachusetts; groups of draggermen sought to relieve restrictions on dragging in the waters under state jurisdiction; and leaders of cooperatives spoke for their memberships on other issues. These groups did not speak of financial hardship among their constituents.[41]

In sum, while the inshore industry had not prospered enough to fulfill all the postwar hopes, the inshore fishery was certainly not the source of trouble in the New England fishing industry after World War II. While the experience in fisheries based on different species varied greatly, changes in the inshore industry could not account for the overall decline in revenues and landings.

CHARACTER OF THE OFFSHORE FISHERIES[42]

The experience of the offshore industry, the other major segment of the fishing industry, contrasted sharply with that of the inshore fishery. Falling revenues, declining wages, and shrinking vessel profits quickly ended postwar hopes in most parts of the offshore industry.

Nearly everyone connected with fishing agreed that sectors of the offshore industry had very serious problems. Beginning soon after the war, fishermen, vessel owners, and some processors campaigned for government relief. A picture of the general character of the offshore industry and the manner in which parts of it changed between 1950 and 1965 helps to explain why those groups were concerned.

The number of boats involved in offshore fishing increased between 1945 and 1950 and then declined somewhat from 1950 to 1965, but unlike the inshore industry, the number of boats was fairly stable. Far fewer boats worked offshore than inshore. From 250 to 300 vessels fished offshore between 1950 and 1965, carrying close to 4,000 fishermen in 1950 and about 2,500 in 1965.[43]

In 1950 boats in the offshore industry ranged in size from the 60 minimum gross tons for offshore work to about 370 gross tons, but more than 75 percent displaced less than 150 gross tons. In 1965 the largest offshore boat displaced 685 gross tons, but it was unique. The boats ranged in length from about 75 to 140 feet. One boat was nearly 170 feet long, but about 70 percent were less than 90 feet.[44]

An offshore boat looks large next to an inshore boat; but if one has not seen many inshore boats, most offshore vessels seem small even at the pier, and at sea they look too fragile to withstand heavy seas. All other kinds of ocean-going vessels dwarf them, including, by the mid-1960s, the distant-water fishing fleets of other nations. The Soviet vessels ranged in length from 95 feet to well over 600 feet.[45]

The offshore vessels can travel to fishing grounds far off the coast. New England boats fish mainly on Georges Bank and in the Gulf of Maine. Some boats travel farther to fishing banks near Canada, Browns Bank, for example, or Middle Bank. Georges Bank, the most important fishing ground for New England, is a vast area of shallow water, 12,000 square miles of it less than 100 fathoms deep. It extends east and south of Cape Cod for about 200 miles. The Gulf of Maine bounds Georges Bank on the north with deeper water and many smaller banks.[46]

As in the inshore fisheries, the size of the boats and the kinds of trips they can make have implications for the markets the boats supply with fish. Trips as far as parts of Georges Bank take about twelve hours from most ports in New England. To pay the costs of such long trips and to fill the larger capacity of the boats, the offshore vessels stay out a week, ten days, and occasionally longer. As a result, offshore boats land fish which can be more than a week old when they reach the dock. These offshore landings supply fresh fish to many areas in New England and beyond; in addition, dealers freeze a share of the catch to sell later or to supply more distant markets.[47]

As in inshore work, successful offshore fishing depends to a large extent on the captain's knowledge of fishing grounds and fish behavior. Since offshore vessels can handle rougher seas, however, their captains have considerable choice about where to fish. Therefore, migration of the fish does not entirely determine composition of the catch. The captain also depends on hunches about the prices different species will bring and his assessment of information about where he and other captains have caught fish. His decisions about where to fish, when to "set out" gear, and how to adjust the gear are especially important in determining the size and composition of the catch.

After World War II new technology improved captains' ability to fish and to navigate. Loran allows skippers to specify the position of the vessel and return to the same spot later. Radios provide communication with other vessels and improve safety because in an emergency captains or crew can contact other boats and the Coast Guard. Radar makes collisions with other boats in bad weather less likely. Electronic fishfinders indicate the depth, although not the species, of schools of fish near the boat.[48]

The expense of changing gear and the need to bring in large loads of fish constrain skippers' freedom in finding fish and in choosing the species to catch. Harvest of different species requires different gear. Vessels outfitted with side or stern trawls harvest bottom-feeding fish, mainly haddock, cod, flounder, whiting, and redfish. Purse seiners fish offshore for adult herring and for menhaden, used for industrial purposes. Vessels equipped with dredges go scalloping. Boats only occasionally use more than one type of gear. In 1959 nine boats, or about three percent of the offshore fleet, had purse seines as well as otter trawl equipment. Six smaller offshore boats converted to scalloping in the summer and to dragging in the winter. By the late 1960s, however, conversion of a dragger from trawling to scalloping had increased in cost to about $15,000 unless the fisherman did much of the work himself, so that few captains made the change. The conversion of a year-old, $480,000, 200 gross ton boat, the "Pat-San-Marie," from scalloping to seining cost $80,000 in 1968, a move so rare that it made news.[49]

Another reason that a captain of an offshore boat cannot pursue the variety of species available to an inshore fisherman is that an offshore vessel must bring in large loads of high-value fish that do not spoil quickly. An offshore captain cannot make a living from less common fish which may bring good prices in small quantities because such fish do not provide enough revenue to cover trip expenses for a large boat.

More fishermen work on an offshore vessel than on an inshore boat. In 1959 the smallest offshore otter trawlers displacing about sixty gross tons employed as few as five fishermen, but the large Boston trawlers had seventeen crewmen, offshore trawlers carried an average of ten or eleven crewmen, a purse seiner employed sixteen fishermen, and a scalloper had eleven men. In 1965 crews on otter trawlers ranged from three to seventeen men, but the average number of eight crewmen was lower than in

1959. Slightly smaller boats in the offshore fleet, changes in boat design, new types of gear, and revision of union rules explained the decline.[50]

Offshore fishermen usually work out of one port and associate with one major kind of fishing. While fishermen often stay with one boat for many trips, many do not have obligations to a boat beyond one trip. They can take a trip off or move among different boats within a fishery. Recommendations of friends or relatives, a reputation as a good fisherman, and friendships with captains have always figured in how easily a fisherman can move from one site to another, although in the 1950s a fisherman who wanted a site usually also had to belong to the Atlantic Fishermen's Union. Fishermen take new sites for many reasons, most commonly to work with family or to improve their incomes. "Highliners," the boats that earn the most income in a year, have less turnover than others.[51]

On the fishing grounds the crew handle the gear and the fish; skills acquired in these tasks are one reason that fishermen tend to stay on one type of boat.[52] The crew of an otter trawler send the net overboard on the captain's orders, manage the "haul back" of the net, dump the fish from the "cod end" of the net into pens on deck, repair the net and gear to send them overboard for the next tow, sort and gut the fish, and pack the fish in ice below deck while the next tow continues. Managing the gear properly is particularly important because if the net tears, frays, or drags incorrectly on the bottom, it brings in few fish. A tear in the net from a "hangup" on the bottom can require hours of fishing time for repair. Knowing how to repair the damaged net or "work twine" at high speed is one of the most important skills. All the work demands strength and speed because the gear is unwieldy, because time spent with nets on the deck costs fishing time and therefore income, and because the crew must clear fish off the deck by the end of the next tow. A job on an otter trawler took longer to learn before the advent of "stern trawling," in which the gear is set out and hauled back over the stern instead of over the side, as in the older "side trawling" method. Stern trawling, introduced in the mid-1960s, made gear handling easier and safer.[53]

Working conditions on an otter trawler are harrowing. All the work except packing the fish is on the open deck regardless of weather, and crews get little rest during trips. Groundfish crews work shifts that continue around the clock unless the captain decides to "steam" to other grounds; repairs on the gear or problems with clearing the deck of fish may mean the crew work more than the twelve hours per day of assigned shifts. Crews on trawlers fishing for redfish usually work during the day because at night the fish come off the bottom and make fishing less productive.[54]

Fishermen on scallopers have the same major responsibilities, but they work with dredges instead of trawls, and they shuck scallops instead of gutting fish. First the crew set out the gear. After the dredges have scraped along the bottom for a while, the crew bring them to the surface to dump the catch on board. The crew shovel rocks, small scallops, empty shells, and other debris or fish overboard, hose off the rest of the catch and cut each scallop open to remove the "meat," the adductor muscle. They discard overboard the rest of the scallop, store the meats in bags and pack them with ice. A reporter along for a scallop trip noted, "Endurance and muscle are the key tools of a top scallop man." The strenuous work continues in shifts twenty-four hours a day.[55]

Work with the gear is hazardous at any time, but in the frequent storms on Georges Bank, the work becomes very dangerous. Lurches of the boat or slipping gear can knock fishermen overboard or take off their fingers, arms, or legs. "Icing," thick build-up of ice on the deck, rigging, and gear, makes a boat so top-heavy that waves can capsize it. Stormy seas can damage a boat even without icing. Long trips make many storms impossible to avoid, but some captains choose to risk fishing during storms because the boat may make more money. Fewer boats work the grounds during a storm so fish are less likely to be dispersed and are therefore easier to catch. At the same time, the price of fish rises as landings fall. Studies of the riskiness of fishermen's work show the result of all these factors; in the early 1960s fishermen suffered more injuries on the job than any other group except coal miners.[56]

The captain's and crew's earnings come from the sale of the fish in port. Auctions five days a week in New Bedford and in Boston determine the "ex-vessel" price of all species landed. An auction also operated in Gloucester for several years after World War II, but since then dealers there have made purchase arrangements with individual boats. All vessels operate under a "lay" system which determines the division of the "gross stock," the total revenue from the trip. The "lay" prescribes which trip costs come out of the gross stock; how the crew and the "boat," or vessel owner, divide the remaining "net stock"; and which costs each group deducts from its share of the net stock. Costs include wharfage fees; charges for scales used in the "weigh out" of the catch; bonuses for the engineer, mate, and cook; fees for the "lumpers" who unload the fish; maintenance of radar and sounding equipment; ice, groceries, water, and fuel; and the captain's share. One of the most common lay arrangements allocates 60 percent of the net stock to the crew and 40 percent to the boat, with 10 percent of the boat's share going to the captain in addition to his share as a member of the crew.[57]

Fishermen, dealers, and vessel owners continually dispute the provisions of the lay and the operation of the auction. Fishermen in Boston, Gloucester, and New Bedford unionized in the late 1930s to form the Atlantic Fishermen's Union affiliated with the National Maritime Union and later with Seafarer's International of the American Federation of Labor. In 1958 New Bedford fishermen broke with the Atlantic Fishermen's Union and formed the New Bedford Fishermen's Union. Through the 1950s and 1960s in all three ports the unions negotiated with the vessel owners over the costs subtracted from gross stock and from each share of net stock, minimum prices for fish, weighing methods, number of fishermen employed on a boat, number of days a boat had to "lay over" between trips, and fringe benefits.[58]

Unlike fishermen in the inshore fisheries most offshore fishermen never own boats. Because of the boats' size and sophisticated electronic equipment, offshore vessels require substantial capital investment. By 1965 an eighty-foot vessel with advanced electronic gear and a modern stern trawling design cost more than $200,000. That was almost double the cost of a boat of about the same size shortly after World War II. Mainly in Boston and Rockland but to a lesser extent in Gloucester and New Bedford during the 1950s, corporations owned offshore vessels and hired captains and crew. Others, like the Boston vessel owner-dealers of the 1940s and 1950s, integrated vertically into packing fish for sale to processors or into simple processing—filleting, skinning, and packing fish for wholesalers. Still others, such as Gorton-Pew Fisheries, later Gorton's of Gloucester, operated such substantial processing facilities during the 1950s that vessel ownership was a minor part of the business. During World War II with demand for fish particularly strong, processors had to rely on their own vessels for a supply of fish; but in the ten to fifteen years after the war, most large processing firms sold their boats. Many now depend instead on imported frozen fish for their processing needs.[59]

These generalizations about vessel ownership apply best to Boston and Rockland. In Gloucester and New Bedford, privately held, family-controlled corporations most commonly own one or more boats, with family members working as captain and filling some of the crew sites. In Gloucester, for instance, the Novellos, the Brancaleones, the Parisis, the Militellos, and others own and captain their offshore boats. Fishing families have also diversified into ownership of gear supply firms, marine railways, fish dealing and processing, and fuel supply.[60]

Immigrants have filled most of the jobs in the offshore fisheries since

World War II. In Gloucester, Portuguese and later Sicilians have made up the largest proportion of boat owners, captains, and crewmen. In Boston, Canadians from the maritime provinces dominated the port for many years. In 1964, 64 percent of fishermen on Boston large trawlers had been born in Canada and 5 percent in Europe. In New Bedford, from 1952 through 1962 two-thirds of the new members of the fishermen's union had emigrated from Europe, usually from Norway, although more recently Portuguese have filled most of the sites.[61]

TRENDS IN THE OFFSHORE FISHERIES: 1945–1965

The large quantities of fish landed by offshore vessels require extensive pier space, unloading equipment, and trucking and processing capacity. Boston, New Bedford, and Gloucester, Massachusetts, as well as Portland and Rockland, Maine, had facilities that filled these needs, so that offshore boats landed nearly all their fish in those ports from 1945 to 1965.[62] Each port served a contingent of inshore boats as well, often as many or more than offshore boats, but the catch from offshore boats dominated the landings.

Fishermen and processors in the major ports specialized in handling different kinds of fish. An otter trawler harvesting redfish landed in Gloucester or in Rockland; a vessel fishing for haddock went to Boston or occasionally to New York to land the catch. Because the ports specialized and adjusted very little to changes in markets for species, they had quite different experiences between 1945 and 1965. Only New Bedford fulfilled the postwar predictions of prosperity. The hardships and decline of the postwar period concentrated in the offshore industry of Boston, Gloucester, Portland, and Rockland.

New Bedford flourished. The value of the catch reached new highs nearly every year in the early 1950s as New Bedford climbed from the fourth rank fishing port in the United States in 1950 in value of landings to third in 1957 to second in 1959. In 1955 the revenue from the New Bedford catch surpassed that of Boston, formerly the major New England port. In 1964 the value of New Bedford landings exceeded that of Boston and Gloucester combined. By 1965 fishermen brought in 147 million pounds of fish and shellfish worth almost $20 million (see Figure 2.1).[63]

Not all species figured equally in New Bedford's growth. Sea scallops provided the largest proportion of New Bedford's fishing income during the twenty years after the war. Landings increased from the 1940s to the early 1960s, but after 1961 they declined until by 1965 landings had fallen

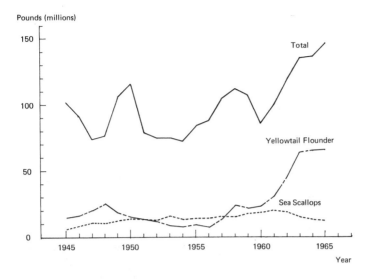

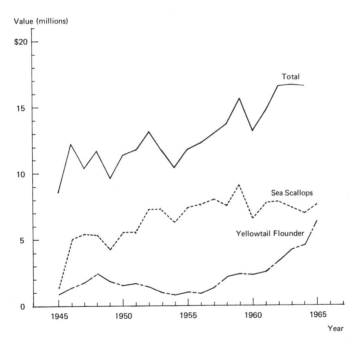

Figure 2.1 New Bedford Landings, 1945–1965. From U.S., Department of the Interior (later Department of Commerce), *Fishery Statistics of the United States*, Statistical Digests (Washington, D.C.: GPO).

to 11.3 million pounds. By 1950, scallop revenue made up nearly 50 percent of the value of all landings, in 1961 more than 50 percent, and in 1965 almost 40 percent.[64]

Yellowtail flounder also added substantially to New Bedford's prosperity, especially after 1958. From the late 1950s, boats that had fished for haddock and cod redirected their effort toward yellowtail. Offshore boats landed nearly 80 percent of the New Bedford yellowtail catch, but small boats also benefited. By 1965, yellowtail produced nearly as much revenue as scallops.[65]

Investment in scallopers and estimates of the crew's share of scallop revenues suggest that at least until 1960, vessel owners and crewmen prospered although their incomes were not extremely high. The number of scallopers in New Bedford declined between 1956 and 1962 from fifty-six to forty-seven boats fishing all year and from seventy-nine to sixty boats working at the peak of the fishing season. Hidden in these figures, however, by 1962, were twelve new, larger boats with more horsepower and up-to-date equipment. The new additions replaced old boats and modernized the fleet so that despite decline in the number of vessels, capital investment increased.

Estimates of the crew share of revenues on scallop vessels in New Bedford from 1956 through 1962 suggest that annual earnings probably were higher than a manufacturing worker's earnings, although a scalloper's crew share paid for more hours of work. A crewman's share, the amount paid to a site in a year, averaged $5,600 to $6,200 in 1956 compared with $4,100 in manufacturing, $7,000 to $7,600 in 1959 compared with $4,600 in manufacturing, and $10,000 to $11,000 in 1967 compared with $6,000 in manufacturing.[66] Most crewmen earn less than a crew share on any vessel because they do not make as many trips as the boat; therefore, a crew share usually goes to more than one crewman during the year. However, the size of the crew share shows that a crewman could earn a very good income if he worked whenever the boat did, although few crewmen would have done so.

Information on a broader group of fishermen working in New Bedford provides little suggestion of unusual problems. Employment declined somewhat between 1952 (when about 940 fishermen worked in New Bedford) and 1953, then increased to about 1,050 by 1962. Large numbers of workers moved in and out of the industry, and many fishermen probably worked part time. Only 775 fishermen worked at least 175 days during two of the three years from 1961 through 1963. The union and the Seafood Producers Association, the organization of boat owners, complained that in New Bedford few young people entered fishing. In 1963, only 21 percent of fishermen who had worked more than 175 days in two of the three preceding years were less than thirty-five years old compared with about 40 percent of the United States male labor force.[67] This trend probably indicated some young people's decisions to work less and others' difficulties in getting sites on boats often enough to accumulate 175 days of fishing in a year, rather than poor wages or deterioration in the fleet. In general, fishermen, vessel owners, and processors prospered.

The trends in New Bedford contrasted with those in other offshore ports in New England, where depression in the fishing industry smashed the hopes of postwar growth. Boston experienced the greatest decline. Landings fell during the 1950s and 1960s after a postwar high in 1947 (see Figure 2.2). The value of landings at Boston Fish Pier also fell, although with great fluctuations, from a high in 1948 of over $16 million to $11.6 million in 1965.[68]

Boston's landings reflected dependence on one species even more than New Bedford's. Boston offshore boats depended mainly on haddock and to a lesser extent on cod landed primarily as bycatch in the haddock fishery. In 1947 haddock made up 60 percent of the weight of the catch from offshore vessels, and cod landings contributed 20 percent. While cod decreased slightly in importance in the total catch, haddock became even more important. By 1950 haddock made up more than 70 percent of the catch, cod 14 percent. By 1965 haddock was nearly 75 percent of the total landings and cod just under 13 percent. Haddock figured as predominately in the value as in the amount of the catch; it brought 60 percent of the revenue to offshore boats in 1947, 72 percent in 1950, and 77 percent in 1965. Cod added 16 percent in 1947, 13 percent in 1950, and 11 percent in 1965.[69]

Activity at the Boston Fish Pier changed dramatically between 1950 and 1965. In 1947 sixty "large" trawlers (over 150 gross tons) fished out of Boston along with twenty-eight "medium" draggers (between 50 and 150 gross tons) and two large line trawlers from days when fishermen left their vessel each day in dories to catch fish with hooks on long lines. In 1965, twenty-six large trawlers and twenty-five medium trawlers remained.[70]

The record of earnings of Boston offshore boats suggested reasons for this decline. Earnings of Boston's largest trawlers over 200 gross tons varied; some consistently made profits while others suffered large losses between 1953 and 1957. Boston large trawlers that displaced between 150 and 199 gross tons suffered losses more generally as their receipts fell. All vessels included in a 1956 survey lost money, and only one out of six in 1957 reported a profit.[71]

The number of fishermen working on Boston offshore boats decreased

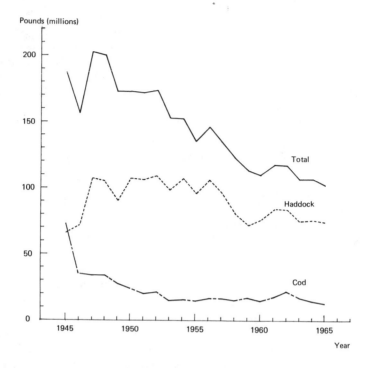

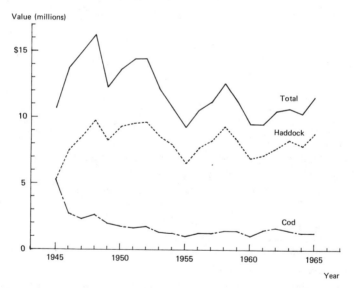

Figure 2.2. Boston Landings, 1945–1965. From U.S., Department of the Interior (later Department of Commerce), *Fishery Statistics of the United States*, Statistical Digests (Washington, D.C.: GPO).

from close to 1,100 men in 1950 to about 730 fishermen in 1964. Most did not earn a good living. In 1964 fishermen generally made about 14 percent more than they had in 1948, but the average earnings of production workers in manufacturing had increased 90 percent in the same period. Between 1951 and 1964 average annual incomes for Boston fishermen on the large offshore trawlers actually declined from about $4,700 to less than $4,200.

Incomes varied considerably, however, with the number of trips and with position in the crew. In 1964 most fishermen who made more than twenty trips per year earned over $6,000, close to the national median for men working full time. This group, about 42 percent of Boston offshore fishermen, worked nearly 270 twelve-hour days, many more hours than most workers. On the other hand, 20 percent of Boston trawlermen did not work as much, making thirteen to twenty trips during the year, and they earned less than $4,000. Eighty percent of these fishermen had no other source of income. The rest of the Boston offshore fishermen made even fewer trips and had lower incomes. The twenty-five captains in the fleet did better than fishermen in other positions. Captains who made more than twenty trips earned more than $13,000, and those who worked between thirteen and twenty trips made about $8,500.[72]

Gloucester's fortunes resembled Boston's. Landings and their value declined erratically after 1951 although Gloucester remained a leading national port in volume (see Figure 2.3).[73]

In the years immediately after World War II Gloucester was the redfish port of the region, landing 73 percent of New England redfish in 1946. In that year redfish landings made up 60 percent of the Gloucester catch in weight, about 54 percent in revenue. Redfish landings declined considerably after the peak year of 1951, however, and the offshore boats bore almost all the impact of the decline.[74]

Unlike the pattern in Boston where haddock remained as important in the catch even though haddock landings declined, redfish in Gloucester became less important. By 1955 redfish accounted for 32 percent of the landings and by 1965 only 18 percent.[75]

The Gloucester fleet turned to other species, the most important of which was whiting. Offshore boats, especially medium-sized trawlers, traveled to the fishing grounds off the Maine coast where whiting were plentiful. Between 1956 and 1957 whiting landings in Gloucester jumped from 44 million pounds to 75 million pounds. The increase saved Gloucester from disaster, stated John O'Brien, a government fishery market specialist. In the late 1950s and early 1960s twenty-eight medium trawlers along with occasional large trawlers fished for whiting from

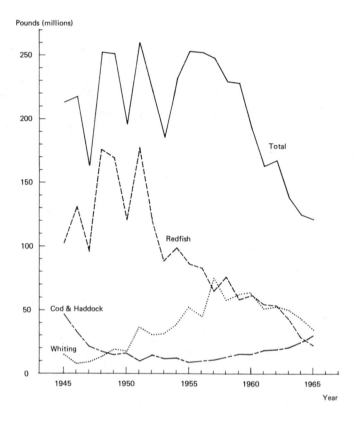

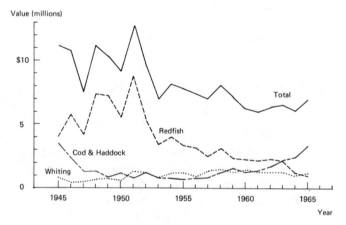

Figure 2.3. Gloucester Landings, 1945–1965. From U.S., Department of the Interior (later Department of Commerce), *Fishery Statistics of the United States*, Statistical Digests (Washington, D.C.: GPO).

Gloucester. In 1960 whiting landings were still high, accounting for a third of the catch and 22 percent of the revenue in the port. Landings declined until 1965, although whiting remained 30 percent of the total catch and brought 15 percent of the port's revenue.[76]

Haddock became more important to offshore Gloucester boats as whiting and redfish declined. In 1960 haddock was only a little over 6 percent of the landings and brought 16 percent of all revenue, but by 1965 haddock landings had doubled, making up 20 percent of the catch and nearly 40 percent of the revenue in the port. The dependence of the offshore boats on haddock was even greater than the Gloucester landings figures indicate because the large boats often took their catch to Boston in search of a better price. In 1963, for example, Gloucester-based vessels accounted for nearly one quarter of the Boston landings.[77]

The changes brought hard times to the Gloucester offshore fleet. The number of offshore boats declined substantially. In 1952 eighty-seven large and medium trawlers that fished primarily for groundfish, mostly redfish but also haddock and cod, landed their catch in Gloucester. By 1955 sixty-seven boats landed fish there. By 1965 probably fewer than sixty offshore boats worked out of Gloucester. The boats in general did alright before 1953, but after that time trawler operations rarely stayed out of the red. Of thirty-five Gloucester trawlers surveyed in the late 1950s eighteen had realized profits and seventeen had lost money in 1953; but total losses were far larger than profits so that the boats showed an aggregate loss. In 1954 and 1955 the situation was much the same. In 1954 twenty-two boats realized profits, and fifteen lost money. In 1955 fourteen profited, and twenty-three had losses.[78]

The number of fishermen working on Gloucester offshore boats undoubtedly declined, too. The number of crew sites declined with the number of vessels from nearly 800 in 1952 to about 650 in 1955. The total number of crewmen, including many inshore fishermen, fell from around 1,640 in 1950 to 1,400 in 1955 to less than 750 in 1965. The average crew share for a site on a boat went down after 1951 from around $7,000 per year to close to $4,500 in 1955; this certainly meant that fishermen's earnings also fell.[79]

In Rockland and Portland, Maine, the other two New England offshore ports, the trends resembled Gloucester's and Boston's although the decline was not as severe. Their fleets depended heavily on redfish and continued to do so longer than Gloucester's. The Rockland and Portland industries were much smaller than those of the two large Massachusetts ports. The value of the landings never reached $3 million in either Maine port between World War II and 1965.[80]

Although offshore vessel owners, unlike inshore fishermen, could not protect their incomes by fishing for different species whenever prices and resource conditions changed, the twenty years after World War II surely offered the fishermen, boat owners, and dealers in Gloucester and Boston enough time to adjust to market conditions so that their fortunes might eventually have resembled New Bedford's. Large numbers of boat owners and fishermen might have left fishing so that the incomes of those who remained did not suffer so much. Even if those in the industry had not considered other types of jobs, they might have moved to other kinds of fishing. For example, owners might have converted their groundfish vessels for scalloping. Captains might have directed more effort toward yellowtail flounder away from groundfish. Crewmen might have moved to New Bedford to get sites on scallopers. Dealers might have marketed more scallops and yellowtail and less groundfish. However, fishermen and boat owners left fishing too slowly to keep incomes from falling. Virtually no one moved to more profitable fisheries. Several characteristics of the industry explain this lack of adjustment.[81]

In Boston some vessel owner-dealers sold their boats and got out of fish harvesting. However, many vessel owners had trouble finding buyers because a new owner would have to spend a large amount of money to convert a vessel for use outside the groundfishery. A few vessel owners and dealers remained willing to take risks to try to revive groundfish harvesting. In the early 1960s dealers pooled resources with others associated with the Boston groundfishery and drew on a federal subsidy to build a new boat for Boston. They wanted the groundfish industry to survive, and they wanted to remain part of it.[82]

While many vessel owner-dealers preferred to leave fish harvesting and concentrate activities in wholesaling and processing, the vessel owner-dealers had few incentives to handle fresh fish other than groundfish. The pressures to get out of wholesaling were not as great as to leave harvesting because wholesaling was more profitable. The dealers had long-term contracts for sale of haddock to retailers and other wholesalers which limited their freedom to decide to sell other species but also sheltered them from changes in the groundfish market for a time. They imported more of the less expensive frozen groundfish to reduce their costs.

Fishermen working on the Boston vessels would have had trouble leaving the industry. They had disadvantages in getting other jobs. By 1964, when many who could leave had done so, more than 60 percent of the fishermen on the large trawlers were over 54 years old. Nearly 70 percent were immigrants, although most came from Canada and therefore spoke English. More than 90 percent had not graduated from high school. Only a third had held a job outside fishing at some time in their careers.[83]

Fishermen in Boston also would have had trouble moving to New Bedford. They did not have the ethnic and friendship ties that would help them get sites. If Boston fishermen had found sites, these positions would have been on low-earning vessels even if the fishermen had worked on better boats in Boston.

In Gloucester the Portuguese and Sicilian families who owned boats wanted to stay in fishing. They came from long fishing traditions and were part of strong ethnic communities centered on fishing. They hung on to their boats through many years of very low earnings. In contrast, vessel owner-dealers in Gloucester sold their vessels or transferred them to Canada.

Gloucester fishermen also wanted to stay in the industry. If they had tried to find other jobs, however, they would have discovered that they were handicapped by lack of education and other work experience and by trouble speaking English. Some found jobs outside fishing through family connections but returned to fishing when incomes in the industry improved.

The Gloucester fishing families had always worked in the groundfishery. Most of them never would have considered leaving groundfishing for other fisheries, according to Susan Peterson, an anthropologist who has studied the fishing industry for many years. "They say they catch what they catch," she said. "They don't want to learn new species. Their identity is bound up in that kind of fish."

A family, not an individual, made the decision to convert a vessel in Gloucester. Even if some believed their family should invest in conversion, others might have thought the impediments and the risks too great and prevented the move.

The barriers to a change were indeed substantial. To convert to scalloping, for instance, a vessel owner had to have money, perhaps as much as 15 percent of the cost of a new boat. Most Gloucester vessels earned too little for owners to finance the conversions themselves. Banks would not lend to the industry, and the loans that the federal government offered would not be large enough to cover the cost of conversion.

Even if a family could overcome the problem of finding money to pay for a boat conversion, the risk of moving into scalloping or yellowtail would have looked very great. The location of scallop beds and concentrations of yellowtail flounder put Gloucester fishermen at a disadvantage. By the early 1960s Canadian vessels were working the scallop beds on the northeastern peak of Georges Bank and making harvesting more difficult for American fishermen. Vessels from New Bedford turned to newly discovered beds off the mid-Atlantic coast, closer to New Bedford than to Gloucester. Yellowtail flounder were most plentiful south of Cape Cod, again nearer New Bedford than Gloucester. The difference in distance meant that New Bedford fishermen could harvest both scallops and yellowtail flounder at lower cost and bring in a fresher, higher quality product. Gloucester fishermen may have wondered how much these differences would reduce their profits compared to those of New Bedford vessels.

Distance alone might not have kept the Gloucester industry out of scallops and yellowtail, but other factors compounded the risk. Gloucester fishermen and vessel owners knew very little about the location and behavior of those species and had no good sources of information. Norwegians and Portuguese who dominated the fisheries in New Bedford would not have shared their knowledge with Gloucester Sicilian fishermen. A Gloucester family that made the very expensive conversion to scalloping would face a long period of low earnings as the captain learned about the resource by trying to harvest it.

The large initial conversion expense and the long period of low income would only have been worthwhile if the profit difference between groundfishing and scalloping remained high. Gloucester boat owners might not have believed they could count on higher profits in scalloping for long, and they hoped that conditions in groundfishing would improve.

If Gloucester families had moved into other fisheries, they would have had trouble finding dealers to buy their catch, further increasing the riskiness of the change. The dealers in Gloucester did not buy and sell scallops and yellowtail in large volume. Vessel owners probably knew that New Bedford markets were hard to enter. Dealers might have refused to handle their catch, and fishermen who wanted to keep the Gloucester vessels out might have sabotaged them, according to Peterson. Nevertheless, a handful of offshore boats did move from Gloucester to New Bedford during the 1950s. Whether families sold the boats to New Bedford interests or moved themselves is not certain, but some Gloucester residents remember that a few Portuguese families did leave for New Bedford.[84]

Gloucester dealers might have diversified into handling larger volumes of yellowtail flounder and scallops, but they did not do so. A few small, family-operated concerns processed only fresh fish at very low profit levels. They could not take the risk of establishing marketing arrangements for other species because they could not be certain of a supply as long as no fishermen made the change. Vessel owners and processors might have agreed to move into other fisheries together, but the fishermen distrusted the dealers and would not have been willing to attempt such a venture.

Individual Gloucester fishermen, like Boston fishermen, would have had trouble moving to another port. If they could persuade a vessel owner to hire them in New Bedford, they would have to work at partial pay for several trips on the lowest earning boats. In addition, by going to New Bedford, they would have left their families and communities, extremely difficult for the first and second generation Sicilians who made up most of the Gloucester fleet by the 1960s.

As a result of these conditions, a sizable group of fishermen, vessel owners, and dealers stayed in groundfishing despite the hard times. They were committed to the fishery and to the community around it, and they faced many obstacles in moving out of the industry. Instead of leaving the fishery, many offered support to political efforts to get help for the industry which they hoped would enable them to stay in business.

END OF POSTWAR OPTIMISM

The postwar optimism about the prospects for the fishing industry faded quickly, well before the trends in the offshore groundfish industry in Boston, Gloucester, Portland, and Rockland had become obvious to many outside of fishing. In 1949 spokesmen from New England and the West Coast who represented fishermen, processors, vessel owners, canners, and seafood workers requested a hearing to call attention to their problems before the House Committee on Merchant Marine and Fisheries. The New England group was worried. John Del Torchio, president of the Gloucester Fisheries Association, an organization of fish processors, called the situation in the Gloucester industry "acute." He told the congressmen, "The fishing industry in Gloucester has been aware of the critical condition facing it for some time." Melvin Bernstein, an attorney representing Gloucester vessel owners, claimed that even the best boats "are right on the ragged edge. Any drop in price and they are done. . . . Something has to be done in the future . . . or the industry will not be there." The mayor of Gloucester warned that without federal action, "Gloucester is destined to become a city of decreasing population, of deserted wharves and a city reduced from prosperity to poverty and bearing the resemblance of a ghost mining town in the West." Gloucester's Congressman William Bates told his colleagues that only the war had saved Gloucester from severe unemployment and business stagnation and that the city could return to Depression conditions. Patrick McHugh, secretary-treasurer of the Atlantic Fishermen's Union, warned of the danger to fishermen "of again living through a period of low earnings, unemployment, and a substandard American way of life." New Bedford voices joined those from Gloucester and Boston to warn of danger to the flounder industry, and one spokesman from Maine pointed to threats to lobstermen's livelihood.[85]

The next few years confirmed the views of some groups that the industry had severe problems. As postwar trends became more apparent, however, New Bedford spokesmen and lobstering interests no longer argued that they were threatened. Rather, groups from Boston and Gloucester called attention to the groundfish industry, those who harvested and processed cod, haddock, redfish, hake, and, less often, pollock and cusk.[86] As leaders from Boston and Gloucester appealed to Congress and to the Tariff Commission for relief in the 1950s, they no longer warned of what could happen; they pointed to what was already happening to the groundfishery.

By the mid-1950s Tariff Commission conclusions and congressional statements reflected a new consensus.[87] In 1949 New England fishing groups were frightened that the industry faced collapse, but they found little sympathy. By the mid-1950s, however, the conventional view in Congress and the press held that the New England fishing industry faced severe problems, epitomized by the difficulties of Gloucester and Boston. Industry representatives campaigned for many kinds of aid. Congressmen, agency officials, and even White House staff agreed that the government should act to cure the industry's ills.

3

Efforts at Revitalization

*N*EW ENGLAND FISHERMEN, vessel owners, and processors in the groundfish industry explained their problems quite simply as they worsened in the late 1940s. Imports of groundfish from Canada, Newfoundland, and Iceland undersold the domestic product, they said, and took over the American market. The fishermen's union, processors' organizations, vessel owners' associations, and seafood workers' union agreed that "increased imports together with decreased exports . . . can only result in the elimination of excess production, either import or domestic. Highly favorably factors for imports must spell the elimination of some domestic production." Imports of groundfish fillets had increased from less than ten million pounds in 1938 to well over fifty million pounds in 1948, they pointed out. In other words, imports of groundfish fillets had increased nearly six times in these years, they said, while United States production of frozen fishery products increased only a little more than 60 percent.[1]

The imports could ruin business, the spokesmen explained, because the imported fish cost less than New England fish at every level of production. Fishing was less expensive in part because fishermen earned lower wages in the other north Atlantic countries. According to Patrick McHugh, secretary-treasurer of the Atlantic Fishermen's Union, "Our fundamental trouble in this industry is caused by the fact that we have to compete with cheap Canadian labor, Newfoundland, and Iceland labor." Not only did Canadian and Icelandic fishermen earn less, but they worked longer hours on the fishing banks, "many times 18 to 20 or 24 hours a day," according to McHugh. And unlike their American counterparts, foreign fishermen had almost no layover time, "just enough to discharge their trip when they are out again." In addition, Canadian fishermen performed tasks not included in American fishermen's jobs, according to Melvin Bernstein who represented the vessel owners of Gloucester:

43

"They paint the boats, they repair the boats." While no one had data to show the differences in earnings, most believed that a Canadian fisherman earned about half as much as an American fisherman.[2]

Foreign vessel owners could realize profits even if they received much lower prices at the dock than United States owners, New England fishery spokesmen said. Fishermen in other countries earned a share of the revenue from the catch, as did New England fishermen, but the lay arrangements differed. According to Bernstein, Canadian vessel owners took almost two-thirds of the gross stock, while in Gloucester, the boat owners earned about 40 percent of the net stock. Foreign vessel owners paid less for equipment and services: "The cost of materials, the cost of netting, the cost of fishing gear, the cost of repairs, particularly, the hourly rate of labor . . . is altogether different than it is here."

Another reason foreign owners' costs were lower was that governments subsidized the fishing industries, the New Englanders claimed. "They have government subsidy for their boats, they get government support, government loans, noninterest-bearing loans," Bernstein said. "In Iceland . . . it is the government buying the boats and giving it to these men. . . . In this country our men have had to build their own boats, mortgage them, finance them. They have high interest rate charges." Thomas Fulham, the president of a Boston vessel-owning corporation, enumerated government help to the fishing industries of Iceland and Canada, which included subsidies and no interest loans for vessel construction and loans for gear and engines. "The result of all these benefits . . . is that our foreign competitors have low-cost producing units enabling them to produce raw material [fish] at a very low base price."

Iceland and Canada financed some of these subsidies, the New England spokesmen claimed, with United States funds. As Congressman Thor Tollefson of Washington phrased the argument, "Our own Federal Government, in many instances, encouraged and assisted in the enlargement and building of a fishing fleet . . . of other nations."

Finally, a few New England spokesmen argued that Canadian vessel owners faced lower costs because they were closer to more prolific fishing grounds. McHugh said, "They may have to steam 100 and possibly as far as 200 miles, whereas we have to steam anywhere from 400 to 700, 800 and 900 miles to reach the same grounds, which means that we must put in 2 to 3 days steaming each trip which means less time . . . when we are producing." The grounds closer to New England had become less productive, McHugh argued. "A few years ago we got for a trip an average of

125,000 to 150,000 pounds," he said. "For the last year or two, it has been around 70,000, 80,000 or 100,000 pounds."

These cost differences had important implications for the operations of the Gloucester boats. Large modern boats in Gloucester, Bernstein said, had earnings of about 6.8 percent of gross stock, an average of about a quarter cent per pound of redfish, when the ex-vessel price of redfish was 4.25 cents per pound. Other boats lost money at that price. If the dealers "cannot pay our boats, our top boats 4¼ cents for redfish, the margin of profit is gone. If all they can pay those boats to compete with Canadian fish is 3.75 cents, almost 4 cents a pound, even these best boats in Gloucester are going bankrupt," Bernstein claimed. For medium-sized draggers, in contrast, the "margin of profit" was smaller. Three out of seven were losing money, and the other four had earnings of about 4 percent of the gross stock. If the redfish price fell from 4.5 cents to 4.1 cents per pound, they would have no profits; below 4.1 cents they would not cover costs.

On the other hand, dealers could not afford such high ex-vessel prices when Canadian dealers paid only 1.5 cents per pound, the amount Bernstein quoted for redfish in Nova Scotia. Canadian dealers started with lower costs of production in paying less for fish, and other factors widened the difference between New England and foreign costs, the New Englanders said. Canadian seafood workers earned less than American workers. Edward Newton, sales manager of the Point Judith Fishermen's Cooperative Association, showed that fish cutters who filleted fresh fish in the United States earned $1.30 per hour compared to $.55 per hour in Canada and $.30 per hour in Iceland. The differentials were similar for skinners, packers, and handlers. Patrick McHugh reported that women in Newfoundland fish processing plants earned $.35 per hour and worked fifteen hours per day. The men made $.60 per hour and worked as long as the employer required. "There isn't any question but those people are being exploited," McHugh said, and by continuing to import fish from those countries, "all we were doing and still doing is making a few fish companies in Newfoundland and Canada rich."

Costs were also lower for Canadian processors because the government had subsidized the building of processing plants and freezers and even contributed to transporting fish, reported John Del Torchio, the president of the Gloucester Fisheries Association. Thomas Fulham listed similar Icelandic and Canadian aid to fish canneries and freezers.

Fulham summarized the influence of all these factors. In 1945 the ex-vessel price of cod had been 3.5 cents per pound in Canada and 6 cents in the United States, Fulham explained. Filleting and skinning left 40 percent of the weight of the fish which meant that the price per pound rose to 8.75 cents in Canada, 15 cents in the United States. Processing labor costs amounted to 4 cents per pound in Canada, 8 cents in the United States. Therefore, the total costs to the Canadian processor were 12.75 cents per pound, but the American processor faced costs of 23 cents per pound.

The result of differences in costs for American and foreign dealers, Del Torchio said, was that Gloucester dealers had to sell fillets for 13 cents that had cost them 20 cents to process. "I think every industry in Gloucester would be very pleased to make as low as a quarter of a cent a pound on every pound of fish handled in Gloucester. . . . They [the Canadians and Icelanders] are just thinking in terms of huge profit. . . . If we go down to 20 cents, they can easily go down to 19 and still make a very fine profit." With exactly the same kind of fish, he said, "They are always just under us."

EFFORTS TO SOLVE THE PROBLEM: THE CAMPAIGN FOR TARIFF RELIEF

Given these explanations of the causes of their difficulties, fishermen, boat owners, and dealers believed their problems would be solved by making imports unavailable or much more expensive. Their views were similar to those of many other businessmen who pushed for higher tariffs on goods competing with their own products. Tariff protection was the most common form of government aid to industry before the 1950s, although, beginning with the Trade Agreements Act of 1934, the Roosevelt and Truman administrations had worked to ease trade restrictions.

Trade agreements effective in 1939 set the duty on groundfish fillets at 1.875 cents per pound on a quota of fifteen million pounds or 15 percent of average annual United States consumption in the three preceding years, whichever was greater. For imports over the quota the agreements set the duty at 2.5 cents per pound. Those tariff levels were insignificant to importers, the fishing industry claimed. When the duties were established, a large share of fish came into the country whole or "in the round," yet by the end of World War II almost all groundfish imports were fillets. Without the head, tail, and bones, the fillet made up only about 40 percent of the weight of the round fish and had much higher value per pound. Furthermore, the price of fillets at the Canadian border nearly tripled between 1939 and 1948. As a result, the tariff on fish above the quota fell from about 33 percent of the price of the fish entering the country from Canada to a little more than 12 percent. The groundfish industry argued that at this low level the tariffs no longer offered protection because foreign and domestic production costs were so different.[3]

Events of the decades before had raised the industry's fears about the effects of too little tariff protection. Many attributed the loss of the Gloucester salt and smoked fish business to inadequate tariffs. In addition, in 1939, General Seafoods, the largest filleting firm in New England, arranged to establish a plant in Newfoundland and ship fillets to the United States duty free. Congress then passed legislation to redefine what constituted an "American fishery" to make such ventures subject to tariffs. Only this action made considerable expansion in Canada unprofitable for the larger New England processors before World War II.[4]

The groundfish industry pressed hard for quotas and for higher tariffs through the late 1940s and early 1950s. A quota would restrict imports of groundfish to the level of a few years before or would at least prevent imports from taking a larger share of the domestic market.

At first the industry's arguments drew little sympathy from the government. For example, in the late 1940s and early 1950s industry representatives argued before the Committee for Reciprocity Information of the State Department that no concessions should be granted on fish products in trade agreements and that more controls on fish imports were needed. The General Agreement on Tariffs and Trade effective in 1948 did not lower tariffs on groundfish, but the United States promised not to raise the duty on fish imported above the quota for the duration of the agreement. In 1949 the House of Representatives responded to pressure from New England interests by asking the State Department to report on the effects of imports on the domestic fishing industry, but the report concluded that the industry did not suffer from the imports. Also in 1949, industry spokesmen argued before the Senate Finance Committee that reciprocal trade agreements legislation should allow the Tariff Commission to hear appeals for relief from injury due to imports. Fishing spokesmen joined lobbyists from other industries in 1951 in pushing for stronger "escape clause" and "peril point" provisions in trade agreements legislation to allow appeals for tariff adjustment and to place restrictions on lowering tariffs if imports harmed domestic industries.[5]

Later in 1951 the Tariff Commission granted the groundfish industry a hearing under the escape clause provisions of the Trade Agreements Extension Act of 1951. The President had authority to make many tariff concessions without consulting Congress or justifying his action. However, the 1951 legislation declared that no tariff concessions should allow imports to injure a domestic industry. Under the escape clause the Tariff

Commission could investigate whether imports harmed or threatened an industry at the request of the industry, Congress, or the President. If the Tariff Commission concluded that imports hurt the domestic industry, they could recommend that the President restrict imports. The President had to explain his decision to Congress if he rejected the Tariff Commission's recommendations.[6]

After studying conditions in the groundfish industry, the Tariff Commission voted three to two not to recommend changes in tariffs. The commissioners who opposed the request for relief argued that the industry's record showed adequate profits, rising wages, and increasing production following the war. The industry had not yet suffered from imports, and the evidence did not suggest that it would in the future, they stated. The two commissioners who supported the New England industry's request believed that the most recent trends showed considerable decline in fortunes and placed the fishing and filleting industry in "an extremely precarious position." Imports threatened the "complete destruction" of the industry, they said.[7]

The New England industry went back to the Tariff Commission for another hearing. In 1954, the Commission ruled in their favor and recommended a limit on groundfish imports of 37 percent of average aggregate consumption for the five years before. They also recommended higher tariffs on that quota.[8]

However, President Eisenhower rejected the Commission's recommendations. In his letter of explanation he stated that after the Commission prepared its report, a new product, fish sticks, was introduced which could help the fishing industry. "I am firmly convinced that it would be a disservice to the long-run interests of the entire groundfish industry to limit the imports of groundfish fillets in these circumstances," the President said. "Such action would reduce raw material supplies of processors of fish sticks. It would create an artificial scarcity and tend to increase price. At the same time it would hamper and limit the development of the market for the product [fish sticks] and jeopardize present prospects for the increase in per capita consumption of fish, which is the key to a real solution of the industry's problem."[9]

President Eisenhower's assessment reflected the hopes of the companies moving into fish stick production. The Birds Eye Division of General Foods had announced the new product in October 1953. Herbert N. Stevens, the Birds Eye product manager, called the development of fish sticks the most outstanding in the fishing industry since the introduction of quick freezing in the 1930s. "We believe this important step in the fishing industry might point the way as a means to help increase the per capita consumption of fish in this country, and thus create an important incentive to the American fishing industry," Stevens said. Fish sticks eliminated problems such as unpleasant odor which consumers associated with handling and cooking fresh fish, Stevens added. Breaded and pre-fried, fish sticks offered uniform quality and the convenience of little or no preparation.[10]

Assessments of the potential popularity of fish sticks proved correct. Fish stick production rose from 7.5 million pounds in 1953 to 63 million pounds in 1955. Almost all fish sticks were processed in New England. Predictions about the effect of fish sticks on per capita consumption were wrong, however. The per capita consumption of fresh and frozen fish, which included fish sticks and groundfish fillets, declined from 6.4 pounds per capita in 1953 to 5.9 pounds in 1955. Because fish stick consumption increased, the per capita consumption of other fresh and frozen products decreased more than the net decline indicated.[11]

The evaluation of the impact that the growth of fish sticks would have on the problems of the fishing industry was also off the mark. Even by 1954 many in the industry were certain that the great popularity of fish sticks would revitalize only some parts of the groundfish industry. The beneficiaries were the most resourceful processing firms, usually the largest, most prosperous ones that still had the capital to invest in new plants and equipment for fish stick production.

Some of these firms, for example, General Seafoods, Gorton-Pew, and Booth Fisheries, had owned fishing vessels in addition to processing facilities before and during World War II. Even before the introduction of fish sticks, however, the vessel operations had become unprofitable enough that the firms had sold some boats and transferred others to Canada where the boats landed fish for the companies' Canadian plants. These companies had turned to imports to supply the raw material they used for processing. Even so, Gorton-Pew Fisheries had announced losses of $237,000 in 1952. In 1954 the large companies still used some fish from their own New England boats, but the development of fish sticks made essential the availability of less expensive, imported frozen "blocks." These blocks were large, frozen slabs of fish pieces and fillets which could be fed into machines for cutting into fish sticks. Local boats could not supply fish at competitive prices, and, stated Frederick Bundy of Gorton-Pew Fishery of Gloucester, they did not supply very much haddock and cod, principal ingredients for fish sticks. Gorton-Pew had three plants in Canada by 1956 that processed fresh fish into frozen blocks for shipment to Gloucester fish stick plants.[12]

Differences in processing costs between Canada and the United States made impossible either the use of Gloucester and Boston fillets in fish sticks or the production of blocks in Gloucester. A Boston fresh fish processor explained that processing fillets and pieces into blocks for fish sticks was a "very exacting business" because fillets had to be completely free of bones and skin and carefully packed in cartons to prevent holes in the finished block. If a dealer paid the vessel owner 5 cents per pound for cod or haddock, lower than the average Boston ex-vessel prices in the mid-1950s, then the cost of the fillets, only 30 percent of the weight of the fish when prepared for fish blocks, would be 16.67 cents per pound. The cost of the cartons and freezing would add 2.5 cents; and labor costs would contribute 6 cents. Even without overhead or profit, the cost of processing fish blocks would total more than 25 cents; but imported fish blocks cost between 20 and 23.5 cents per pound. "Now I ask you what possible chance is there for the fisherman or processor to share in this new field?" questioned the Boston processor. Indeed, Birds Eye had tried to process fish into frozen blocks in Boston but had found it financially impractical.[13] The dilemma was clear. Higher tariffs on imported fish could disrupt the fish stick business because fewer consumers might buy fish sticks at higher prices. But to hope to take advantage of the fish stick boom, fishermen, boat owners, and smaller fresh fish processors had to have higher tariffs on those raw materials.

No sophisticated analyses of fish stick market prospects contributed to the President's decision not to limit imports, but pressures from fish stick processors did. During the hearings before the Tariff Commission in mid-1953 fishermen, boat owners, and processors had testified in favor of higher tariffs on groundfish fillets. By the time the Commission completed its investigation and sent its recommendations to the President, however, the growth of the fish stick market had encouraged the firms moving into fish stick production to qualify their support of higher tariffs. Some of them sent a telegram to President Eisenhower the day before he was to make his decision in order to "appeal to you to rule on the problem in such a way as to permit fish blocks to be imported outside any quota."[14]

The clout of the fish stick producers became more evident during 1954 in the success of their own campaign for tariff protection despite the administration's policy of lowering tariffs. When a regional customs official placed fish sticks in the same category as "preserved" fish, covered by a low, flat-rate tariff, rather than "processed" fish, protected by a higher ad valorem fee, the fish stick industry appealed through Senator Leverett Saltonstall of Massachusetts to reverse the decision. The Bureau of Customs ruled, however, that the duty would remain low. Fish stick spokesmen pressed for legislation to raise the duty. Senator Saltonstall proposed an amendment to a tariff bill to place an ad valorem tariff of 20 percent on uncooked fish sticks and similar products "if breaded, coated with batter, or similarly prepared" and an ad valorem tariff of 30 percent on cooked fish sticks. Under existing regulations, Congressman William Bates told the House, the tariff on fish sticks was lower than the tariff on raw fish. The domestic fish stick industry made every attempt to help itself, he said, but it needed protection from imports, and the bill would ease some of the strain from foreign production.[15] Congress approved the amendment. The fresh groundfish industry had pressured publicly for years for higher tariffs without success despite its financial problems, yet the fish stick interests obtained very high tariffs on fish stick imports without ever appearing in a public hearing, testifying before a congressional committee, or demonstrating that the industry suffered harm.

President Eisenhower's statement reflected the lobbying of fish stick processors, but his decision on groundfish tariffs in 1954 undoubtedly had more to do with traditions that favored reduction of tariffs and with his administration's policy of free trade. As Solomon Sandler, spokesman for the Gloucester Vessel Service Association, pointed out, the processors' telegram "was all that was needed by the President to have something to hang his hat on so that he could reject the Tariff Commission's recommendation" for increased tariff protection.[16]

Easing of tariff barriers had begun with the passage of the Trade Agreements Act of 1934. Congress authorized the President to lower tariffs by as much as 50 percent of the 1934 levels in reciprocal trade negotiations. After World War II Congress gave the President permission to reduce the tariffs even more, to half the 1945 levels. The United States joined the General Agreement on Tariffs and Trade (GATT) to lower tariffs in joint negotiations with a large number of countries. Although in the late 1940s and early 1950s Congress restricted the President's authority through the escape clause and peril point provisions, the Eisenhower administration continued to reduce tariffs. Freer trade was vital, President Eisenhower stated repeatedly, in strengthening the free world against communism.[17] Higher tariffs on groundfish, almost all imported from Canada and Iceland, were inconsistent with his policy.

In addition, the countries exporting groundfish protested—and the administration responded. After the groundfish industry appealed to the Tariff Commission for the second time, the Canadian government warned the United States in a note to the State Department that any increase in import restrictions on groundfish fillets would have "serious implications." Canada's development of fisheries depended on the United States market. The State Department reassured the Canadian government that a recommendation from the Tariff Commission need not be accepted by the President.[18]

The importance of foreign policy concerns became more explicit when the New England groundfish industry appealed to the Tariff Commission a third time. In late 1956 the Commission ruled unanimously that imports caused serious injury to the domestic industry and recommended higher tariffs. Again the recommendation went to President Eisenhower. By this time no one suggested that the new fish stick production would aid the fishing and filleting sector, but the President rejected the recommendation. In his explanation, he wrote that he had to consider "all other pertinent factors bearing on the security and well-being of the nation." The administration sought to encourage the expansion of trade among free nations, he said. He was especially reluctant to impose trade barriers because "the other nations concerned are not only our close friends, but their economic strength is of strategic importance to us in the continuing struggle against the menace of world communism." Instead, the industry should seek other ways to improve its competitive position, without the imposition of trade restrictions which "might discourage needed improvements."[19]

On one hand, the President's position was not surprising. Between 1948 and 1955, there were 59 applications for relief under the escape clause. In 15 cases the Tariff Commission recommended stiffer import restrictions. The President approved the recommendations only five times. On the other hand, the decision on groundfish attracted wide attention because the reasons for rejecting the Tariff Commission's recommendations were unusual and because the administration could use the same argument to deny tariff relief to almost any other industry. In a similar case in 1952 President Truman had rejected the Tariff Commission's recommendation to raise garlic duties. He had argued that Italy, the principal producer, needed to earn more dollars and that United States tariffs would be harmful to "our mutual security." The groundfish case was the first, however, in which the President responded to a unanimous ruling of the Tariff Commission by taking the position that the economic health of allies had higher priority than the survival of a domestic industry. In the earlier decisions on groundfish industry tariffs the question had been whether or not imports were hurting the domestic industry. Now the President did acknowledge very serious injury, but no tariffs would be altered.[20]

More international considerations were involved in the groundfish decision than the President's statement admitted, however, which meant the same decision was less likely for other industries. Iceland had demanded that the United States close its military base in Iceland, but four days before the President announced his decision on tariffs, Iceland cancelled its request for the withdrawal of United States troops. While those outside the efforts to get changes in tariffs speculated about whether this action had anything to do with the President's decision on groundfish tariffs, fishing industry representatives knew it did. James Ackert, a leader in the Atlantic Fishermen's Union, said, "We were told point blank in the White House that the fishing industry is not worth a NATO base."[21]

In the next ten years the industry occasionally tried again to get tariff relief. In 1961 Gloucester interests appealed directly to President Kennedy for higher tariffs. In 1963 the Gloucester Fisheries Commission, alarmed at the possibility of greater imports of fresh irradiated fish, passed a resolution calling for quotas on fresh groundfish. Irradiation promised to extend the shelf life of fresh fish so that Canadian fresh fish could compete with the United States product despite the time in trucking the fish from Canada. In 1964 the New England Association for the Preservation of the Groundfish Industry, which represented over 75 percent of the processors, dealers, and boat owners in New England, argued before the Tariff Commission against reduction in tariffs on groundfish. Groundfish were excluded from GATT negotiations, and tariffs remained the same.

In 1967 Congressman William Bates introduced a bill at the request of the Gloucester Fisheries Commission to increase tariffs on fresh irradiated fish. "The New England fisheries lost the frozen fish industry to imports," said Salvatore Favazza, the executive secretary of the Gloucester Fisheries Commission, "but hopes by these means to hold on to the major part of the fresh fish industry." Also in 1967, most of the Massachusetts congressmen from coastal communities introduced legislation to increase tariffs on all groundfish in response to pressures from those who were not satisfied to concentrate on fresh fish. Neither measure passed Congress.[22]

Although the New England fishing industry continued to pay attention to tariffs, no efforts after 1956 equaled the three appeals to the Tariff Commission either in single-mindedness or in hopefulness. Much of the effort after 1956, even in calling for higher tariffs, aimed merely at keeping the problems of the fisheries in front of Congress and the Tariff Commission so that the United States would not make still more concessions on groundfish. The efforts were directed also at making sure that foreign countries obeyed the trade regulations that kept products from coming in at even lower prices.[23]

OTHER ATTEMPTS TO SOLVE THE PROBLEMS

In the years that followed, from the mid-1950s through the late 1960s, fishermen, boat owners, and processors turned their energy to improving their fortunes without tariff relief. They directed most of their appeals to the federal government, but they also explored what they could do for themselves and what help they could get from state and local governments.

For example, vessel owners in Gloucester cooperated for a few years to find ways to reduce insurance costs. Boston dealers organized a short-lived cooperative during the late 1950s to work on marketing and advertising. At other times Boston dealers and vessel owners tried to work together on marketing, but the efforts "were always ad hoc and never lasted long," according to Thomas Fulham, one of the dealers and vessel owners who participated.[24]

These were insignificant efforts. During the early postwar troubles, fishermen, boat owners, and dealers could have chosen many ways to forestall the hard times, especially if they had worked together with willingness to compromise. Donald J. White, an economist who studied the New England fisheries for several years, pointed out ways that groups in the industry might begin to build a foundation for cooperation. Given such cooperation and the leadership of the fishermen's union, he said, "coordinated, systematic research, market development, and improved industrial practices" might provide answers to the fishery's problems. Francis Sargent, director of the state fisheries office in Massachusetts during the 1950s, agreed with White. He urged the industry to resolve their disputes and to find ways to take advantage of new technology.[25]

Industry groups did not settle their differences enough to work closely on problems; perhaps it was unreasonable to hope that they could do so. In the opinion of many involved, the 1946 fishermen's strike in Boston demonstrated the intransigence of the union, which would not compromise, they believed, even to keep boat owners in Boston from going out of business. Even within groups with shared interests—fishermen, vessel owners, or dealers—cooperation was difficult. Individuals feared that others in the group might gain more from joint efforts than they would themselves. Because compromise seemed so impossible, industry leaders were convinced from the start that they could do little to help themselves.[26]

By the mid-1950s the industry had missed the best opportunity to act. Most processors, boat owners, and fishermen no longer had the financial resources for joint efforts to help the industry or for changes in their own plants or boats which might increase profits. The processors with the capital and the foresight turned to fish stick production.

As their troubles developed, the groundfish industry appealed to state and local governments for help. The states responded in several ways. All continued to sponsor research on fishery resources and cooperated through the Atlantic States Marine Fisheries Commission to plan research, to coordinate fishery regulations, and to protect the states' authority over fisheries from federal government incursions. In the early 1950s, Massachusetts Governor Paul Dever established a fisheries promotion committee which recommended ways to aid the industry. In 1954, also in Massachusetts, Governor Christian Herter set up a commission to promote the interests of the fishing industry and to study its problems. The commission included representatives from the state government and all parts of the offshore industry and met for several years. In 1960 Governor Foster Furcolo of Massachusetts established the Marine Fisheries Advisory Commission to help formulate a fisheries policy for the state, to make recommendations for improving state programs, and to consider proposals for state action related to marine fisheries. Later in the 1960s Massachusetts Governor John Volpe appointed yet another group to study the fishing industry's problems.[27]

These and other efforts touched the offshore groundfish industry very little. Most state actions instead affected the inshore industry because the state had jurisdiction over fishing activity and resources within three miles of shore. The Marine Fisheries Advisory Commission, for example, considered inshore fisheries problems almost exclusively. State officials devoted considerable time to resolving gear conflicts in state waters between draggermen and fishermen with fixed gear. The states sponsored research and debated resource management measures for inshore species, principally shellfish and lobsters.

The few state efforts which aimed specifically at helping the offshore industry had little effect. The governors' commissions that were charged with considering the problems of the offshore fisheries produced reports and recommended action, but very little happened as a result. In 1968 Governor Volpe announced that the state would purchase only domestically caught and processed fish. State fishery officials estimated in the 1970s that the state did not buy much fish and concluded that the effort did not last long.[28]

The state commissions did offer a setting for representatives of the fishing industry to meet to discuss common problems and goals and to plan efforts to get federal action. One Massachusetts commission was a source of pressure for the first postwar legislation to aid the fishing industry in 1954. Francis Sargent used the commission meetings to get industry opinion about the position he should take on state legislation and in dealings with federal and state fishery officials. The commissions did not usually have this effect, however, because industry groups had too many differences among themselves, in the opinion of Thomas Fulham, who served on several governors' commissions. Gloucester draggermen fishing for redfish and whiting had trouble working with the owners of the big Boston trawlers that fished for cod and haddock. The fishermen's union, vessel owners, and dealers could not cooperate in this arena either.

All in all, the New England states made few efforts to help the offshore fishing industry. Their governments were in no position to do much, recalled Sargent. The states' departments with responsibility for fisheries had few staff and very small budgets that were committed to fulfilling the states' traditional role in fisheries, research on coastal species and regulation of the use of some coastal and estuarine resources. In addition, state legislatures were unlikely to appropriate the sums of money which the departments might require for significant programs. "The industry was viewed as dying," Sargent said. "Most of the legislators [in Massachusetts] did not care much about the industry." In any case, a move to set up substantial programs to revive any industry would have been virtually unprecedented for the states.

Local government actions to help the offshore groundfish industry were even more limited than state efforts. Gloucester made the most noteworthy attempt. The Gloucester City Council established the Gloucester Fisheries Commission, according to Mayor Beatrice Corliss, "to follow continually the progress of the fishing industry and to recommend such action as becomes necessary to further the prosperity of the fishing industry and, thereby, Gloucester as a whole."[29] The Commission became more than that due to the leadership of executive secretary Salvatore Favazza during the 1960s. Favazza became, in effect, a paid, full-time leader for political efforts, vital when other spokesmen could do political work only as extracurricular activity. The Gloucester Fisheries Commission helped organize the fishing industry in Gloucester to press for federal legislation. The Commission initiated legislation through Congressman William Bates, lobbied on fishery issues, provided information on the industry, and generally led Gloucester efforts to solve fishery problems, largely those of the offshore groundfish industry.

Even as state and local governments set up commissions and planned research, fishing industry leaders were convinced that state and local efforts could offer them no more than their own efforts. They believed that state officials saw the offshore groundfish industry as the responsibility of the federal government because state jurisdiction extended only three miles from the coast. The fishing industry also believed that their problems were the domain of the federal government although national fishery jurisdiction also extended only three miles. Although in 1967 Congress increased it to twelve miles, this was still not far enough to include the fishing areas of the offshore boats. Virtually none of the industry's ideas for government aid depended on fishery jurisdiction at this time. Fishery leaders also perceived that state government officials did not care what happened to the offshore industry, despite the work of state fisheries directors on the industry's behalf. "The state government had no money and no interest," said Thomas Fulham.

With no hope of success in industry-sponsored efforts to revive the fisheries or of significant aid from state and local governments, fishing industry leaders saw the federal government as the best source of help. "It was a matter of grabbing anything that floats by in order to survive," said Thomas Fulham. Congress seemed receptive to the pleas of industry. Government had provided aid to industry during the Depression, and indeed, the Gloucester fishing industry had applied for farm credit and for loans from the Reconstruction Finance Corporation. As their troubles deepened after the war, fishing leaders noted the extensive federal aid for farmers. "Agriculture rightly has had the support of the Federal Government," believed Patrick McHugh, secretary-treasurer of the Atlantic Fishermen's Union, but "the fisheries has similar needs." During the 1950s Congress was considering the problems of other troubled industries and debating ways to assist them. These included textiles, shoes, mining, farming, and plywood manufacturing.[30]

By the mid-1950s the fishing industry's own experience with the federal government suggested they might succeed in getting help from Congress and the administration. During years of appealing to Congress and to government agencies for stiffer trade restrictions, industry spokesmen had made contacts with congressmen and agency officials and learned a good deal about lobbying and testifying that could be useful in looking for other types of federal aid.

Furthermore, as fishing spokesmen pointed out, President Eisenhower himself in 1956 had suggested that the industry look for other ways to obtain help from the federal government when he rejected recommendations for higher tariffs. Congressmen whose districts were affected by the decision favored that approach, and they asked fishing industry leaders what Congress could do for them.

The industry's experience in the tariff appeals strengthened their belief that they ought to get government aid. The tariff rulings had proved imports hurt the groundfish industry. "Why should one industry bear the burden of providing for the nation's security?" industry spokesmen asked. The rest of the country, they argued, should shoulder some of the load through tax-supported programs to help the groundfishery.

The federal government engaged in other activities, less publicized than the tariff decisions, that added further to the fishing industry's troubles. The industry believed the government should compensate the fisheries for that harm. As part of war reconstruction programs, for example, the United States government provided funds to other nations to rebuild their fisheries. Some of those industries then exported fish to the United States, which hurt New England fishermen, boat owners, and processors. In another example, the Jones Act and court decisions made fishermen eligible for large payments from boat owners in case of injury or death. Boat owners argued that the settlements greatly increased insurance costs. A 1792 law to help the boatbuilding industry prohibited the use of foreign-built vessels in the fisheries, but vessels constructed in the United States cost about twice as much as boats built in other countries.

The fishing industry believed that these were all reasons that government should help because the same reasons legitimized government intervention on behalf of other troubled industries during the 1950s. Spokesmen for the textile industry, for example, explained that farm programs made their raw materials—wool, flax, and cotton—far more expensive. Therefore, they argued, the federal government should provide programs or raise tariffs to help the textile industry overcome this disadvantage.

Finally, fishing industry spokesmen knew that the governments of other countries, including Canada and Iceland, were already helping their fisheries. If non-socialist nations were providing their industries with subsidies and loans, then perhaps the United States would do so.

The groundfish industry could consider several kinds of federal assistance. They could push for price supports that would guarantee a price regardless of levels of production and demand. The industry could campaign for programs to expand the market for fish. If demand were greater, price and revenue would rise. Because income was a share of the revenue from the catch, New England producers might be better off unless imports increased enough to hold prices at the same level, below the point where many boats could remain in business. Federal or state government purchases might increase the demand for New England fish, however, without expanding the market for fish from other countries.

The fishing industry could also seek programs to lower the costs of fishing so that the amount subtracted from gross stock would be smaller and the incomes of fishermen and boat owners would be higher even if price and total revenue remained the same. These programs could aim to lower specific costs of harvesting or to increase the efficiency of boat operators. Programs could also attempt to lower the costs of production for processors.

The industry tried first to get price supports for fish. As early as 1947 Patrick McHugh stated the union's position that the farm price support system should extend to fish. In 1948 Gloucester's mayor wrote to Congressman Bates, "In view of the difficulty [vessel owners and fishermen] are having in making their expenses and fish being a food product, they are wondering whether or not there is any possibility of price laws being passed covering fish products, particularly redfish." Congressman John Kennedy introduced a bill in 1950 to set up a $3 million price support program for the fisheries. In 1954, shortly after President Eisenhower rejected the tariff recommendations, fishery leaders sought to persuade congressmen to add a rider to a farm bill to support the price of fish. Fishing spokesmen suggested that the Commodity Credit Corporation provide loans and make purchases to raise prices to 90 percent of the 1942 average. "The Federal Government has in similar and related instances touching on both the production of (1) food and other agricultural commodities, and (2) other natural resources commodities (copper, lead and zinc) provided price supports through Federal agencies," argued Patrick McHugh. All these efforts failed to get fishery price supports.[31]

The groundfish industry's timing was wrong for seeking price supports. Through the early 1950s congressmen faced growing public dismay over the expense of the farm program and the problems of storage and disposal of the agricultural surplus. New England congressmen told industry spokesmen that, as a result, the fisheries would never get congressional backing for price supports and therefore they should come back with proposals for other ways the government could help.[32]

After 1954 the industry expressed most concern about their costs and paid less attention to the market for their product. Soon after the 1956 tariff decision, the New England Committee for Aid to the Groundfish Industry outlined a four-point program. They asked for aid to reduce the cost of vessel insurance; long-term loans to dealers and processors for modernization, expansion, and working capital; aid to equalize the cost of vessel construction here and overseas; and funds to eliminate the differential between the cost of domestic fillet production and the price of imports.[33] With a few changes, this remained their agenda.

When bills included provisions for loans or subsidies to processors, many processors outside the fresh groundfish sector opposed the legislation. The National Fisheries Institute, the processors' lobby, stated that its members were "violently opposed to Government controls and to Government interference of any kind," which they feared would result from a bill supported by the groundfish industry to pay processing plants up to a third of a cent per pound of fish handled. "Soft loans," they said, could also be a "Pandora's box" beginning extensive federal government involvement. C. L. Stinson of Stinson Canning Company, one of the largest sardine packers in Maine, opposed payments to firms because too many plants already processed herring. The tuna canners considered it "unthinkable" that the federal government would aid their competitors.[34] Loans and subsidies to boat owners, on the other hand, met almost no opposition from the industry.

FEDERAL PROGRAMS TO HELP THE FISHING INDUSTRY

The industry's assessment of the federal government as the most promising source of help proved correct. All the significant aid programs for the offshore groundfish industry came from the federal government. Starting in 1954 and continuing through the late 1960s Congress enacted a large number of laws, and agencies directed programs to address fisheries problems.

The first programs had little direct effect on the lives of the fisherman, the boat owner, or the processor. The early laws provided funds for research and reorganized the administration of fishery affairs. In 1956 legislation offered loans to vessel owners that involved more direct contact between government and business. Enormous government subsidies later placed significant constraints on those who received them. Under a 1960 program of vessel construction subsidies, government officials examined boat owners' finances; and boat operators who applied for funds had to follow regulations about vessel construction, fishing activity, and crew hiring practices that interfered with their accustomed autonomy.

Likewise, although early programs cost the government almost nothing, successive programs increased in cost. An early law transferred funds from the Department of Agriculture. A later one provided a loan fund. Finally, subsidies during the 1960s amounted to millions of dollars per year, a large expense for fisheries aid although small compared to other federal government activities.

The programs that began in 1954 covered a range of approaches. Some aimed to increase the demand for fish; most were intended to decrease the cost of harvesting.

Increasing the Demand for Fishery Products

Industry concern about inadequate demand for fishery products contributed to passage of the 1954 Saltonstall-Kennedy Act to "encourage the distribution of domestic fishery products." The legislation diverted from the Secretary of Agriculture to the Secretary of the Interior a percent of the revenues from duties on fishery products. The funds were to be used to promote distribution of domestic fish products through education and research, to develop markets for domestic products, and to conduct other fisheries research.[35] Most efforts to increase the demand for fish received funding under this legislation.

Under Saltonstall-Kennedy, the Bureau of Commercial Fisheries established voluntary guidelines for sanitation and for product inspection which would improve the quality of fish landed by New England boats. The industry and the Bureau believed that consumers' experience with deteriorated fish kept demand low; if quality were improved and were more uniform, people would buy fresh fish more often. Starting in 1957 Bureau staff widely publicized the new guidelines, visited processing plants, and went to sea on fishing boats to show processors and fishermen how they could improve their methods of handling fish.[36]

Some fisheries agency officials believed that fish handling improved as fishermen and processors learned more about its effects on quality. While some practices may have changed as a result of the program, visits to Boston and Gloucester fish piers as late as 1978 showed that many of the Bureau's recommendations were not in practice. The suggestions had little effect on the behavior of most fishermen and processors, according to Jacob Dykstra, president of the Point Judith Fishermen's Cooperative Association; only minimal requirements enforced by the Food and Drug Administration and state inspectors in shore plants influenced operations.

The failure of such efforts to change behavior showed most clearly when in 1967 congressmen introduced bills to increase inspection and grading of fish to protect consumers from food poisoning. They argued that improvement in quality would also make fish more attractive to consumers and would, therefore, help the fishing industry. According to Dykstra, the legislation would not provide substantial consumer benefit or increase the movement of domestic products. Lobbyists from most other fishery groups joined him in opposing the bills.[37] The opposition to required standards suggested that fishermen and dealers rarely observed the voluntary ones.

Efforts to increase demand took other directions. Research, most of it under Saltonstall-Kennedy, sought to learn more about the markets for fish. For example, surveys reported on fish preferences and consumption patterns in different areas of the country by demographic groups. These studies did not include recommendations for ways to increase demand, but the industry could use the reports to decide on the best strategies for advertising.[38]

Other efforts were more direct. For example, the Bureau of Commercial Fisheries contracted for a study of problems in the marketing of New England fishery products, the results of which were turned over for action to the New England Committee for Aid to the Groundfish Industry. The Bureau of Commercial Fisheries also ran market development programs and offered information to food specialists and consumers about new types of fish and ways to prepare fish.[39]

The fishing industry tried to persuade the federal government to purchase more domestic fish. After President Eisenhower rejected the Tariff Commission recommendations in 1956, the Veterans Administration announced that it would use more frozen fish fillets in hospitals. Some Saltonstall-Kennedy funds were earmarked for the purchase of fish for school lunch programs.[40]

The Defense Department has no records of its purchases of fish during the 1950s. However, Thomas Fulham remembered that the Veterans Administration did buy more fish. By the mid-1960s, all Defense Department purchases of cod, haddock, ocean perch, and whiting fillets were small, close to $2.8 million for about 6 million pounds of groundfish. If all the fillets had come from New England fishermen, the sales would have amounted to only about one percent of the landings of those species in 1966. The contribution to demand for New England fish was even smaller, however, because a large proportion of the fillets had undoubtedly been originally imported. Defense Department purchases of cod and haddock portions, processed by fish stick companies from imported fish, amounted to almost $1.6 million for 3.2 million pounds.[41]

The Fish and Wildlife Service worked with schools to encourage the use of fish in the school lunch program. However, the Department of Agriculture, which administered the program, left decisions about purchases up to the school districts and never required that school districts buy domestically caught and processed fish. In Massachusetts, where domestically caught groundfish would have been easier to buy than in any other state, the school districts bought fish sticks. "We never had success with the fresh fish," recalled one administrator, despite some promotion efforts in cooperation with the New England industry.[42]

Reducing the Costs of Production

Federal programs to reduce the costs of fishing played a far more important role in attempts to solve fishing industry problems than the efforts to expand the market for fish. Most of the energy of the industry lobbyists and most congressional debate focused on cost reduction through the 1950s and the 1960s. By the mid-1960s the industry had been the beneficiary of safety programs, training for fishermen, research and development, loans, and vessel construction subsidies.

Groundfish industry boat owners were particularly concerned about the rising costs of insurance for boats and for crew. By 1957 almost 95 percent of New England vessel owners believed the federal government should step in to solve their insurance problems. In 1957 the Gloucester Fisheries Commission decided to concentrate all its attention on getting government relief from high insurance rates. As their premiums rose as much as 100 percent in one year, Gloucester vessel owners met to draft proposals for the Secretary of the Interior on ways to deal with insurance problems. Governor Herter's committee studying the industry's problems discussed high insurance premiums and the difficulties of obtaining any coverage at one of its earliest meetings.[43]

In response to industry concern, the Fish and Wildlife Service sponsored a study under Saltonstall-Kennedy authority to find out the reasons for accidents and to explain the high insurance rates. In 1959 they developed a vessel safety program for New England which provided information on how to operate boats and handle gear more safely and how to make rescue from boat sinkings more likely. Following these recommendations might reduce the number of injuries and damage to the boat and, therefore, might hold down insurance premiums. The Bureau of Commercial Fisheries, which succeeded the Fish and Wildlife Service, demonstrated safety equipment, issued safety bulletins on a range of subjects, and worked with the Department of Labor to develop a safety education course in fishermen training programs.[44]

According to the Bureau of Commercial Fisheries, these programs led to safer fishing practices, installation of more safety equipment, and fewer injuries. John Murray, the Bureau's New England fishing vessel safety officer from the early 1960s through 1973, said that eventually many boat owners "carried through with" the safety measures although he could not say whether the changes affected the cost of insurance. Among the ports least receptive to the Bureau's program were Gloucester and Boston, the centers of the groundfish industry. As a result, the Bureau concentrated its efforts elsewhere, most notably in New Bedford.[45]

Perhaps the Bureau of Commercial Fisheries' safety programs slowed the increase in insurance costs, but expenses did continue to rise for the groundfish fleet. By 1964 insurance was about 50 percent of the fixed costs of vessel operations in the Boston groundfish fleet, about the same as the cost of provisions for the crew. Older vessels had greater increases and higher insurance costs than newer ones. Wooden vessels had higher rates which increased faster than those of steel boats.[46] Groundfish vessels were generally old and constructed of wood and therefore bore some of the highest insurance costs in the New England fleet.

Whatever the influence of the safety programs on the costs of insurance, fishermen and boat owners in the groundfishery continued to cite insurance costs as one of their most important problems. They did not succeed in getting financial assistance from the federal government to cover the insurance, although Congress debated bills to provide lower cost insurance.[47]

Groundfish boat owners believed that another factor which raised costs was a shortage of young men in fishing. "This prospective field of employment has been sadly neglected," said Thomas Rice on behalf of Boston vessel owner-dealers. "We are suffering today because of this neglect. The average age of the fishermen working out of the port of Boston is 59 years of age." Younger fishermen with special training in fishing skills would make fishing more efficient, he and others said, but young people did not seek such jobs.[48]

In 1956 Congress passed legislation that provided money for vocational education for fishermen. Drawing on some of these funds, the Gloucester school department set up a three-year fishing and vessel management course for high school students. The director of the program estimated that between four and six students per year might become fishermen, about half the students who enrolled. In Maine, state and federal funds helped support training of fishermen at the Marine Vocational Technical Institute.[49]

In 1963 the Atlantic Fishermen's Union arranged on-the-job training under the Manpower Development and Training Act to prepare fishermen for the groundfish fleets in Boston and Gloucester. By 1965 almost 50 out of 110 enrollees had graduated from the training program, not a bad record according to some, because at least one of the courses took place during stormy fall months. Fifty percent of the men who graduated, however, quit after a few trips. Very few of those who stayed in fishing continued to work on offshore groundfish vessels.[50]

Vessel owners and processors believed that the industry would benefit if the federal government paid for research and development in fisheries. In 1954 the New England Fisheries Committee, made up of representatives of fishery associations and state and local government agencies, outlined a lengthy research agenda. The list included biological and oceanographic research to find ways to sustain the yield from fish stocks; a statistics program to improve information for biologists and provide market news to the industry; exploratory fishing and gear development to find new concentrations of fish resources and more efficient ways to harvest them; and a search for better ways to preserve, process, distribute, and market fish and for new uses of underutilized species and fish wastes.[51]

Before 1954 the Fish and Wildlife Service had already completed a substantial amount of research, which was traditionally its most important role. The most highly publicized studies that touched the groundfish industry in the early postwar period began to develop technology for freezing fish at sea.[52]

With passage of the Saltonstall-Kennedy Act in 1954, the federal government provided more funding for such research projects. Appropriations for research on fisheries rose during the mid-1950s; the Saltonstall-Kennedy program supplemented those funds with well over $1 million per year. Furthermore, funding for exploratory fishing and gear development and for "technological studies" rose only slightly through regular appropriations, but Saltonstall-Kennedy allocations doubled the funds available. In the next few years, market news and statistics coverage expanded; biologists studied the growth and spawning characteristics of important commercial species and the influence of environmental conditions on the abundance of Atlantic groundfish; Bureau of Commercial Fisheries research vessels investigated the effects of larger mesh on the composition of the catch; biologists and engineers continued experiments on technology for freezing fish at sea; and economists looked at the feasibility of freezing fish at sea.[53]

Other programs added to the research capacity provided by Saltonstall-Kennedy. In 1956 legislation provided funds for training researchers and technicians in fishing-related work. The Commercial Fisheries Research and Development Act of 1964 offered federal funds to match state money. In 1966 Congress passed the National Sea Grant College and Program Act to promote research, education, training, and advisory services related to use of ocean and coastal resources. The fishing industry tapped other sources of funds, such as the Economic Development Administration, for support for applied research.[54]

Following 1954, government-funded research contributed to most changes in vessel technology, use of new species, and innovations in fish handling. Most parts of the fishing industry benefited. For example, state-funded research in Maine developed better lobster holding pens. Researchers from the National Marine Fisheries Service (successor to the Bureau of Commercial Fisheries) cooperated with firms entering the new red crab industry to provide biological information and to test new types of gear.[55]

Research touched the groundfishery as well. Government studies along with a boat builder's experiments evaluated the efficiency of stern trawling compared to traditional side trawling for groundfish. Because stern trawling was more efficient and safer, it became the most important innovation in groundfishing during the 1960s. However, although the research results were complete, few groundfish vessels used stern trawling until the mid-1970s. Fishery biologists learned about the nature of groundfish stocks and suggested ways to increase yields, but fishermen and boat owners acted on scientists' suggestions to increase fish yields only when government regulations directed them to do so.[56]

The most ambitious efforts to reduce costs for the groundfish industry addressed the expenses of vessel construction and repair. In 1956 industry representatives argued that while higher tariffs would solve their problems permanently, they needed loans for vessel repair and maintenance in the meantime. No bank would make loans to boat owners because, bankers had told them, "We don't want to own the boat and we know the minute we loan you the money we are eventually going to own the boat."[57]

After the President rejected the 1956 Tariff Commission recommendations, the fishing industry sought larger subsidies for boat construction. Thomas Fulham explained to congressmen that even when boat operators made a profit, they would not purchase new boats because "a fishing trawler cannot be operated profitably on the base cost of a new vessel." At the same time, the greatest hope for the industry's revitalization depended on new boats. Director of the Bureau of Commercial Fisheries Donald McKernan believed that if boats were up-to-date, the industry might be able to compete with imports. Insurance and repair costs would be lower for new vessels; therefore, boat owners could meet operating expenses more easily, spokesmen for the industry argued. However, the industry stated, construction of vessels cost so much more in the United States than in foreign countries that vessel owners had to have help to pay for new boats.[58]

The Fish and Wildlife Act of 1956 provided loans for financing the operation, maintenance, replacement, and repair of fishing vessels and gear for boat owners who could not obtain loans elsewhere. Boat owners had to be able to pay back the loans in ten years, and interest rates were not subsidized.[59] In other words, Congress believed a capital shortage existed for the fishing industry; conventional financing did not fill the demand from good credit risks because private market suppliers overestimated risk and because the strict terms of private financing made repayment too difficult.

In the early years of the program, the loans did serve the offshore groundfish industry whose difficulties had been a major argument for passage of the legislation. In 1958 representatives of the fishing industry told Congress that the loans were a good stopgap measure. Gloucester boat owners had made extensive use of loans to keep their boats going until the federal government could do something more that would really help. According to Mayor Corliss of Gloucester, "If it had not been for this, the fishing industry would have been in one chaotic mess. Without it, we would not have held on this long." The Bureau of Commercial Fisheries agreed; its director, McKernan, said that Gloucester had received more funds than any other port and that more loans had gone to New England than to any other region. New England boat owners received 85 loans which made up a third of the total loan principal.[60]

By 1965 the record of loans showed that the program was no longer touching the groundfishery as much. The Bureau of Commercial Fisheries had approved 166 loans for $4,380,000 in New England, with Massachusetts boat owners receiving 102 loans totalling $3,600,000. About 50 percent of the loans had been under $10,000. The loans helped large numbers of small vessel operators, according to McKernan.[61] Small vessel operators were inshore fishermen, who did not face severe problems as a group and who had had no role in lobbying for the legislation. The largest share of the loans were, therefore, not dealing with problems of the offshore groundfish industry.

The full record of the program showed the extent of these tendencies. The fishery loan fund served approximately 350 boat owners in New England between 1957 and 1973, but only 75 to 100 of the loans went to offshore boats, and somewhere between a quarter and a third of these offshore boats came from the prosperous scallop and flounder fisheries of New Bedford. The majority of loans in New England aided the construction of small boats, especially for Maine lobstermen.[62]

Individual groundfish boats did profit from the loan program. Some boats earned more than they would have without loans, according to a National Marine Fisheries Service study, because the loans went for boat renovation or new gear which made fishing more efficient.[63]

The Fish and Wildlife Act of 1956 also authorized the Bureau of Commercial Fisheries to provide mortgage and loan insurance for construction, reconstruction, or reconditioning of fishing vessels. The Bureau of Commercial Fisheries did not implement the program until 1960. By 1965 eight large vessels in the New England groundfish industry had received mortgage insurance to cover financing worth nearly $870,000, always in combination with a vessel construction subsidy. Two scallopers had also received mortgage insurance.[64]

In 1960 Congress passed legislation which provided vessel construction subsidies to cover the difference between the costs of boat construction in the United States and abroad up to a third of the total cost of the vessel. The law required that any subsidized boat operate in a fishery that imports harmed or threatened.[65] As a result, only New England groundfish vessels were immediately eligible for the funds. However, from 1960 through 1963 only six applications for funds were approved. Three subsidy boats fished out of New Bedford, two out of Boston, and one out of Rockland, Maine. No Gloucester boat owners had even applied for subsidy.[66]

In 1964 Congress passed the Fishing Fleet Improvement Act which amended the 1960 legislation to provide a larger subsidy, up to 50 percent of the cost of construction. The new law allowed owners in any fishery to use the subsidy as long as new boats would not "cause economic hardship to efficient vessel operators" already in the fishery. The law required subsidized vessels to be of advanced design and equipped with new kinds of gear to allow them to operate in "expanded areas."[67]

By 1969, 32 boats had been constructed under the new subsidy program. Fifteen of these operated out of New England ports, of which ten entered the prosperous New Bedford scallop fishery. Five went into the groundfishery: one each in New Bedford, Gloucester, Boston, and Rockland and one for a company in New York City which planned to operate the boat out of Gloucester.[68] The total addition to the groundfish fleet was very small, nowhere near the original goal to completely replace the offshore groundfish boats.

By the middle to late 1960s no one any longer assessed the subsidy program against its original goal of replacing the offshore groundfish fleet with vessels whose cost compared favorably with that of foreign vessels. Programs to help the industry "meet foreign competition" meant something new, and the goals of the subsidy program had changed accordingly. In the 1950s meeting foreign competition had meant enabling the fishing industry to realize a profit despite the low cost of imported fish. By the mid-1960s the phrase meant helping the United States fishing fleet to regain preeminence among world fisheries. "We were formerly in second place among the fish producers of the world," Donald McKernan emphasized. "We are now in fifth place. Our share of the world catch has dropped from 13 to 7 percent in the years since 1956. By way of comparison, since 1947 the Soviet Republic has more than doubled her fish catch." By 1969 such concerns were even more prominent. Edward Garmatz, chairman of the House Committee on Merchant Marine and Fisheries, opened hearings on extension of the Fishing Fleet Improvement Act. "Since the 1940s the United States has slipped from first to sixth place among the leading fishing nations of the world," he said. "We are now outranked by Peru, Japan, Red China, Russia, and Norway, respectively. In view of this deteriorating situation, it is imperative that the Fishing Fleet Improvement Act be extended."[69]

This new perspective in Congress and in the administration led to the construction of "Seafreeze Atlantic," the most famous of the subsidized vessels. In 1966 American Stern Trawlers, a New York-based subsidiary of American Export Industries, applied for subsidies for two factory trawlers. One, later called "Seafreeze Pacific," was to operate in the bottomfish industry of the north Pacific. The other, "Seafreeze Atlantic," would go to Gloucester for the groundfish industry. Both vessels would use stern trawling, and they would process the fish on board, something no American boat had done successfully.

The Maritime Administration and the Bureau of Commercial Fisheries approved subsidies for the boats over objections. Other groups planning to build vessels complained about two boats' taking all the subsidy funds for one year. Boat owners already in the industry feared competition from the new vessels, and owners and fishermen suspected that the company would hire foreign fishermen as crew. Joseph Slavin, the director of the Gloucester Laboratory for the National Marine Fisheries Service, warned McKernan that construction of enormous factory ships took United States fishery development in the wrong direction. The strength of the fleet was in coastal fisheries except for the tuna industry, he pointed out, and building on that strength made most sense. Furthermore, he warned, England's factory vessel "Fair Try" was losing money, an experience that did not bode well for United States efforts with factory boats.[70]

The attractiveness of boats as advanced as any foreign vessel won out over this opposition. "These vessels would be a real test as far as the U.S. fishing fleet is concerned," said Harold Crowther, successor to McKernan as director of the National Marine Fisheries Service. "We hear many claims of the need for the U.S. fishing industry to get out on the high seas and compete with foreign fleets such as those of the Soviet Union, Japan, Canada, and others."[71] These other nations had factory ships which processed large quantities of fish to be transported home months later.

"Seafreeze Atlantic" and "Seafreeze Pacific" each cost close to $6 million by the end of construction in late 1968 and early 1969. Both received subsidies of about $3 million, the entire appropriation for the program the year the boats received funding. As of 1969 "Seafreeze Atlantic" cost more than six times as much as the second most expensive subsidy boat in New England. It cost more than ten times as much as every other subsidized boat in New England.[72]

"Seafreeze Atlantic" was a huge vessel 296 feet long. Only one other New England fishing vessel compared with it in length, the "Saint Patrick" of Portland, which was 240 feet long. Other boats in the fleet were less than half the length of the new boat. The "Seafreeze Atlantic" displaced 1,593 gross tons. The "Saint Patrick" displaced less than a third as much, and the next largest boats were only 320 gross tons. Even these were the giants of the fleet. Most offshore boats displaced between 60 and 150 gross tons.[73]

"Seafreeze Atlantic" had the newest stern trawling gear. Only a few New England boats, mostly other subsidy boats, were built for stern trawling. Their gear operated on the same principles but was a fraction of the size. "Seafreeze" could adjust the gear for traditional bottom fishing or for midwater trawling for pelagic fish such as herring. Modern foreign boats had such technology, but it was nonexistent in the New England fleet.

The second deck of "Seafreeze Atlantic" was a fish processing factory equipped with more modern equipment than a processing plant on shore. Baader machines from West Germany could gut and behead fish at the rate of twenty to thirty per minute. Other Baader machines filleted and skinned the fish. The wastes went to a completely automatic fish meal and fish oil plant in the ship's hold. Because of this processing capacity, "Seafreeze Atlantic" could stay at sea for sixty to ninety days.[74]

"Seafreeze Atlantic" was christened in September 1968 with considerable fanfare. The wife of Governor John Volpe of Massachusetts broke the champagne bottle over its bow. Clarence Pautzke, acting assistant Secretary of the Interior for Fish and Wildlife, praised American Stern Trawlers "for their courage in facing many unknown factors in designing, constructing and operating a vessel so different from anything ever built or used by the U.S. fishing industry." Donald McKernan, by then special assistant for fisheries and wildlife to the Secretary of State, compared the venture by American Stern Trawlers to those of the seventeenth-century London merchants who developed trade with the Americas, India, and the East Indies. Harold Crowther and others saw the effort as much more than a test of businessmen's judgment. "If this doesn't succeed, we might as well stay on the continental shelf," Crowther said.[75]

In a move to hire an outstanding captain as well as to minimize union opposition to "Seafreeze," American Stern Trawlers called James Ackert from his post as head of the Atlantic Fishermen's Union to skipper the ship. He would command seventeen other officers and fifty-six crewmen, twelve of them fishermen and the rest factory workers. Ackert felt cautious but optimistic. "I thought it would work at first," he says now. At the time he told a reporter, "We will have to learn our way with this equipment. Much of this equipment American fishermen have never seen before, and there will be some mistakes and some will cost a lot of money."[76]

"Seafreeze Atlantic" began its career, however, with several disadvantages. American Stern Trawlers offered $8,000 per year to fishermen and $5,200 per year to processing workers with bonuses for extra production of fish. At those salaries, both fishermen and processing workers could find jobs on conventional boats or in plants ashore. Only a few fishermen applied for jobs. "I tried to get them to offer more," Ackert said, "but the accountants said that was the amount the company could pay." Most of those hired, according to Ackert, had never been on a fishing boat before.[77]

The management of American Stern Trawlers decided that the ship should follow the foreign fleets in search of groundfish, principally cod, and process the catch into frozen blocks. For most of the year this meant working among icebergs off Iceland, Greenland, and Labrador. Ackert told the managers that he thought the boat should stay on the banks off the United States shores. He recommended that "Seafreeze" harvest herring on Georges Bank to avoid the problems of extremely cold weather in the far north and to make shorter trips possible if necessary. United States fishermen had never exploited Georges Bank herring because its quality would have been too poor by the time they landed it. "Seafreeze" might harvest the herring profitably for foreign markets because the vessel's freezing capacity solved the problem of quality, Ackert believed.[78]

"Seafreeze" left for its first trip off Labrador in late fall 1968 to spend several months in the Arctic with untried gear and inexperienced crew. The night before he went, Ackert visited a friend who worked for the National Marine Fisheries Service. "It's going to fail, isn't it?" Ackert said. "Yes, it is," the friend answered.[79]

Ackert termed those first "Seafreeze" shakedown cruises "disastrous." The crew had trouble with the gear among the ice floes, which Ackert had anticipated because such difficulties occurred on any boat using new equipment. Usually the crew could adjust the gear, change the way they operated it, or recommend engineering changes.

The problems Ackert saw as insurmountable had to do with the crew. Work was difficult with so many inexperienced workers. In addition, because the fishermen and processing workers did not want to stay at sea for so long, they complained and worked badly. Each time the boat came into port, almost all the crew resigned.

Captain Cecil Benson of Kennebunkport, Maine, took over the boat after the shakedown trips, but conditions did not improve. On a trip that began in late March 1969 confusion about who did what deck work exacerbated problems with the gear. Morale among the crew was extremely low. German officers directed the fishing, but most of the fishermen were immigrants who could not understand the officers' instructions. One crewman had the impression of continual "screaming and hollering" from the captain's loudspeaker and of a nervous crew jumping to do whatever they could without thinking. Large amounts of fish left ungutted too long in pens had to be discarded. One fisherman was badly injured when he was pinned by the gear. Toward the end of April a crewman from Gloucester died when a falling block hit him in the head.

The processing workers and some of the fishermen refused to work after the death. When the boat docked in Saint Pierre, a French island south of Newfoundland, to put the body ashore, the crew "mutinied," in Ackert's words, and went on a rampage of vandalizing the boat. "I've been 22 years at sea," Benson said. "What happened on this ship, as far as I'm concerned, just doesn't happen on any ship." The crew was the most unruly Benson had ever seen. "It was a continuous battle to get them to work," he said. Most of the crew left the vessel in Saint Pierre.[80]

Ackert recruited another crew and took them north to the "Seafreeze" to assume command of the boat again. This time the boiler broke down at sea, and Ackert and eight other members of the crew caught pneumonia. The boat docked in Canada, and Ackert went home.[81]

Nearly every trip in 1969 and all but a few of the others ended as "brokers" in which income did not cover expenses. "Seafreeze Atlantic" returned from its seventh trip in February 1971 and tied up permanently in Norfolk in April 1971. By the time the American Stern Trawlers sold out to new owners in 1974, the company had lost $11 million.[82]

The Groundfish Industry's Success in Getting Help from the Federal Government

By the late 1960s the federal government had a substantial record of efforts to help the New England fisheries. The attention and energy lavished on such a small industry seem remarkable. In 1950 all fishermen in New England, inshore and offshore, made up at most one-half of one percent of New England workers. New England's major employers, the shoe and textile industries, were also in trouble and asking for aid. If Congress had dismissed the difficulties of the fishing industry as inconsequential in comparison with more pressing regional industrial problems, that action would not on the surface have seemed surprising. A number of factors accounted for the fishery's success in getting help from the federal government despite its size.[83]

Compared to their difficulty with self-help efforts, industry groups cooperated best in lobbying for federal legislation, which required a smaller investment of time and money from individuals than self-help. Getting federal assistance required no compromises among industry groups; if boat owners received subsidies, for example, fishermen would not have to sacrifice. Even so, lobbying groups rarely cut across interests in the industry, to include fishermen and dealers, for example; and many groups came together for only a short time to push for one type of legislation. The effectiveness of lobbying groups depended on the commitment of leaders rather than on the work of large numbers of members. The fishing industry had a handful of capable leaders to push for legislation and to insist on response from federal agencies.

The efforts to get tariff assistance had heightened the political savvy of the fishing industry spokesmen. In 1949 they had been novices in efforts to influence government decisions. By 1956 they were well known to the legislators on the committees that handled fishing-related bills, and they knew the administrative routes for accomplishing their aims.

In the efforts to get help from the federal government, the industry could rally support from state and local government officials. Directors of the states' divisions of fisheries worked for federal legislation, and one or two became leaders of the industry movement. State legislators from fishing districts were happy to testify before Congress on behalf of federal legislation even though they could not persuade their own legislatures to help the industry.

The organizing and lobbying skills of industry leaders served the fisheries well in part because of the mood of Congress in the mid-1950s. The industry's appeals to the Tariff Commission had documented the problems of the groundfishery. In 1949 few outside the industry had felt concern about the difficulties of the New England groundfishery. By 1954, however, many in Congress believed the industry's claims that imports caused loss of jobs and income for fishermen, vessel owners, and processors. By 1956, nearly everyone agreed that the fishing industry faced serious problems that could worsen. With those issues settled, Congress could debate whether the government should help the industry and, if so, in what ways.

Some congressmen were predisposed to sympathize with the industry's plight and to believe Congress should help. Although fishermen were a very small percent of the regional labor force, the industry could easily employ between 15 and 20 percent of the work force in coastal communities. Industry spokesmen claimed the percent of the labor force in fishing-related jobs in those towns was even higher: 30 to 40 percent. Because the fate of the fisheries affected a large share of the constituents from coastal towns, their legislators supported fishery bills. Senators and representatives from other New England districts usually favored aid for the industry also, despite the lack of strong public concern about the industry in the region during the 1950s and 1960s.

The design of specific legislation broadened the constituency beyond the groundfish industry and New England in all but one case. Representatives and senators from the rest of the East Coast, Gulf, West Coast, and Great Lakes states supported bills because their fishery constituents wanted the legislation, too.

A number of influential congressmen supported the fishing industry's efforts. Their backing helped explain the passage of fishery legislation, said Francis Sargent, director of the Massachusetts fishery division through the 1950s. In the House, for example, the sympathetic John W. McCormack of Boston was majority leader during the 1950s and Speaker of the House from 1962 through 1970. William Bates, representing the district which included Gloucester, was an influential member of the House Committee on Merchant Marine and Fisheries. Senators John Kennedy and Leverett Saltonstall of Massachusetts pushed the industry's cause in the Senate during the 1950s. Early in the 1960s Senator Edmund Muskie of Maine became a leader on behalf of fishery interests. The congressmen from New England joined others from the rest of the country. Most notably, Senator Warren Magnuson of Washington chaired the Senate Committee on Interstate and Foreign Commerce during most of the fishing industry's appeals for help. He worked on behalf of fishermen in the Pacific Northwest and allied with the New England congressmen to push for legislation.

The fisheries cause gained leverage from the fact that other troubled industries were seeking aid at the same time. "I pray that when we come along with the farm program," said Representative Toby Morris of Oklahoma, "if we make a good, reasonable case and show that farmers are entitled to it, help us out. We need it, just as the fishing industry needs it."[84] Congressmen who had introduced bills to subsidize mining in the upper Midwest voted for the fisheries subsidies.

Proponents offered many arguments to persuade more congressmen to support fishery aid legislation and to lessen the opposition. Government should not bail out an industry which could have done more for itself, they implied; however, the fishing industry deserved help. "Has the industry been remiss?" asked Senator John Butler of Maryland. "Obviously not. The fishing industry is composed of many individuals and small companies which lack the resources to carry on coordinated research activities of the proper and essentially broad scope." The New England fishing industry had been "sick" for many years, but "not because New England fishermen lack ingenuity, initiative or the will to do hard work," argued Congressman Edward Boland of Massachusetts. The people in the fisheries, said Massachusetts Senator Leverett Saltonstall, were "working hard and earning their livelihood by the sweat of their brows."[85]

Congress could not expect the states to offer more help in the industry although the states had traditionally conducted fishery research, congressmen argued. "The state government and the industry itself . . . are working to the utmost of their ability to join in the research problems," stated Senator Magnuson. "One thing is certain," declared Senator James Duff of Pennsylvania. "Neither the impoverished industry nor the tax-starved states can alone finance the extensive research that must be conducted if our national fisheries are to be preserved and expanded."[86]

Furthermore, comparison of federal aid to the fisheries with aid to other industries showed that the fisheries were receiving much less assistance. Senator John Pastore of Rhode Island complained, "It strikes me that every time the word 'agriculture' is mentioned in this body it is like mentioning the sacred cow. There are other people in distress. There are fishermen in my section of the country who are out of work." All that the fishery legislation would provide, he and many others emphasized, was "equity and justice." The Saltonstall-Kennedy bill, for instance, would merely offer fishermen a little bit of what farmers had received for many years.[87]

While the contrast with agriculture showed the neglect of fisheries most clearly, congressmen easily found other examples. "National policies have been established in the case of many of our great industries—and rightly so; but our fisheries have always been neglected in that respect," argued Senator Magnuson. Senator Saltonstall contrasted fishery aid with merchant marine programs: "Why should merchant vessels, which carry freight, be given a construction cost subsidy, whereas fishing vessels, which serve one of our great industries, with the people in it providing food for all of us . . . be deprived of a construction subsidy?"[88]

Not only did the fisheries receive substantially less attention and aid than other industries, congressmen stated, but the federal government had actually hurt the industry in some cases. They agreed with industry spokesmen that the government should compensate the fisheries for this harm. Congressman Bates emphasized, "The damage done to our fishing industry at home by direct and indirect, or lack of action by our Government. . . . is an incredible, fantastic and unfair story that has brought this 300 year old industry to its knees." He described the history of tariffs on groundfish. He pointed to the Jones Act. In addition, the Navy had taken many fishing boats for military use during the war, he said, just when the fishermen had the best prospects for making money. In providing generous foreign aid, the United States had built fishing boats for Iceland, a major New England competitor, and had equipped the vessels with the latest radar and sonar. Fishermen paid twice as much for boats constructed in domestic yards rather than overseas, but law forbade the use of boats built in other countries. "Let this great Nation assume its own responsibility and carry its own load and remove it from the fishermen who have been hurt too often and too hard," Bates urged.[89]

Aid to the fishing industry served the national interest, congressmen stated. The government should help the fishing industry "to continue to make its important contribution to national prosperity," argued Senator Butler and others. "The commercial fishing industry is a vital and important part of our national economy," emphasized Senator Magnuson. It employed thousands of workers directly and additional thousands in related businesses, as well as paying millions of dollars in taxes to state and federal governments. The fisheries, Magnuson said, had "contributed so much in making the United States of America the most powerful nation in the world." The condition of the fisheries was important not only because the industry added to the gross national product but also because fishery problems could "adversely affect our independence for protein food from foreign sources during periods of international emergencies," pointed out Senator Frederick Payne of Maine. Furthermore, the Defense Department considered fishing vessels vital for use in war; a program that subsidized their construction would strengthen the nation's defense. Fishery programs constituted "a vital part of our national defense and security structure" even without war, Magnuson argued. "Our intelligence sources tell us, that as part of the strategy employed by the Russians in this cold war, they . . . are presently implementing a long-range commercial fishery program designed to make Russia the leading fish-producing nation in the world by 1965." It was crucial that the United States help its industry to stay ahead, congressmen repeated.[90]

While the Soviet Union's investment in its fishing industry was particularly alarming, other nations had subsidized their fisheries, too, congressmen pointed out. Only the United States had not done so. Representative Bates pointed out the aid to fishing industries in "practically every country of the world." "While the American fishing industry was operating with no more than Yankee ingenuity the fisheries of other nations were being actively sponsored by the governments of those nations," emphasized Senator Payne.[91]

Opposition from congressmen, the administration, and interest groups had molded the bills that made it to the floors of the Senate and the House as supporters sought to increase chances of passage by taking opponents' arguments into account. Some congressmen still argued against the bills. Many opposed government intervention on behalf of any industry. "I just wonder whether we should not at least stop and take a look to see not just what this particular bill does, but where it takes us in the long run," said Congressman John Byrnes of Wisconsin. Senator Frank Lausche of Ohio warned, "We have a repetition here of the old and well-established rule: 'If the camel's nose once gets under the tent, no matter how slightly, eventually his whole body will enter it.'" If the government subsidized the fishing industry, he said, then there was no reason not to subsidize the pottery, scissors, machine tool, bicycle, and athletic equipment industries. "I cannot approve of the argument that since Red Russia is spending money for that purpose, we should do so also," Lausche repeated frequently. "If that argument is sound, we might as well throw overboard our system of government and adopt the economy of Red Russia." "We shall have to kick the camel out," said Senator John Williams of Delaware. "Today the taxpayers are confronted with the highest debt in the history of the country." "Are we going to subsidize the textile industry?" asked Senator Strom Thurmond of South Carolina. "Are we going to subsidize the plywood industry? Are we going to subsidize the automobile industry? . . . our Government cannot afford to inject itself in order to save . . . industry."[92]

Supporters of fishery legislation responded to these arguments. Bills to help the fisheries were not setting a precedent for subsidies to other industries. In some cases, the precedent was already there. The fishing industry wanted the same kinds of programs that agriculture and the merchant marine had enjoyed for many years. In other cases, the legislation was not just a subsidy for an industry. "This is a food resources program . . . rather than an industrial program," claimed congressman Thor Tollefson in debate on legislation to train personnel for the fishing industry.[93] Defense needs called for a vessel subsidy, other congressmen argued; therefore, this program differed markedly from subsidies other industries might want.

The fishery programs were also temporary, congressmen told opponents of the legislation. The Saltonstall-Kennedy legislation was an "experimental, emergency" program to be reconsidered within three years.[94] The first vessel subsidy bill expired in three years, the second in five years.

Furthermore, the programs would cost almost nothing. Saltonstall-Kennedy would transfer funds from the Department of Agriculture to the Department of the Interior. Loans to the fishing industry would be repaid with interest. "It is a very small bill moneywise," said Congressmen Torbert MacDonald of Massachusetts about the first vessel subsidy. "The cost of this program per year does not reach the cost of the storage program for surplus crops . . . for a single day." Congressmen Stanley Tupper of Maine added that under the second vessel subsidy, "The average vessel would pay back the subsidy in the form of taxes within 5 years."[95]

While these arguments convinced some congressmen to support fishery legislation, other opponents remained who occasionally succeeded in amending legislation. Congressmen who opposed any government aid to industry received support in arguing further that the proposed programs were not the right way to help the fisheries. Congressman Byrnes of Wisconsin did not see how training fishery technicians and fishermen would solve the industry's problems because "all it involves is the matter of promoting education and training professional personnel." Others argued that reciprocal trade agreements should be changed before Congress subsidized an industry hurt by imports. The American fishing industry already had too many boats, charged Congressman

Thomas Pelly of Washington, adding that the new subsidy bill "will not materially change the situation faced by the American fishing industry."[96]

Groups opposed specific bills on other grounds. Some congressmen fought the transfer of funds from the Department of Agriculture to the Department of the Interior proposed under Saltonstall-Kennedy. The measure could be "the first step toward chipping away from money . . . for sustaining an adequate farm program in the United States," warned Senator George Aiken of Vermont. The fishery research program ought to rely instead on direct appropriations, he and others argued.[97]

Conservation groups, sport fishermen, and wildlife organizations opposed the Fisheries Act of 1956 which would have created a separate agency at a higher level than the Fish and Wildlife Service to handle the problems of the commercial fishing industry. Their congressional supporters amended the legislation which became the Fish and Wildlife Act of 1956 to preserve "a proper balance between all these programs."[98] The new Bureau of Commercial Fisheries that resulted was not much more important than the Fish and Wildlife Service had been.

The large number of fishery aid programs of the 1950s and 1960s were the product of these forces. By the late 1960s, however, the concerns of the industry and of Congress had changed; new alliances were forming to back different kinds of support for the fishing industry.

PROGRAMS TO REDUCE COSTS OR INCREASE DEMAND IN THE 1970S

"Seafreeze Atlantic" was the last great effort of the subsidy programs. Few new subsidy boats were built after "Seafreeze," and by the time the factory ship started operations, very little money remained for vessel construction. The new programs Congress did set up promised to be less expensive in direct outlays if not in tax expenditures. The Federal Ship Financing Act of 1972 replaced the mortgage insurance program with the "fishing vessel obligation guarantee" which allowed more flexible financing. The Merchant Marine Act of 1970 set up a capital construction fund allowing fishermen to defer federal tax payments on income from the operation of fishing vessels if that income were used for the construction, reconstruction, or purchase of a fishing vessel. In 1970 the National Marine Fisheries Service launched a marketing program to promote pollock, an underutilized groundfish.[99]

These new efforts notwithstanding, the energy that had gone into the programs of the 1950s and 1960s was nearly spent by the end of the decade. Industry spokesmen, Congress, and agency officials turned their attention to new difficulties and to quite different ways of dealing with the fisheries' problems. Before looking at those new efforts, however, it is important to consider how the older programs affected the groundfishery and why the programs did or did not succeed in helping the troubled industry.

4

The Shortcomings of Intervention

*T*HE FISHERY AID PROGRAMS provided some benefits for people in the groundfish industry. For instance, the construction subsidies helped pay for eleven new boats for the groundfishery. Between 50 and 75 offshore groundfishermen received loans for repair or replacement of gear and boats. The Department of Defense purchased some groundfish from New England. Perhaps the activities of some programs prevented some problems and slowed the decline of the offshore groundfish industry or stimulated growth in other sectors of the fishing industry. They may have also provided technical understanding and sophistication in political work that helped the industry to handle new problems later.

By the late 1960s, however, the fishery programs had failed to solve the problems of the offshore groundfish industry. In 1954, the year of the passage of the first federal aid legislation, Boston fishermen had landed 141 million pounds of groundfish worth almost $10 million. In 1965 they landed only 96 million pounds valued at $10.8 million. If Boston's groundfish revenues had kept pace with inflation and growth in the rest of the economy, the revenues from the catch would have reached $18 million by 1965. In Gloucester the picture was much the same. Landings of groundfish declined from 115 million pounds in 1954 to 58 million pounds in 1965. The value of the groundfish catch fell from nearly $5 million to $4.6 million. In Boston, fishermen earned an income comparable to the national median for full-time male workers only if they worked at least 50 percent more hours than other workers. Few boats stayed out of the red. The numbers of fishermen and boats in the groundfish industry fell steadily during the 1950s and 1960s.[1]

Fishing industry spokesmen, congressmen, and officials of the Bureau of Commercial Fisheries offered many explanations for the continuing troubles of the New England groundfishery and the failure of the aid

81

programs to turn industry fortunes around. For many in the industry, the lack of tariff protection explained the difficulties, and no other program could overcome the import problem. As Patrick McHugh, the secretary-treasurer of the Atlantic Fishermen's Union, stated, "There is no doubt in my mind that this whole industry has been sacrificed for the national defense." Others claimed the efforts to help were too small. Senator Leverett Saltonstall of Massachusetts declared in 1965, "Our fishermen have been unable to meet the demand because basically they have been unable to keep abreast with technological advances. . . . Our tariff protection is not adequate . . . we must provide the tools so that our own fishermen may compete with the modern foreign fleets being built by other countries." Harold Crowther, director of the Bureau of Commercial Fisheries, told fishermen that subsidy funds were far too small to rebuild the fishing fleet. Crowther felt fatalistic: "The continued existence of many problems . . . has become a way of life in the fisheries and we must learn to live with it."[2]

Exactly what the programs did for the industry is hard to uncover in part because records of the programs' accomplishments are very poor. The Department of Defense did not distinguish between purchases of imported and of domestic fish or between fish sticks and fillets. The Bureau of Commercial Fisheries often discarded records of the fishery loan fund after boat owners repaid loans. Other records were lost when the office administering the loan program moved. The loan application records which have survived in Washington or in Gloucester do not usually show the actual amount of money fishermen received. If a loan application was approved in Washington and a fisherman said he had underestimated his needs, the local office increased the amount of the loan without going through the lengthy approval process again.[3] The most important obstacle in assessing results of the programs precisely, however, is determining what would have happened without the programs: how much boat investment would have taken place without loans and subsidies; how much research scientists could have accomplished without the federal funding; how fishermen would have fared without some of the government-financed research findings; and what the demand for fish would have been without market development efforts. In most cases, it is impossible to tell what would have been.

Despite these problems in analyzing the efforts to aid the fisheries, it is certain that the programs did not cure the industry's difficulties by the late 1960s. Further, the operation of the programs and the dimensions of the problems that faced the offshore groundfish industry suggest many reasons for the programs' failure. These reasons were more varied and more complicated by the late 1960s than the industry, congressmen, or agency officials realized. The programs had few effects on the groundfish industry in part because they were too small or were not the right kinds of programs, as some people stated, but the programs they thought would have solved the problems could not have done so either. The programs to increase demand for groundfish and to decrease the costs of fishing had few effects on the groundfish industry because they were incorrectly conceived, badly implemented, and too small to cope with very large problems.

INCREASING THE DEMAND FOR FISH

A look at the attempts to increase the demand for fish reveals several reasons that fishery aid programs did not revitalize the groundfish industry. Although some programs may have had a small effect on the New England groundfishery, the major efforts were so flawed in execution and design that they could not have influenced groundfish fortunes.

Fish buying programs rarely touched the groundfish industry. The school lunch program bought fish sticks, not New England-caught groundfish. Although the message to buy more fish reached the local level, the buyers in the school districts did not receive instructions about the kinds of fish they should use. Indeed, the administrators in Washington who made the allocation decisions for the Saltonstall-Kennedy fund may not have understood that the problems of the New England fisheries were in the groundfish industry and that therefore the school lunch programs should buy groundfish.

Several factors helped to explain the lack of direction in the school lunch buying effort. As the New England groundfish industry allied with other parts of the nation's fishing industry in order to push Congress to pass fisheries aid legislation, they also blurred the identity of the groups with the problems. The impression that fishery problems had a broad constituency helped to get fishery legislation through Congress, but it interfered with getting officials to direct programs in ways that might actually deal with groundfish problems. In addition, Washington officials were listening to the appeals from other sectors in the New England industry and from fisheries in other parts of the country. In New England the fledgling fish stick producers, for example, worked to provide a product attractive to government purchasers. As early as 1953 they were selling large quantities of fish sticks to schools.

Fish sticks suited the goals of the local school districts better than fresh groundfish. "They took the easy way," said an administrator of the

Massachusetts school lunch program. Fish sticks were easier to handle and prepare than fresh fish, and children liked them. No government agency suggested that the goal of stimulating demand for New England groundfish should supercede any of the objectives of the school lunch program.[4]

When the government did buy New England groundfish products, the efforts were much too small to help, if data on Defense Department purchases of fish in the mid-1960s are an indication of the amounts bought during the 1950s and early 1960s. In addition, a share of the groundfish bought by the Defense Department came from importers of frozen fillets, so that the total effect of the purchases on New England fishermen and fresh fish processors was negligible.[5]

While implementation problems in large part explained the failure of government buying programs to aid the industry, other programs to increase the demand for fish were improperly conceived. The promotion of higher standards for handling fish reflected incorrect assumptions about the motivations of fishermen and dealers. The program assumed that if workers in the fishing industry knew how to improve the quality of fish, they would handle fish differently and purchase the equipment needed to do so. However, as late as the mid-1960s, many plant operators felt that they could make as much money selling bad fish as good and did not care about quality, according to an expert on nutrition from the Massachusetts Institute of Technology.[6]

Every consideration encouraged the individual boat owner or dealer not to make changes in operations to improve quality, especially if the changes cost money. The behavior of one fish dealer or boat owner could not influence consumer attitudes about fish. Changes in the way he handled fish would not affect the price he received because the quality of fish was very difficult to judge at the dock and because pricing rarely took quality into account. If a dealer or boat owner followed the recommendations of the Bureau of Commercial Fisheries, he would have to spend money on new boxes and other equipment, and crewmen and processing workers would have to take on more time-consuming tasks in handling the same amount of fish. Furthermore, if many fishermen and processors did upgrade their handling procedures, those who did not spend the money and time would still benefit if demand for fish increased.

Opposition to inspection and to mandatory standards for handling fish showed further that fishermen and dealers did not share the conviction of some congressmen and agency officials that better standards would lead to higher quality fish, that a better product would encourage people to eat more fish, and that the additional purchases would raise fish prices and revenues enough to make up for the higher costs. "It is our experience," stated Jacob Dykstra of Point Judith, "that regulation and restriction can only result in increased costs of harvest and production thereby reducing our ability to compete in the marketplace." The Gloucester Fisheries Commission observed that "unnecessarily high standards" would force many vessels out of business especially because foreign fishermen would not face the same restrictions and would continue to produce fish at the same low price. As late as the mid-1970s Louis Ronsivalli, director of the Gloucester Laboratory of the National Marine Fisheries Service, ran marketing experiments to try to prove to fishermen and dealers that guaranteed higher quality would increase demand and therefore prices and revenues. "I can't understand the opposition to improving quality," he said.[7]

The programs to improve the handling of fish erred also in assuming that boat owners and dealers were able to make the recommended changes. Even if they had approved of the program's goals, hard-pressed vessel owners and processors in the groundfish industry would have found it nearly impossible to bear the additional costs of new equipment and more time-consuming procedures.

If implementation problems and difficulties in conception had not interfered with their effectiveness, programs still would have faced a complicated task in stimulating demand for groundfish. The National Marine Fisheries Service's unsuccessful effort in the early 1970s to develop a market for pollock, an underutilized groundfish, illustrates the dilemmas of fish promotion efforts. Although the National Marine Fisheries Service promoted the product, consumers who decided to try pollock would have had trouble finding it in their stores. The landings remained far below those of haddock or cod because its price was about a third of the price of haddock and about two-thirds of the price of cod; furthermore, the price spread widened rather than narrowed during the promotion effort.[8] Although most consumers could not have found pollock, they had to buy more before the price would rise enough to attract fishing effort.

While these programs attempted without success to influence demand for groundfish, changes in the market for fish were causing large shifts in demand. These changes make the efforts look particularly feeble and show what a massive task the programs faced. Along with the cost disadvantages which the industry cited, the fall of demand for fish was a major cause of the industry's trouble. The failure of even better designed, more skillfully implemented government programs would have been understandable.

As World War II started, the federal government began to purchase large quantities of fish for the armed forces and for the allies. By 1943 one quarter of canned fish went to the Lend Lease program, and about 35 percent fed the armed forces. The government bought 15 percent of all fresh and frozen fish. The New England groundfishery benefited not only from these larger government purchases but also from greater civilian consumer demand. Groundfish was not rationed, and consumers who could not get meat turned to fish. Prices and incomes in the fisheries went up with the large increase in demand and with reductions in the New England offshore groundfish fleet's capacity.[9]

When World War II ended, however, the groundfishery lost the basis for its great prosperity. The government sharply reduced purchases of fish, and consumers began to buy more meat and poultry in place of fish as those products became available again.

An increase in imports helped slacken demand for groundfish as well, although, contrary to the industry's belief, imports alone did not explain their troubles. Between 1941 and 1946 imports of groundfish fillets had quintupled and in 1946 exceeded 49 million pounds. By 1953 imports of groundfish fillets approached 90 million pounds. Wholesalers who had bought frozen groundfish from New England processors turned to foreign suppliers who offered the product at lower prices. The Boston fishermen's strike of 1946 accelerated this trend, many dealer-vessel owners believed. Wholesalers who depended on New England fish sent representatives to Newfoundland and Nova Scotia during the strike to show plant operators and workers how to prepare the product they wanted. The New England industry's St. Louis customers, for example, turned permanently to Canada, said Thomas Fulham. "The ability to process fish was transferred to Nova Scotia and Newfoundland during the 21 weeks of the strike," he said.[10]

How much the imports contributed to the fall in demand for the New England product as compared with other postwar factors is hard to say. Imports competed with the New England frozen fish market; fresh fish from outside the country spoiled before reaching domestic markets. However, United States processors froze more than 70 percent of domestically harvested groundfish during the late 1940s and early 1950s.[11] Nevertheless, if consumer demand for groundfish had remained strong after World War II, imports probably would have seemed much less important to the industry.

The decline in demand for groundfish made prices and revenues fall and left fishermen and boat owners stranded. Many fishermen had never held other jobs and had few alternatives outside fishing. A large proportion were immigrants with little education and with trouble speaking English. A big offshore trawler was a particularly durable capital investment that had no use in other fisheries in New England or in other parts of the country without expensive conversion. Boat owners therefore had very few opportunities to recapture the capital they had invested. One incident showed how eager they were to get out of vessel ownership. "In 1947 Uncle Sam put out a flier to our industry stating that he was interested in purchasing some fishing trawlers for delivery to Germany," said John Fulham, a vessel owner-dealer from Boston. "Practically our entire fleet of fishing trawlers was offered to Uncle Sam to buy. . . . we all, even in 1947, wanted to get out of the business, because the fleet owners could see the handwriting on the wall." The government bought only the twelve vessels which met the government's specifications.[12]

Although the departure of boats and fishermen from the industry was slow during the late 1940s and early 1950s, the incomes of those who remained might have been expected to improve. Population increased in the Northeast, the major market for New England fish; and, although growth was slower than in the rest of the country, demand for groundfish would have increased for the smaller number of boats and fishermen if no other market conditions had changed.

But other conditions did change. Beginning in 1954, the new market for fish sticks undermined demand for New England groundfish again. By 1955 at least 55 percent of households in the Northeast—New England, New York, New Jersey, and Pennsylvania—were using fish sticks, a much larger percent of households than in any other region of the country. In addition, a quarter of the households in the Northeast which consumed fish sticks said that fish sticks had replaced some or all of their purchases of other fish. Two-thirds of these households consumed less fresh fish. Ninety percent bought less fresh and frozen fish, all of which meant less New England-caught groundfish.[13]

Imports of frozen groundfish fillets leveled off. They fluctuated between 85 million and 114 million pounds from the mid-1950s through the mid-1960s. In contrast, imports of frozen blocks and slabs of groundfish for fish sticks grew enormously; by 1964 they exceeded 165 million pounds. To what extent imports contributed to the problems of the groundfish industry by continuing to hold down or decrease demand in ways other than through the market for fish sticks is difficult to say. For the period from 1957 through 1967, analysis failed to show that imports influenced the ex-vessel price of groundfish.[14]

The development of fish sticks and frozen blocks was not the last change to undercut demand for New England groundfish. In 1966 Pope

Paul VI and the conference of bishops in the United States ruled that American Catholics no longer had to abstain from eating meat on Fridays except during Lent. Dealers and fishermen in the groundfish industry, serving a market where 45 percent of the population were Catholics, feared more hardships as they lost a guaranteed market for fish. "You know the Cardinal," a group of processors and boat owners said to Thomas Fulham, a long-time leader in efforts to help the fishing industry. They pressed him to try to get the new ruling rescinded. Within the next two years, their fears about the immediate effects of the change were confirmed. The new rules probably held down the ex-vessel prices of haddock, cod, and redfish.[15]

The federal government's programs to increase the demand for groundfish seem remarkably small and ineffectual in comparison with these much larger forces influencing demand. Even if programs could have been designed better and if implementation problems could have been solved, government efforts would probably have had to be much more extensive to outweigh these other trends. Massive government purchases might have been the only way to increase demand sufficiently, but Congress would have been unsympathetic to a buying program or to any other type of effort which would inevitably have cost a great deal of money.

Decreasing the Costs of Fishing

Programs to lower the cost of fishing suffered from problems similar to those of the efforts to increase the demand for fish. Implementation of the loan fund, research and development programs, and the vessel construction subsidy benefited other parts of the fishing industry, but rarely the offshore groundfishery. Incorrect assumptions about the causes of problems and about the motivations of fishermen and boat owners prevented other programs from solving the fishery's problems.

In large part because of poor implementation, the fishery loan fund hardly touched the groundfish industry. Most of the government's fishery loans went to inshore boat owners; a large number of others went to the prosperous New Bedford scallop and flounder fisheries, both inshore and offshore. The owners of offshore groundfish boats received only between 15 and 20 percent of approximately 350 loans to New England boat owners between 1957 and 1973.

This distribution of loans had a plausible explanation. Boat owners who found the program most attractive may already have been considering new construction, major repairs, or rehabilitation of their boats.

Groundfish boat owners were rarely in this group. The fishery in which boat owners received the largest number of loans, inshore lobstering, prospered during the 1950s and 1960s. Many lobstermen who applied for loans for new boats withdrew their applications when they saw the paperwork required, and paid for their boats out of family resources. Although many could not get a loan from another financial institution, as required for program eligibility, they could and did buy new boats without the loans.[16]

Neither legislation nor regulations directed administrators to award loans to some fisheries more often than to others. The financial statements of boat owners from prosperous fisheries must have looked better to loan officers than those of most groundfish boat owners, who were bad risks even for the fisheries loan fund. Because the law required that the loans be repaid, the loan fund had "not been soft enough to help many fishermen and boat owners in New England. . . . There was not enough chance of repayment to take the chance on giving them a loan," said Donald McKernan, director of the Bureau of Commercial Fisheries.[17]

As with the fishery loan fund, neither legislation nor regulations directed program administrators to favor research and development projects which addressed groundfish industry problems. Therefore, as biologists and economists in the fishery agencies and outside the government decided on research questions, they did not give special thought to studies that would help the groundfishery; and most research did not look at groundfish problems.

The vessel subsidy programs set up after 1964 also benefited other groups more than the groundfish industry. As with the loan fund, a particularly prosperous sector of the New England fishing industry, this time the New Bedford scallop fleet, took advantage of the funds most often. Boat owners probably would have built most of the subsidized scallopers without the federal money, but as they planned to purchase new boats, they found they could reduce their costs by taking advantage of the subsidy. Before the 1964 revision in the subsidy law which opened the program to boat owners outside the groundfishery, one New Bedford boat owner had protested that New Bedford did not need subsidies, in part because about four new boats entered the city's fleet every year. As of 1975 eighteen offshore boats operated out of New Bedford that had been built between 1960 and 1964 before the subsidy became available to scallopers. In the groundfish industry, in contrast, only a few boats entered the fishery without subsidy.[18]

Even if all the vessel construction funds had gone to the groundfishery, however, the program would not have replaced the offshore groundfish fleet as originally intended. The program never received enough funding to do so. Spokesmen for Boston's groundfish industry, Thomas Rice and Thomas Fulham, estimated in 1959 that replacement of the groundfish fleet over ten years would cost $10 to $15 million. A group of Boston Fish Pier leaders had announced in 1958 that they would try to build twenty new offshore trawlers of 180 gross tons for Boston over ten years at a cost of $200,000 each. Rice and Fulham's estimate drew on that plan and included the replacement of many more boats from Boston, Gloucester, and Portland.[19]

Congress authorized $2.5 million per year for three years in the 1960 subsidy legislation. Assuming the estimates of Rice and Fulham were correct, that level of funding would have allowed for construction of about ten boats per year, a substantial number of new vessels for the groundfishery. However, in response to the small requests from the Bureau of Commercial Fisheries, Congress appropriated only $750,000 from 1961 through 1964. Furthermore, the Bureau spent much less than the appropriation in every year: in 1961 no funds went for boat construction; in 1963 only about $93,000 went for subsidies; and in both 1962 and 1964 the Bureau spent between $400,000 and $500,000 for boat subsidies.[20]

Congress authorized $10 million per year after 1965 under the expanded vessel construction subsidy. Appropriations again amounted to much less, although they met the Bureau of Commercial Fisheries' requests. The first year under the expanded program, 1965, Congress allocated $2.5 million for construction subsidies, but the Bureau used only $157,000 for boat payments out of a total subsidy program budget of $395,000. The Bureau used the congressional appropriations of between $3 million and $6 million from 1966 through 1969, never close to the authorized $10 million. Director of the Bureau of Commercial Fisheries, Harold Crowther, explained that his agency had never asked for the full authorization because the Nixon administration's "austerity program" placed a ceiling on the funds the Bureau could request.[21] The vessel construction program was not high enough among the Bureau's or the administration's priorities to receive support for more funding.

Even if the subsidy program had used the authorized funds to pay for vessels for the offshore groundfishery, the program could not have achieved the original goal of replacing the groundfish fleet. By the 1960s, the cost estimates of Rice and Fulham were too low. A subsidized boat which a group of Boston groundfish interests brought into the fishery in 1962 cost $462,000 even under stringent cost controls, although the vessel displaced 239 gross tons, a third more than the boats planned in 1958. A boat designer estimated in 1965 that a 100-foot steel boat cost about $400,000, a 100-foot wooden on $280,000. The requirements of the subsidy program accounted for part of this increase in boat costs. Features such as mine detectors, which the Navy wanted for the boats' use in war, added to the expense. Inflation in the cost of steel and other inputs added substantially to boat costs in the 1960s. By 1970 the same boat cost at least 50 percent more than it had in 1960.[22]

The funding problems that interfered with the vessel construction programs were a symptom of the lack of agency and administration commitment. As the director of the Fish and Wildlife Service pointed out in 1955, the original purpose of the fisheries agency had been scientific. The "backbone" of the Fish and Wildlife Service, he said, was "the development of knowledge and information based upon scientific studies and statistics, and making that information available both to the Service and to outside agencies to enable them to better manage the fishery and wildlife resources of the Nation." That tradition continued to dominate the agency's activities as Congress added the assistance programs for commercial fisheries to their responsibilities. In one typical year, said Ed Raymond, administrator of financial assistance in the Northeast region from the 1960s through the 1970s, funding for one study of plankton was more than double the allocation for financial assistance. Joseph Slavin, a fisheries administrator whose career began in the 1950s, argued that one could not fault the Bureau of Commercial Fisheries or its successor, the National Marine Fisheries Service, for failing to solve the groundfish industry's problems because the agencies had never aimed to do so.

This strong tradition, as well as administration views, accounted in large part for the Bureau's lack of response to the very clear intention of Congress that the fishery programs should solve industry problems. Fisheries troubles were virtually ignored in the agenda of every President until the late 1960s.[23]

More common than difficulties in implementation were problems with program conception. The safety programs, training for new fishermen, the fishery loan fund, the first vessel construction subsidy, research and development programs, and "Seafreeze Atlantic" were all based on incorrect assumptions about the industry that meant these efforts could not solve the problems of the groundfishery.

The Bureau of Commercial Fisheries safety program assumed that boat owners could take advantage of the changes the program advocated. The few owners who could build new groundfish vessels also had money to pay for the new safety features. The majority of boats in the groundfish fleet, however, had very low revenues. They could not afford to make extra expenditures for safety equipment when they could not even keep their boats in good repair. As the Bureau's vessel safety officer for New England observed, in New Bedford where the fishing industry was more prosperous, boat owners were more receptive to the Bureau's program than in Gloucester and Boston.[24] The safety program could not reduce insurance costs for hard-pressed groundfishermen if boat owners could not adopt new methods.

Even if boat owners had used new safety equipment, insurance costs might not have gone down, although program administrators assumed they would. Other factors were very important in determining insurance costs. The cost of insurance declined for groundfish vessels with the best profit records between 1953 and 1957 among one sample of boats. All the vessels with consistently poor operating experience had substantial increases in insurance costs. Marine insurance brokers said that they considered earnings along with the level of boat maintenance, loss record, and quality of management in negotiating new insurance contracts. Insurance companies used profits as an indicator because vessels with better earnings made fewer hull insurance claims. Perhaps boat owners with deficits postponed important maintenance expenses or intensified fishing operations to raise receipts and, therefore, had more claims. In addition, owners in financial difficulty may have seen the insurance contract as a way to recoup some losses. If they damaged or sank their boats, they could realize some gain as they went out of business.[25] All these facts meant that if a hard-pressed groundfish boat owner adopted some of the safety measures which the Bureau suggested, his insurance costs would drop very little if at all. Furthermore, none of the basic reasons for his financial troubles would be solved because high insurance costs were a symptom of the problems in the industry, not a cause.

The training programs to attract young men to the groundfish industry suffered from similar deficiencies. The program supporters assumed incorrectly that the groundfish industry suffered from a shortage of crew. They believed, in addition, that training programs would make fishing jobs attractive to young men. Implicitly, advocates of the training programs assumed that training could overcome the disadvantages of lack of experience which they appeared to believe kept young men out of fishing. The major argument for the training programs was that younger men would be more productive than older workers and would therefore lower the costs of fishing for the New England groundfish fleet.

The groundfish industry did not have a crew shortage. In the mid-1950s when industry representatives pressed for funds for training, Boston still had so many fishermen looking for work that the union supervised rotation of crewmen to spread jobs among more people. By the mid-1960s boats with the lowest incomes had trouble finding crewmen even though younger and less reputable fishermen generally did not work full time. The vessels with higher earnings had no problems finding experienced crew.[26]

Training programs could not make young men more willing to accept the fishing jobs which paid the lowest wages and offered the most uncomfortable and most dangerous working conditions, the only sites open to any newcomer. Nearly all the trainees had the flexibility to leave fishing for other jobs or to leave groundfishing for other kinds of fishing. The groundfish fleet looked particularly unattractive. A fisherman who went through the program run by the Atlantic Fishermen's Union under the Manpower Development and Training Act said, "I started in Gloucester on groundfish boats. It took me less than a year to realize the money to be made at the time was in the New Bedford yellowtail flounder industry . . . and I joined."[27]

Very low wages and dangerous conditions probably accounted for the small number of young fishermen; no other barriers kept young men out of fishing, but training programs did nothing to raise salaries. Like the vessel safety efforts, training programs dealt unsuccessfully with a symptom of the industry's problems but did nothing to counteract the causes of the problems.

Even the major argument for the training programs is hard to justify. Young men would not have increased fishing productivity, if the preferences of boat owners and captains are an indication of labor quality. Older men worked most often and held the better sites, those of captain, engineer, or mate, or of crewman on a higher-income boat. Boat owners saw the older men who had known reputations as the most desirable captains, and captains often preferred to hire older men whose work they knew would be good. No union regulations kept the older men in the best positions in the fleet.[28]

The fishery loan legislation also reflected incorrect assumptions. Congress and the industry believed that a shortage of capital hurt the groundfish industry, that boat owners who could repay loans could not get financing from private lending sources. Banks overestimated the riskiness of loans to individuals based on the problems of the industry as a whole, supporters of a loan fund believed.

The experience of the fishery loan fund suggests, however, that the shortage of capital was much smaller than either congressmen or the industry had thought. Program administrators had trouble finding groundfish boat owners who they felt confident could eventually repay the loans, according to the director of the Bureau of Commercial Fisheries. When the Bureau did make loans, groundfish boat owners often failed to pay back the money. The list of loans foreclosed by the Bureau of Commercial Fisheries by 1961 showed that all the New England defaults came from the offshore groundfish ports, Boston and Gloucester. In 1972 National Marine Fisheries Service analysts found that 20 percent of the loan fund's losses came from New England boats. About a quarter of all loans were in foreclosure, but at least a third of loans to New England groundfish boats were among these. The most common reasons for default were low catches, high insurance rates, crew problems, and the need for more extensive repairs, some of the same general problems which groundfish boat owners had cited for years. In an ironic twist considering that the fishery loan legislation had passed in response to groundfish industry problems, the National Marine Fisheries Service study recommended that loans be denied to boats in fisheries with resource problems, such as the New England groundfish industry.[29]

The 1960 boat construction subsidy also reflected incorrect assumptions. Congress and the industry underestimated the amount of money the government would have to promise a boat owner before he would invest in a new groundfish vessel. The subsidy program assumed that if the cost of a new boat were lowered to the cost of construction in a foreign boatyard, boat owners would purchase new vessels. However, very few boat owners built groundfish vessels under the program; no Gloucester boat owner even applied for funds. Salvatore Favazza, executive secretary of the Gloucester Fisheries Commission, believed Gloucester fishermen and boat owners had not shown interest in the program because of "misunderstandings as to the working of the subsidy." Certainly some Gloucester families did not want government help; they took pride in paying for vessels themselves. One new boat entered the Gloucester offshore groundfish fleet during the years of the first program, and it was not subsidized. Gloucester fishermen had used the loan fund, however, and Gloucester interests had lobbied for the subsidy legislation. More likely than "misunderstandings," most fishermen and boat owners could not raise their share of the capital; or the income prospects for groundfish vessels did not seem good enough, even with the subsidy, to make new investment worthwhile. In contrast, in New Bedford where very few boats engaged in groundfishing but fishermen and boat owners had more capital, more boat owners used the first subsidy program.[30]

Thomas Fulham and others formed the Boston Fishing Company to build the "Massachusetts," the first new boat in Boston in fourteen years. Fish dealers, cold storage operators, oil suppliers, gear and equipment suppliers, restaurant owners, and mechanics and other tradesmen who knew about fishing joined the venture. The new boat's arrival in Boston in 1962 attracted considerable attention. The vessel indicated "a new day dawning" for the fishing industry, proclaimed one press report. According to Fulham, "Headlines ran the gamut from small effort to answer to the Red threat."

However, the experience of the Boston group confirmed that the one-third subsidy for vessel construction under the 1960 program could neither assure a return on investment nor allow for innovation in boat design and fishing gear. "I doubt seriously," Fulham said, "if any group in the country could duplicate the cost control exercised in this venture." He explained their methods: "In all respects, she is an excellent vessel built from a proven design, constructed of improved materials and modernized machinery. . . . There is nothing new or exciting, nor are there any unique features which will enhance our national prestige or aid us in assuming a proud posture among the fishing nations of the world. In short, to do that would have been so costly that the project would never have gotten off the ground. . . . None of the customary legal fees, travel, office expense, management, or promotional expenses were paid. The vessel design, which is normally a significant percentage of the cost, was provided at no cost. Even the shipyard owner was persuaded to build a sister ship for a company in which it had an interest to lessen further the costs of construction." In addition, the Fulhams had control of the company which owned Boston Fish Pier. They received income from the sale of ice and the rental of fish pier space, both of which would increase with the operation of a new boat at the pier; they could invest more in the new boat as a result. Few groups, Fulham pointed out, would be willing to repeat the Boston group's effort. "She is a vessel launched by cooperative desperation," he said. "People work and invest because they anticipate a wage or return on their investment. The people who nurtured the 'Massachusetts' received no wage and its stockholders are hoping, but do not anticipate a return on their investment."[31] Under such conditions, it was not surprising that few boat owners already in the groundfishery tried to use the subsidy.

The proponents of research and development programs assumed too optimistically that the fishing industry could and would benefit from the information and technical knowledge which the programs produced. However, much of the research had no relation to the groundfishery, and few could move to other fisheries to take advantage of the information. Even when research dealt with the groundfishery, the findings had little to do with the actual work, although the new knowledge could offer benefits over the long run. Greater understanding of the nature of groundfish stocks and of the behavior of groundfish species had little relation to the welfare of the industry before the mid-1960s. When research did have applications, few in the groundfish industry had the money to take advantage of the findings. They rarely built new boats or rehabilitated old ones. Therefore, they could not use the new technology of stern trawling, although its financial advantages were obvious. Boat owners in the groundfish industry were very slow to adopt new technology even when they had the money to do so, however. During the 1960s and 1970s most new vessels were built for side trawling. In other cases, research developed technology that would not have been profitable even if groundfish boat owners could have paid for it. Freezing fish at sea, for example, would not have provided an adequate return on investment during the 1950s and 1960s.

Although research and development programs could not turn the industry's fortunes around, the work did make valuable contributions to understanding the fisheries and to developing new technology over long periods of time. During the late 1960s and early 1970s, for example, knowledge that had accumulated over many years of research about the size and behavior of fish stocks became particularly important for efforts to manage the resource. By the late 1970s many of the new boats were designed for stern trawling, and some fishermen who believed that freezing a few species at sea would be profitable looked at the results of experiments conducted during the 1950s.

The "Seafreeze Atlantic" failure exhibited the worst misconceptions about the way the groundfish industry operated. The venture's most serious problems grew out of incorrect expectations about the behavior of fishermen. New England fishermen were accustomed to trips of seven to ten days or two-weeks at the longest, but "Seafreeze" was built for trips that would last three months. New England fishermen earned a share of the revenues from the catch and controlled the size of their incomes to some extent. They could always hope to earn more if they became more skilled in catching and handling fish or if they worked harder. In contrast, "Seafreeze" offered wages, not even particularly good wages. Most New England fishermen were used to developing relationships with the rest of the crew over many trips; these ties became impossible on the factory vessel. Most fishermen never considered taking a "Seafreeze" job; and most of those who did work on the vessel left after a short time because they could not tolerate the long trips, bad crew relationships, fixed wages, and the work with unskilled crewmen when the boat could not attract enough experienced fishermen. The "Seafreeze" owners, congressmen, and agency officials had not expected the clash between New England fishing traditions and the vessel's arrangements. Because their perception of the industry's character was wrong, their vision of the results of the "Seafreeze" effort was not fulfilled.

Unlike the rest of the boat subsidy program, the "Seafreeze" venture had not aimed to solve the fishing industry's problems or to help fishermen and boat owners. The purpose had been to raise the status of the United States among fishing nations, to show that this nation could harvest more fish with more advanced technology than other countries.

Poor implementation and inaccurate assumptions about the nature of the industry and its problems were not the only reasons the efforts to lower costs failed to solve the groundfish industry's difficulties. The programs faced a larger task than the industry or agency officials realized.

Even if programs had lowered the costs of fishing, they might not have slowed the departure of boats from the groundfish industry during the 1950s. Portuguese or Sicilian families with strong traditional ties to fishing owned many of the Gloucester boats and would stay in fishing if they could earn enough income to cover costs. During the hard times in the 1950s and 1960s they did whatever they could to keep boats going. In contrast, many of the vessel owner-dealers based mainly in Boston would leave the fishery if their income did not match the return they could get from other investments and if they could find a way to recapture at least part of the capital their boats represented. These vessel owner-dealers often were part of companies with broader fishing and processing interests or were subsidiaries of corporations with substantial investments outside fishing. Even moderately successful aid programs would have had difficulty reducing the costs of fishing enough to stop the departure of this group from the harvesting of groundfish in New England.

In 1950 dealers and processors owned nearly all the boats in Boston's offshore fisheries, and dealer-owned trawlers brought in up to 80 percent of Boston's annual landings. Vessel owner-dealers had traditionally chosen to maximize the profits in fish dealing rather than in vessel ownership, but after 1950 vessel operation earned even lower profits. In addition, as many dealers increased their purchases of less expensive imported frozen fish, they no longer needed a guaranteed supply of caught fish, a compelling reason for boat ownership during World War II.[32]

The development of fish sticks made boat ownership more unattractive. The five vessel owner-dealers that produced fish sticks by 1955 had owned about twenty-five of the Boston offshore boats in 1949, two-thirds of the trawlers over 150 gross tons. The fish stick producers used imported fish blocks rather than New England-caught fish. During the 1950s the fish stick processors and other dealers sold their boats to fishermen in Gloucester or Maine or transferred their boat operations to Maine or Canada. By 1960 fish stick producing firms owned very few of the boats in Boston.[33]

As some Boston dealers' reliance on Boston fresh fish weakened, they not only sold or moved their boats but also moved their processing operations out of Boston to new or expanded plants in Canada, Maine, and Gloucester. "This shows clearly that the problems are not in the overall marketing of fishery products, but that producing these products at Boston is difficult under present cost conditions," stated a long-time observer of the Boston fishing industry from the Market News Office of the Bureau of Commercial Fisheries.[34] Most likely, the trend showed that when a firm expanded into fish stick operations, sold its vessels, and depended heavily on imports, land and labor costs and access to foreign shipments of fish made Boston unattractive compared to other locations. Fish stick firms did not need to stay on Boston Fish Pier.

The vessel owner-dealers rarely stated that their location needs had changed when they went into fish stick production. Instead, vessel owners and some union leaders claimed that Boston's industry declined because of the intransigence of the fishermen's union. The union would not allow changes in the lay arrangements to provide a larger return on investment for vessel owners. As a result, many in the Boston industry argued, owners sold their boats or moved to ports where wages were lower. In Maine where the union was weak and in Canada where the fishermen had not unionized, the owners could do better. The president of Gorton-Pew, later Gorton's of Gloucester, a vessel owner-dealer-processor, expressed the prevailing view in 1956: "The crews in general on these Gloucester boats [Gorton-Pew's] are faring very well. It is the companies that are not faring very well. . . . the fishermen have the owner into a position that is completely untenable in view of present-day operating costs."[35]

On the other hand, most fishermen believed they were not well off. In the early 1950s when crew shares compared favorably with the incomes of Boston manufacturing workers, fishermen pointed out that they earned less than a full crew share because they did not go on every trip a vessel made. They worked more hours and, they said, therefore earned less per hour than their annual salaries suggested. Even when many fishermen did earn more per hour than manufacturing workers, the hard, dangerous work on the north Atlantic made the earnings low in terms of effort. Through the 1950s and early 1960s, fishermen's earnings declined while other workers' incomes rose so that by the early 1960s fishermen on the large boats in Boston usually earned much less than the national median income. Those who did earn incomes of about the national median level worked many more days than other workers in New England and held sites on the most prosperous boats.[36]

The departure from Boston of General Seafoods, the Birds Eye Division of General Foods, illustrates the importance of a vessel owner-dealer's profit calculations, growth of imports, fish stick production, and labor disputes in Boston's problems. At the end of World War II, General Seafoods was the largest boat owner-dealer in Boston. In 1945 after the company had refitted ten boats returned from the Navy, its Boston fleet totalled eighteen vessels, fifteen company-owned and another three chartered, at least twice as many boats as any other vessel owner-dealer. All the boats were large offshore trawlers, displacing between 160 and 320 gross tons.[37]

By the late 1940s, General Seafoods felt the slump in vessel profits. In 1946 the new contract between fishermen and vessel owners in Boston, agreed upon after a five-month strike, gave fishermen a raise of about 25 percent at the expense of vessel owners through changes in the lay arrangements. General Seafoods appealed to the union to relax rules about the number of days boats could stay at sea. Boats could not make enough money without longer trips, and the company would have to leave Boston if the rules were not changed, the management told the union. The threat caused heated debate in the union. Its head, Patrick McHugh, was "anti-capital," a group of younger fishermen claimed, and they campaigned against him to convince union members to grant General Seafoods's request. After long floor discussion the membership voted by a narrow margin to refuse to make the changes the company wanted.

Over the next few years General Seafoods sold or transferred its boats, eliminating jobs for about 300 fishermen. In 1949 the company sold some boats to the Army for use in Germany. By the end of that year the company had reduced its fleet to five Boston trawlers and four trawlers operating out of a new Rockland, Maine, redfish plant. Over the next few years the company transferred more boats to Nova Scotia and to Rockland. The 1946 Boston fishermen's strike was part of the reason for the decision to reduce the fleet, management said, but not the only one. The company had been able to protect itself during the strike by pushing production in its Canadian plants to record highs. The company could also move its boats to Canada or to Rockland to avoid the unfavorable lay arrangements in Boston. Rather, management reported, trawler ownership was simply not profitable anywhere.

In 1953 General Foods developed the first fish sticks. The company produced fish sticks from domestically caught fish in Boston for a short time but found that processing imported blocks and slabs from its plants in Canada was more profitable. The following year the company sold three large Boston trawlers to another Boston firm and transferred the rest of its vessels to Rockland. The processing operations, which had filleted and frozen Boston-caught fish, moved to Gloucester and Rockland. The company reacquired half a dozen vessels from the Army for operation out of Rockland and Halifax, Nova Scotia.

Jim Ackert, one of the younger fishermen who wanted to go along with General Seafoods's request in the late 1940s, remembered that many believed that if the union's vote had gone the other way, General Seafoods would not have left. Most likely, however, General Seafoods would have stayed in Boston as long as the company could press the union into making concessions, at least before the development of fish sticks; but when the union could give no more, the company would have moved its boats or sold them anyway, especially after fish stick production began.

Indeed, despite freedom from Boston labor problems, General Seafoods sold its fishing operations in Rockland and Nova Scotia to National Sea Products, the largest fish processing firm in Nova Scotia, in early 1957. "From a cost standpoint," General Foods reported, "Birds Eye has found it advantageous to purchase its requirements for fish and to limit its activities to processing and distribution." National Sea continued to operate General Seafoods's processing plants and boats in the ocean perch fishery from Rockland, Maine.

As General Seafoods's decision to build and expand its Rockland redfish plant suggests, cost considerations were different in the redfish (ocean perch) fishery than in haddock and cod. Labor problems may have been more significant in explaining Boston's losses in the redfish industry. Only ocean perch could be processed from New England-caught fish as cheaply as from imported Canadian fillets, the president of Gorton-Pew reported in 1956. Large companies continued to own boats in the ocean perch fishery and to process fish from the boats, but they moved their operations from Boston to Maine. In addition to General Seafoods, F. J. O'Hara and Sons moved a large share of operations from Boston to Rockland as early as 1939 to fish for redfish and process it. Both companies had transferred remaining Boston-based boats to Rockland by the 1960s. The boats' trips to the ocean perch fishing grounds were shorter from Rockland than from Boston; but, probably as important, the fishermen's union was weak, and the companies faced none of the disputes over the lay agreement and the operation of the auction that they did in

Boston. General Seafoods paid fishermen wages on the Rockland boats, which removed fishermen's concern about fish prices, a very unusual move in the New England fisheries.[38]

In Boston the fishery aid programs had no apparent effect on the decisions of the vessel owner-dealers whose behavior accounted for the largest part of Boston's decline in number of boats and in volume of landings. Congress and the fishery agencies assumed a constituency of fishing interests who wanted to remain in harvesting or in processing of New England-caught fish. In Boston that group did a small share of the business. The vessel owner-dealers' requirements for boat profitability were probably too high for even successfully designed and implemented programs to meet, given the scale of efforts Congress had intended.

The forces that encouraged boats to leave Boston ran their course. In the 1960s, however, the vessel construction subsidy program aided the purchase of a few boats for a new organization of industry around the core of firms which had hung on through the hard times. Thomas Fulham pointed proudly to the fact that his group had built two new boats despite predictions by at least one fishery expert in the early 1950s that no one would be able to bring a new vessel into the industry. By the 1970s nearly all Boston landings came from the subsidized boats and from Gloucester vessels whose captains hoped to get a better price in Boston than in Gloucester. The port had become a center for fish wholesaling. Boston's dealers handled fresh fish from all over New England along with Canadian frozen fish.[39]

THE DILEMMA OF HOW TO REVITALIZE THE INDUSTRY

Programs to increase the demand for fish and to reduce the costs of fishing failed to make the industry prosper in part because of implementation problems and incorrect assumptions about the character of the industry. Most programs would have been too small to solve the industry's problems even if some of the efforts' other difficulties had been resolved.

Certainly some programs could have made the industry prosper. Massive government purchases of New England groundfish could have raised prices enough to enable most boats to operate in the black and most fishermen to earn adequate wages. Boat operations would have become profitable under programs which successfully lowered insurance costs and repair, maintenance, and gear replacement expenses to Canadian levels. Subsidy programs of such a scale would have involved large and continuing government expenditures, between $5 and $10 million in 1957 alone.[40] Buying programs and subsidies would also have meant an extensive government role in the industry to monitor costs and activities to determine subsidy levels. No one in the industry wanted so much government interference in his affairs. Congress and the administration also opposed such a large and expensive government role in private enterprise except in the special case of agriculture. While the troubles of other, larger industries more central to the national economy might eventually overcome misgivings about government intervention in the private sector, the fishing industry's difficulties could not do so during the 1950s and 1960s, especially without the industry's support.

The government could have relieved groundfish industry troubles by buying the boats of vessel owners who wanted to get out of fishing and by helping fishermen move to jobs outside fishing. The boats and fishermen who chose to stay in the industry would have earned more satisfactory incomes as the quantity of fish landed declined and prices rose. No one in the fishing industry or in the federal government ever proposed such an effort, however. The industry pushed for programs that would enable boat owners and fishermen to stay in the industry. Congress was unlikely to agree that government should assume private losses on capital investment in boats, even if the industry had wanted it.

In contrast, the programs on which the industry placed its best hopes could not have solved the industry's troubles. Neither the higher tariffs recommended by the Tariff Commission in 1956 nor more extensive vessel construction subsidies could have assured a prosperous future.

The industry and Congress alike believed that higher tariffs would solve the offshore industry's problems. If other difficulties remained, they felt, the industry would be able to handle these troubles under the protection of higher tariffs. "We believe very sincerely that the actual solution, the real solution, is the correction or restriction of the imports," Solomon Sandler of the Gloucester Fisheries Commission stated in 1956. Mayor Corliss of Gloucester wrote, "A permanent solution, in our opinion, is the acceptance of the Tariff Commission recommendations." If the President had agreed to these, Congressman William Bates of Gloucester was asked in 1958, "would that have remedied the conditions?" "Yes sir. I believe that perhaps it would have done so," Bates answered.[41]

In 1956 the Tariff Commission recommended increases in the duties on groundfish fillets to remedy the "serious injury to the domestic industry." The Commission suggested that the duty on fish under the quota— the first fifteen million pounds of groundfish imported in a year or 15 percent of average domestic consumption for the three preceding years, whichever was greater—be raised from 1.875 cents per pound to 2.8125 cents per pound. They recommended that the tariff on the remainder of groundfish imports increase from 2.5 cents per pound to 3.75 cents per pound.[42] This tariff increase would have been too small to solve the problems of the groundfishery.

In 1956 imported groundfish cost much less than New England-caught fish. Cod landed at Boston Fish Pier in 1956 averaged 7 cents per pound, or the equivalent of 18.4 cents per pound of filleted weight. Haddock earned Boston fishermen and boat owners 7.3 cents per pound, or about 18.3 cents per pound of filleted weight. The price of imports of groundfish blocks was about 18.7 cents per pound in 1956 not counting freight charges, duties, and insurance. Transportation costs from Nova Scotia to the Gloucester fish stick plants were less than 1.5 cents per pound. In other words, species landed at New England ports which were suitable for fish stick ingredients cost only half a cent less per pound than the processed imported fish, about 2 cents less than a foreign price counting freight charges. With additions to the New England ex-vessel price to cover labor, capital costs, and profit margins in filleting and freezing into blocks, the United States price for the processed product would have been much higher than the cost of imported blocks. The ex-vessel prices of the Canadian fish that went into the groundfish blocks were only a third to a half of the prices at the Boston Fish Pier.[43] Even if the tariffs had added the full cent or so of the increase in duty to the cost of the blocks and slabs, New England-caught fish would not have been inexpensive enough to substitute for imports.

The prices of imported cod and haddock fillets were also much lower than the prices of domestic fish. In 1956 the price of imported frozen cod fillets not counting duties, insurance, and transportation was 18.6 cents per pound. Imported frozen fillets of haddock, hake, pollock, and cusk cost 20.8 cents per pound. These prices were at most 2.5 cents per pound higher than the prices of unprocessed fish landed at Boston Fish Pier. Seen another way, the landed price of cod in Nova Scotia plus transport costs plus the new tariff would have been at most 14.2 cents per pound of filleted fish if tariffs had increased price by the amount of the increase in duty. The price of cod landed in Boston, converted to filleted equivalent, was over 4 cents per pound more than that Canadian price. Because processing workers' wages were lower in Canada than in the United States and filleting used the same technology in both countries, the difference in costs was probably even larger. The cost of Nova Scotia haddock would have been about 13.9 cents per pound of fillets after transportation costs and tariffs were added to ex-vessel prices. In Boston the ex-vessel value of filleted haddock was nearly 4.5 cents per pound more.[44] Even with the higher tariffs therefore, the domestic producers would have bought more imported frozen fillets.

For redfish, in contrast, the new tariffs would have encouraged dealers to buy more of the domestic product because foreign and domestic prices were nearly the same. The cost of Nova Scotia redfish fillets, counting ex-vessel price, transport costs to Gloucester, and the full amount of the tariff, would have been at most 13.3 cents per pound in 1956. The ex-vessel price of redfish fillets in Gloucester was 13.5 cents per pound, virtually the same, although with differences in processing costs, Nova Scotia would have gained a greater advantage.[45]

When they could not get higher tariffs, the industry campaigned for subsidies to reduce their costs, their next best hope for staying in business. The major attempts to reduce costs during the 1960s aimed to lower the expense of vessel construction. The few vessel owners who took advantage of the subsidies profited, but if all offshore groundfish boats had been replaced, as the program originally intended and as the industry had hoped, the results for owners would not have been favorable.

The subsidized boats made money, probably more than most other boats. Owners who had used subsidies returned to apply for funds to build more boats. The group of fishing interests led by Thomas Fulham built two boats under the first subsidy program, and another group that included Fulham and others constructed two more boats with funding from the second subsidy program. O'Hara and Sons of Rockland, Maine, built two boats under the first program, three under the second. "The fishboat subsidy has been a great help to our company," one boat owner reported. "Many of the highline New England vessels have been built under the program, and while the red tape has been a bit rough, it's been worth it." According to Frank O'Hara of O'Hara and Sons, "The fishing industry had a good thing [in the subsidy]."[46]

In 1966 the three Boston boats constructed with funds from the first program performed better than most older vessels. Of sixteen Boston boats of about the same size, only two made more trips and brought in more fish than the subsidized vessels, and only one of the older boats generally had larger loads of fish per trip.[47] The three subsidy boats were certainly among the five highest earners of boats their size in Boston.

While owners usually argue that boats of the same size have the same costs, the new boats probably had lower costs than the two older boats which brought in more fish. Both of the latter boats had been fishing thirty years, about as long as a boat was normally expected to last. They probably had higher repair and insurance costs because those expenses rose with the age of the boat. Compared with boats of about the same size which harvested less fish, the subsidy boats probably had the additional advantage that they attracted better captains and crew who knew they could make more money on the new boats, which were also safer and usually had more comfortable living quarters.[48]

If many more offshore groundfish boats had been replaced with boats similar to the Boston ones, the effects on all owners would not have been favorable. In 1959 about eighty large boats, over 125 gross tons, and about ninety-five medium-sized boats, 60 to 125 gross tons, fished offshore for groundfish out of New England ports.[49] With replacement of many of these by the late 1960s, the volume of landings would have gone up for a few years. Prices for groundfish would have fallen, and revenues would have been higher for the fleet as a whole. For the remaining older boats, however, incomes would have been lower unless they could have brought in more fish to compensate for the lower price. New boats would have benefited most from the higher fleet revenue, and their incomes would have been satisfactory for a short time.

Profits would have declined within a few years, however, because the added fishing effort would increase costs. Biologists now believe that production from the stocks of cod and haddock was around the highest possible sustainable yield in the 1950s on Georges Bank and in the Gulf of Maine. New England vessels harvested the bulk of that catch.[50] With additional larger, more efficient boats, landings from the banks would have gone up for a while and then fallen to a lower sustainable yield from a depleted stock. Eventually, boat owners' costs would have risen as they had more difficulty harvesting fish. Then boat owners would have been vulnerable again to increases in other costs or to decreases in demand.

This scenario could not have been played out quite this way, however. In the mid-1960s foreign fleets began to fish heavily on Georges Bank for groundfish species, especially haddock. In 1964 the combined international harvest was 64,000 metric tons of haddock from Georges Bank; in 1965 the amount more than doubled to nearly 150,000 metric tons. United States vessels had harvested 73 percent of the Georges Bank haddock landings in 1964, but in 1965 they brought in only 35 percent of the total. By 1969 Georges Bank haddock production had fallen to 22,000 metric tons. Landings per day fished, an indicator of the condition of the haddock stock, fell from 5.6 metric tons in 1965 to 2.8 metric tons in 1969. In other words, boats brought in half as much fish for the same amount of time on the grounds.[51]

As haddock became badly depleted, groundfish boats turned more effort toward cod. Total yearly landings of cod had fluctuated between

11,000 metric tons and 39,700 metric tons but rose to 57,300 metric tons in 1966 with large catches by foreign boats. Landings declined considerably after that.[52]

Redfish had shown symptoms of depletion even without much foreign boat activity. The catch per unit of fishing effort declined from 1950 through the late 1960s in the fishing areas closest to the United States, and boats traveled farther, to banks off Nova Scotia and Newfoundland, to find better stocks.[53]

By the late 1960s the severe fishery depletion had distracted fishermen, boat owners, congressmen, and agency officials from their earlier explanations for troubles and from the programs designed to solve those problems. New perceptions evolved of the causes of the groundfish industry problems; and as foreign fleets fished heavily on the offshore banks, the industry and the government developed new proposals to deal with the difficulties.

5

Foreign Fleets and Questions of Fisheries Control

*I*N SUMMER 1960 New England fishermen sighted trawlers from the Soviet Union on the offshore grounds for the first time. The boats attracted only passing interest, perhaps because they stayed about 160 miles offshore and fishermen rarely saw them trawling. Defense Department officials, in contrast, expressed considerable concern, for they suspected that the trawlers doubled as spy ships. According to Navy observers, a Russian trawler, unusually clean for a fishing vessel and with no fishing gear in sight, viewed the maneuvers of a Polaris submarine off Long Island. A Soviet defector told Congress that intelligence units commanded the Russian trawlers off the New England coast. Congressman John W. McCormack of Massachusetts declared that well over 200 vessels equipped with a "forest of radar nests and electronic gear" were massing in the Atlantic to spy on the United States fleet.[1]

In 1961 when Russian vessels returned to Georges Bank to fish more heavily, New England fishermen reacted much more strongly. The fishing activity constituted a "Russian invasion" and "a second 'Berlin Situation.'" Russians used illegal small-mesh trawl nets, the fishermen charged. American boats had to leave the areas where the Russians fished in order to avoid being run down by the large Russian vessels, complained offshore fishermen from Boston, Gloucester, and New Bedford. "We're thinking of asking the Coast Guard to give us protection," a fisherman on one of the largest Boston groundfish trawlers said. Russians violated international regulations by "charging around at night without running lights," fishermen complained. In their "deepest penetration" of coastal waters, the Russians sent 60 vessels to the fringe of Nantucket Shoals where inshore draggers commonly fished. Fishing violations and interference were not the Russians' only sins, the fishermen suggested, in support of Department of Defense allegations about spying. Vessels that

107

showed little sign of fishing activity, they said, carried sophisticated electronic gear and came within a few miles of the New England coast.[2]

NEW CONDITIONS: THE GROWTH OF FOREIGN FLEETS

In 1961 at most 100 foreign fishing vessels, nearly all from the Soviet Union, fished on Georges Bank. They offered only an inkling of what New England fishermen would see in the next few years. As a result of the foreign fleets, revolutionary changes would take place in the use of New England fish resources before the end of the decade.

In August 1963 nearly 300 Soviet vessels, more than the entire New England offshore fleet, were fishing on Georges Bank and other New England grounds, many within a few miles of Cape Cod. By 1964 five nations besides the United States and Canada were catching significant amounts of fish off New England: Great Britain, the Soviet Union, Poland, Norway, and Spain. The number of Soviet vessels on New England grounds at the peak of the season decreased, but the boats were larger than ever before, and they greatly outnumbered those of every other foreign fishing nation working in the region.

The numbers impressed those who viewed the fleet. A New England congressman who flew over the Russian fleet said, "It was an awesome sight. It stretched from one horizon to the other." According to a Gloucester offshore fisherman, "Some days it's like New York City out there." "If you were to be present on this scene at nighttime," a boat owner reported, "it would look to you just the same as a large city with thousands and thousands of lights as far as one can see over the horizon."[3]

The size and technology of the foreign vessels fishing the traditional New England grounds were as impressive as their numbers. The foreign vessels were much larger than New England boats, usually displacing from 500 to 2,500 gross tons, ten times the displacement of New England side trawlers. More importantly, however, by the mid-1960s the foreign vessels used newer technology, stern trawling, and could adjust their gear to fish at different depths in order to direct effort toward a variety of fish stocks, something no New England vessel could do. Many stern trawlers immediately processed the fish they caught. Accompanying the trawlers on the grounds were a variety of big support ships that could process fish, take on processed fish for transport to home ports, provide fuel and other supplies to the boats, repair equipment, and offer medical services and recreation to crews.

American observers were amazed. The Russian fleet, said Congressman Hastings Keith of Massachusetts, "looked like a Navy task force, or perhaps like the great echelons of self-propelled combines we see pictured in Kansas wheatfields." According to John Cronan, chief of the Division of Fish and Wildlife in the Rhode Island Department of Natural Resources, the foreign fleet was "Ford, General Motors, and all the rest at sea, rather than in Michigan." The Russians were "sweeping Georges Bank with all the thoroughness of a naval mine sweeping operation," according to one reporter.[4]

Foreign fishing strategies differed considerably from those of the New England industry. The fleets stayed at sea for months. In the north Atlantic they fished the banks off Norway, Greenland, Iceland, and Canada as well as Georges Bank and areas off the coast of the mid-Atlantic states. Fishing techniques varied somewhat among countries, but usually groups of vessels fished together. Soviet vessels coordinated their trawling to cover an entire area of ocean bottom and moved together to new grounds at the decision of a chief on one of the vessels in the group. They practiced "pulse" fishing, working intensively on one stock of fish until it was too depleted to make further fishing worthwhile.[5]

According to fishermen and their spokesmen, these techniques were remarkably effective. After the Russian fleet passed, one captain reported, fishermen found the "bottom clean as a whistle." According to a fisherman's wife, the foreigners "vacuumed" the grounds.[6]

The foreign fleets soon harvested a large share of the catch from the New England fishing banks (Figure 5.1). In 1960 before the foreign boats arrived, United States fishermen landed almost 90 percent of the fish harvested from Georges Bank, all the fish caught off southern New England, and more than 96 percent of the catch from the Gulf of Maine. Most of the remainder of the harvest from Georges Bank and from the Gulf of Maine went to Canadian fishermen. In 1965, however, American fishermen caught only 35 percent of the harvest from these areas, and Canadians caught only another 7.5 percent. The Soviet Union took 56 percent of the total harvest off the New England coast that year. On Georges Bank, the American fishermen brought in only 38 percent of the total catch. By 1972 they caught only a little over 10 percent of the harvest from Georges Bank and about 12 percent of that from southern New England. Only in the Gulf of Maine did New England boats continue to dominate fishing activity; there they harvested about 77 percent of the total.[7]

At first the foreign fleets, dominated by the Soviet Union, directed their fishing efforts toward species that the New England fishermen had never harvested in large quantities. In the early 1960s the Russians fished for adult herring and whiting on Georges Bank. Then they harvested red

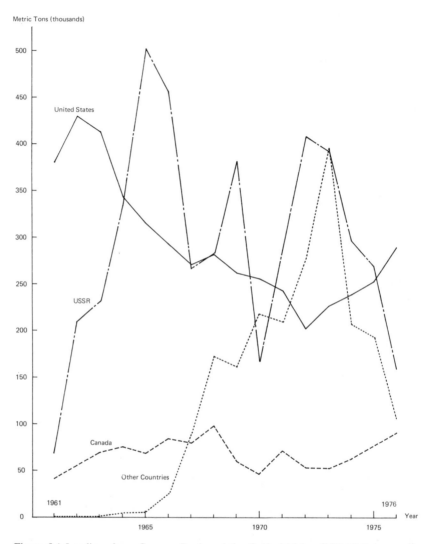

Figure 5.1 Landings from Georges Bank and the Gulf of Maine (ICNAF Sub-area 5), 1961–1976. From Leah J. Smith and Susan B. Peterson, "The New England Fishing Industry: A Basis for Management," Technical Report 77–57, Woods Hole Oceanographic Institution, Aug. 1977, Table I.4 from ICNAF Statistical Bulletin.

hake, used for industrial purposes in the United States. In 1965, however, when the strong 1963 "year class" of haddock (the fish spawned in 1963) became large enough to be captured in considerable quantities in fishing nets, the Soviet vessels turned their attention to that stock, the most valuable to New England fishermen. The foreign catch of Georges Bank haddock more than quintupled, jumping from 17,600 metric tons in 1964 to nearly 97 thousand metric tons in 1965, while the domestic catch rose only slightly, from 46,500 metric tons to almost 53 thousand metric tons. The Soviet Union announced that its catch in 1969 of yellowtail flounder equaled two-thirds of the domestic harvest. Yellowtail, like haddock, was especially important to New England fisheries.[8]

The fish stocks could not withstand these pressures for long without problems. Whiting fishermen off southern New England had trouble finding enough fish to make a trip, and fishermen who caught red hake for industrial production noted low abundance on their traditional grounds. The worst fears centered on the haddock and yellowtail flounder resources. Bureau of Commercial Fisheries biologists warned that no strong new year classes would follow the 1963 cohort of haddock that was so heavily exploited. By 1970 stocks were so low that fishermen, biologists, and government officials talked about a haddock "crisis."[9]

New Perceptions of Reasons for Groundfish Industry Problems

As the foreign fleets increased their fishing pressures on New England's traditional grounds, New England fishermen, processors, and boat owners in the groundfish industry slowly formed new perceptions about the causes of their problems. In the early to mid-1960s they continued to complain that the foreign fleets interfered with fishing operations in outrageous ways. For example, James Ackert, head of the Atlantic Fishermen's Union, reported that Russian patrol ships "come up right alongside of you and put the spotlight on you and just keep nudging you off" the fishing grounds. Fishermen alleged that the fleets used gear that was illegal under international regulations. Furthermore, the foreign vessels were unfair competition. Seventy-five percent of the boats in Gloucester were over twenty years old, run-down, and outmoded, according to Manuel Lewis of the Gloucester Fisheries Commission. "Can we expect this type of vessel to compete with the modern Soviet and Japanese fishing vessel? . . . the Soviet fishing fleet. . . . subjects one's own to humiliation by their size and age and equipment of the most modern types."[10]

Although the complaints were new, none constituted a redefinition of the causes of the New England groundfish industry's problems, but rather reflected fishermen's competitiveness. The ambition to be "highliner," one of the high earning boats in a port, drove the most capable captains to perfect their ability to catch fish; it motivated many crew to improve their skills, to seek sites on the best boats, and to aim to become captains. The desire to earn money was rarely separable from the "big bag mentality." Even when prices were low, captains wanted the satisfaction of locating large quantities of fish and bringing in the largest loads.[11]

Until the early 1960s, boat owners and captains could compare their performances with each other and with Canadians. Canadian boats were similar to their own. Beginning in the early 1960s, however, they watched the Russian boats hauling in enormous quantities of fish, with no hope of doing so well with their own boats. Fishermen felt the competition even more keenly because the foreign boats and fishermen were Russians, the Cold War enemies who were blockading Berlin, setting up missile bases in Cuba, and competing with the United States in space exploration and in arms development. The larger boats' bullying tactics only increased their frustration and contributed to their fury. They filed charges with the State Department and with the International Commission for the Northwest Atlantic Fisheries (ICNAF) that the Russian boats were not operating under the internationally negotiated gear constraints that limited fish-catching ability, but the accusations were never proved. The officials concluded that the small-mesh nets New England fishermen found on the banks and labeled otter trawl nets were probably drift nets and gillnets for which there were no mesh size regulations, although fishermen said they found such nets laced into otter trawls.

Along with their other arguments, spokesmen for the groundfish industry did warn that the Russians were depleting the fish stocks. These points were not important, however, to spokesmen who urged Congress to pass vessel subsidy legislation that might allow New England fishermen to take larger amounts of fish from the same grounds. Indeed, no groundfish industry voices spoke up in 1966 when New Bedford and Point Judith groups first called for a 200-mile zone for United States fisheries jurisdiction in order to restrict foreign fishing activity and prevent more severe depletion. Not a single representative of fishing interests in Gloucester, Boston, or Maine lobbied for extension of fishery jurisdiction to even twelve miles in 1966.[12]

From the mid to late 1960s, however, a new definition of the causes of the groundfish industry's problems began to evolve. As early as 1964 James Ackert told congressmen that the industry was greatly concerned that the Russians would deplete the fishing grounds. Few others joined him, however, until the depletion of the fish stocks began to hurt New England fishermen. In 1969 the landings of haddock declined to only 38 million pounds, just two-thirds of the previous year's catch and the lightest harvest anyone in the fishing industry could remember. Foreign fleets' increased fishing effort and the failure of all year classes after 1963 caused the depletion, the New England industry said. By the early 1970s, fishermen, boat owners, and processors envisioned a future where they would not be able to locate enough fish to stay in business. Rising costs and imports still worried them, they said, but none posed the threat that the foreign fleets did. Salvatore Favazza, executive secretary of the Gloucester Fisheries Commission, explained that the New England fisheries suffered from two basic problems, foreign competition in the marketplace and for the resources on the fishing grounds. Before 1960, he said, market competition had been most important, but after that, competition for the fish became most critical "with the foreign fleets raping our resource."[13]

By the early 1970s New England congressmen and elected state officials had also adopted a new, clearcut assessment of causes of fishery problems. "The decline of the Massachusetts fishing industry can be traced directly to the increase in the number of foreign vessels fishing off the New England coast. . . . the New England fishing industry is being savaged," said Lieutenant Governor Donald Dwight of Massachusetts. Congressman Silvio Conte of Massachusetts stated, "Boats lie idle and the fish markets are sparsely stocked. . . . The supply of haddock, yellow-tailed flounder and herring may be depleted so badly that it is unrecoverable unless we stop this decimation immediately." "The decline of our fishing industry due to foreign overfishing and the massive invasion of the foreign fleets during the early 1960s is well documented," Congressman Peter Kyros of Maine reported. Senator John Pastore of Rhode Island told his colleagues, "Hundreds of fishermen were driven from their livelihood on the sea as foreign fleets virtually exterminated haddock. For years the fishing fleet of Gloucester, once the greatest fishing port in America, struggled for survival." Furthermore, congressmen repeated often, the fish harvested by foreigners from New England banks returned to the United States for consumption. "Much of this foreign catch is then exported to the United States where it often sells for less than that which is caught domestically," Congressman William Cohen of Maine said.[14]

A few industry voices joined those of the public officials, but for the most part, groundfish spokesmen knew that the foreign fleets had not caused all the economic problems of the 1950s and 1960s. Members of the groundfish industry also knew, although elected officials may not have, that the foreign fleets depleting the fish resources did not supply groundfish to American markets. Those nations, primarily Canada and Iceland, fished their own traditional grounds and were waging their own struggles with the same distant-water fishing fleets.

Furthermore, those in the groundfishery knew that the problems were disappearing for which they and their predecessors had sought cures for so many years. During the early 1970s fishermen's earnings and the profits from boat and plant operations rose. In 1973 Gloucester landings brought higher revenues than in any year since 1951. While total Gloucester fishing revenue fell somewhat in 1974, offshore groundfish industry fortunes improved greatly. Between 1974 and 1976 the total Boston and Gloucester offshore boat earnings rose more than 35 percent, well ahead of the rate of growth in the rest of the economy. During the early 1970s the number of offshore groundfish boats had continued to decline. According to one account, eighty boats from Gloucester and Boston fished the offshore banks for groundfish in 1971; only sixty-five worked in 1974. Therefore, the larger revenues meant even greater increases in income for individual boats. The number of crew working on each vessel had declined, too. In some cases, the new technology of stern trawling made boat operation possible with fewer crew than older side trawling methods. Even for side trawlers, however, lower catches per fishing day as the stocks became depleted meant that fewer men could clean and pack the fish. Therefore, crewmen's earnings rose even faster than boat incomes. By 1974 a crewman on a Gloucester offshore boat earned more than ever before, $15,000 to $20,000 per year.[15]

The numbers of fishermen and boats in the industry had declined considerably from the 1950s into the 1970s. Virtually unaffected by government efforts to help, the industry gradually did better by contracting. As fishermen and boat owners left the fishery, individuals' earnings rose to a level that allowed boats to realize profits and fishermen to earn attractive wages.

The depletion of the fish stocks added to the costs of harvesting and slowed economic recovery, but growth in the demand for fish pushed revenues up. During the early 1970s fish became more attractive to a growing number of consumers who wanted low-cholesterol, low-calorie, nutritious foods. Further, in the opinion of Thomas Fulham, Boston boat owner and fish dealer, the papal ruling that allowed Catholics to eat meat on Fridays made a positive change in consumer tastes possible. "Get ready for a luxury business," he had told other Boston dealers. Fish would no longer be a penitential food. When consumers did not have to eat fish, they would become more receptive to its attractiveness. By the mid-1970s, nearly all good restaurants in New England offered fish on their menus, a complete change from the 1950s and 1960s, according to Fulham.[16]

As their incomes rose, fishermen, processors, and boat owners in the groundfish industry saw the foreign fleets taking the fish that they felt would allow them to earn even more, to purchase new boats, and to expand their plants. Despite the economic uncertainty and their complaints about foreign fishing, some fishermen planned expansion to take advantage of the good times. In Gloucester a few fishermen ordered expensive new vessels after 1973, the first since one order in 1970 and indicative of more new investment than at any time since the early post-World War II years.[17]

The prosperity of those in the groundfish industry made them more like the other groups who worried about the foreign fleets' activities off the New England coast. Beginning in the early years of foreign fishing, well before the groundfish industry redefined the source of its problems, better-off segments of the industry voiced anxiety about the future of their prosperous fisheries. One of the first groups to take their concerns to Congress was the Point Judith Fishermen's Cooperative Association, made up of inshore fishermen. Traditionally, said Jacob Dykstra, the president of the coop, Point Judith fishermen had ranged over the continental shelf from Nantucket Shoals to Virginia and occasionally as far as Georges Bank with no competition from foreign vessels. They had "maintained a steady and prosperous fishery," but the huge foreign catches would destroy the fish resources on which they depended. In 1966 the fishermen in Point Judith already felt the effects of depletion and pressured the State Department to restrict foreign fishing. The prosperous New Bedford industry also protested the foreign fleets' activities because they feared harm to their fisheries as they observed the difficulties of other groups.[18]

In the early 1970s as new opinion in the groundfish industry took shape, virtually every other New England fishing group also expressed anger and alarm at the foreign fleets' activity and its effects. Offshore lobstermen complained vociferously about the foreign fleets during the early 1970s. After 1966 several small companies had purchased gear, invested in boats, and learned the new technology to exploit recently discovered offshore lobster stocks. Immediately they had run into conflicts with the foreign fleets that by the early 1970s had developed into an "offshore gear war." The lobstermen set hundreds of traps on lines along the edge of the continental shelf, on the outer edges of Georges Bank, and returned to pull their traps and remove the lobsters a few days later. Frequently, however, they discovered that fishing vessels had towed through their gear and cut off the lines. They lost thousands of dollars worth of equipment on the ocean floor or in the nets of trawlers which lobstermen presumed were foreign. On many occasions they watched groups of foreign trawlers run across their lines. Richard Allen of the Atlantic Offshore Fish and Lobster Association warned, "Few of our fishermen dare to carry guns on their vessels for fear that they would use them as they watch their livelihoods being destroyed."[19]

In the early 1970s catch rates declined 20 to 30 percent per year. Many offshore lobstermen blamed the foreign fleets for harvesting large quantities of lobsters. The drop in the catch rates in the fishery "could not be explained by an analysis of the U.S. fishing effort," according to Allen. He reported rumors of substantial landings of lobsters in foreign ports. Regardless of their views on the extent to which foreigners harvested lobsters, nearly all fishermen and state fishery officials feared that the foreign boats might turn their efforts toward the lobster stock at any time and virtually wipe it out.[20]

Partyboat captains also protested the foreign fleets. They reported that Russians had decimated sea bass, porgies, and fluke, the backbone of charter and partyboat business in southern New England and the mid-Atlantic states. "The only reason that the Russian slaughter didn't destroy the partyboat business was that each year we enjoyed tremendous runs of bluefish," said Allan J. Ristori, chairman of the Emergency Committee to Save America's Resources, the partyboat captains' new organization. "What will happen to the hundreds of party and charter boats dependent of this fishery if the bluefish disappear?"[21]

Successful political organizing reflected the breadth of the concern and the strength of the feelings among fishing interests. In 1971 diverse New England fishing interests formed the New England Fisheries Steering Committee at the initiative of Gayle Charles, manager of the Provincetown Cooperative Fishing Industries. The Steering Committee eventually included representatives from every major port and every type of fishing. The organization aimed to influence federal policy toward fisheries because "New England fishermen and fishing communities have been a marginal consideration where national policy is concerned," Charles said. In the following years, most of the group's energy addressed problems with the foreign fishing fleets.[22]

During 1973 ten fishing organizations representing approximately 8,000 fishermen formed the eastern division of the National Federation of Fishermen. While the national organizers spoke of general "fishery interests" and "common problems," most groups joined because of their concern about foreign fishing, and groups opposed to government action to constrain foreign fishing did not join.[23]

Both the Steering Committee and National Federation of Fishermen drew strength from long-established organizations of boat owners and processors, fishermen's unions, and cooperatives. In addition, some local groups formed around the foreign fishing issue. In Gloucester in 1971, for example, boat owners and a handful of processors asked James Ackert, formerly head of the Atlantic Fishermen's Union, to lead a new organization, the New England Fisheries Association, which would present a unified position on foreign fishing and other industry concerns.[24]

The broad base of industry concern in New England made new efforts to get government aid distinctly different from those of the 1950s and 1960s when the groundfish industry had nearly always suffered and protested alone. Indeed, the concern came from a constituency much broader than New England interests. Fish stock depletion was much worse off the New England coast than anywhere else, and the stocks hardest hit were haddock and yellowtail flounder with herring a close third. However, fishermen in the mid-Atlantic states felt depletion caused by the fleets fishing south of New England. On the West Coast foreign vessels had arrived in the Bering Sea in large numbers in the early 1960s to fish for bottomfish and, in some cases, salmon. Fishermen from Washington, Oregon, and Alaska had begun to protest the presence of the foreign fleets by the mid-1960s; and the National Federation of Fishermen started on the West Coast. As fishing pressures drastically reduced the fish stocks in the northwest Atlantic, the fishermen on the Gulf Coast worried that the foreign fleets would move to their own traditional fishing grounds.

EFFORTS TO RESTRICT FOREIGN FISHING

The solution to their difficulties with the foreign fleets seemed clear to New England fishermen, boat owners, and dealers. Ideally, they wanted to see foreign fishing prohibited on their traditional grounds. If that were not possible, they wanted foreign fishing efforts restricted. The New England industry saw two major ways to try to accomplish these aims. First, they could attempt to influence multilateral fishing agreements under which New England fishermen would share the resources with foreign fishermen. The International Commission for the Northwest Atlantic Fisheries could restrict fishing on the New England stocks. South of Rhode Island and Connecticut, outside the ICNAF area, the State

Department could negotiate agreements with individual nations to reduce fishing activity. Control of fisheries was a major issue in the negotiations at the United Nations Law of the Sea conferences; the outcome of the deliberations could profoundly affect foreign fishing rights off the United States coast.

Second, the fishing industry could press for domestic jurisdiction over coastal fishing grounds to give New England fishermen first claim to the resources and to exclude or reduce foreign activity. New England fishing interests preferred this approach. Jacob Dykstra of Point Judith and spokesmen from New Bedford called for extension of fishery jurisdiction to 200 miles in 1966. Wives of Gloucester fishermen traveled to Washington in the late 1960s to demonstrate for a 200-mile limit.[25] However, the New England spokesmen found little support and considerable opposition from the administration. They decided to get what they could from multilateral negotiations as long as those were the only promising directions.

International Commission for the Northwest Atlantic Fisheries[26]

The most obvious forum in which New England fishing interests could influence decisions about control of foreign fishing was ICNAF. It had been founded in 1950 to bring fishing nations together to cooperate in "the investigation and conservation of fishery resources in the Northwest Atlantic," according to Secretary of State Dean Acheson and his delegates to the international fishery meetings of the late 1940s.

The need for such an organization had become apparent in part because of the depletion of important fish stocks. "The number of marketable-sized haddock is now at an all-time low," Acheson wrote. "Fishing for rosefish [redfish] has been very heavy in recent years and the abundance of this fish has been gradually reduced to the point where United States vessels have found it necessary to travel much farther from port in order to find commercial quantities. The catches of cod from the New England banks are likewise reduced and an increase in the number of lengthy and expensive trips to the Nova Scotian banks has become necessary. Catches of halibut have gradually dwindled through the years." Furthermore, the pressures on the threatened stocks could increase. The postwar domestic otter trawl fleet was larger than at any other time. The North Sea and other European fishing grounds were badly depleted, and foreign fleets in search of more plentiful resources might make the trip to the New England banks.

ICNAF, its founders hoped, would provide for international cooperation in the collection and analysis of fisheries information for the northwest Atlantic Ocean. ICNAF might also provide ways for governments to cooperate to sustain the yield from the fish stocks, explained the delegates to the conference which drafted the fisheries agreement. "In the long run," the delegates noted optimistically, "it provides a means of meeting a situation . . . before [it] reaches a crisis stage."[27] Eleven nations signed the convention: Canada, Denmark, France, Iceland, Italy, Newfoundland, Norway, Portugal, Spain, Great Britain, and the United States.

Each member country appointed one to three commissioners to serve on ICNAF along with experts to assist them. Each nation could set up an advisory committee of fishermen, boat owners, and others well informed about fishery problems. Separate "panels" of commissioners were to look at the problems of fisheries in different areas of the northwest Atlantic, could recommend that the commission undertake scientific investigations of fisheries in their areas, and could propose commission decisions on joint government actions to keep stocks at levels which would permit the harvest of maximum sustained yield. The commission set up the Standing Committee on Research and Statistics made up of scientists from member countries. The committee was responsible for recommending better research programs and statistical procedures and for providing the commission with regular assessments of the fish stocks. ICNAF was to meet annually to consider the condition of the fish resources as described by the committee of scientists. The commission could take action on the recommendation of a panel with the support of two-thirds of the member countries.[28]

In its most important decision for New England fishermen before the arrival of the foreign fleets, ICNAF regulated mesh size in the haddock fishery. Even before World War II, fishery biologists and some parts of the industry had agitated for regulations requiring larger mesh for the haddock fishery to reduce the destruction of very small fish. Other industry groups opposed controls on American fishermen without restraints on Canadians and other foreigners who might fish for haddock. Mesh size agreement through ICNAF dealt with those objections by regulating the actions of fishermen in several countries. The mesh rules took effect in mid-1953, more than two years after the United States commissioners had proposed them at the first ICNAF meeting.[29]

Fishermen and boat owners generally accepted the rules because they discovered that they saved considerable work if they did not have to clean or discard large numbers of small fish. Fish and Wildlife Service biologists estimated that over twelve million baby haddock were saved from the Boston fishing fleet in the first year of mesh regulation. Fishermen actually caught more haddock with the larger mesh, the biologists said, because they caught marketable fish rather than very small ones that were discarded at sea. In the years that followed, ICNAF occasionally revised and extended the mesh rules to improve enforcement, to cover more fishing grounds, and to take account of haddock caught in fisheries directed at other species.[30]

For the most part, however, ICNAF functioned as a center for scientific communication and data gathering. The organization became an invaluable source of data on the harvests of northwest Atlantic resources and of studies about the character and abundance of those resources and the potential effects of greater fishing effort. Therefore, the work at the meetings held little of immediate interest to fishermen, boat owners, or dealers.[31]

ICNAF worked smoothly for more than fifteen years because, despite the concerns of State Department officials, fishery biologists, and some industry spokesmen, fish stocks were not in trouble. New England and European trawlers did not continue to increase their fishing effort and therefore did not threaten to cause the depletion that ICNAF's founders had feared. ICNAF had no controversial decisions to make and no crises to handle. The idea of managing the use of fish resources through international organizations was farsighted in the 1940s, but the drafters of the ICNAF agreement could not have foreseen the complexity of international fishery politics or the urgency of action to reduce fishing pressures when new technology and investment in large numbers of vessels would add to the speed with which countries could exploit a fish resource. In 1950 no one had tried to manage the use of fish resources on such a scale, and no one had thought very much about the economic, biological, and political considerations in such an undertaking.

In the early 1960s as the foreign fleets began to fish heavily on Georges Bank, ICNAF faced its first major challenge and failed to prevent severe fishery depletion. Certain conditions in the ICNAF agreement kept the organization from acting effectively. Although it could make rules about the use of the fish resource, the convention made no provisions for enforcement of decisions. Therefore, by default, the nations whose vessels fished in the ICNAF areas had responsibility for assuring that their fishermen followed the rules. Legislation to implement the treaty defined United States enforcement procedures. Other nations could adopt quite different measures or none at all or could neglect to carry out the enforcement procedures they had adopted. Commissioners from the coastal fishing nations and their industry advisors suspected that distant-water fishermen ignored the rules and that their countries had no enforcement programs. ICNAF commissioners faced the prospect that no matter what they decided, few fishermen might be required to abide by the rules.

ICNAF's limited authority to regulate fishing activity also handicapped the organization. The convention specified the types of regulations ICNAF could put in place. ICNAF needed more flexibility and a broader mandate in order to hope to act effectively in the complicated management of international use of fish resources.

The procedures for implementing ICNAF decisions meant that a proposal became a regulation only after several years, if at all. Jacob Dykstra of Point Judith, an industry advisor to ICNAF, was exaggerating only a little when he described the process: "When the member nations decide that there is something that needs attention, the first thing they do is try to agree that there is a problem, and they say they will go back to their member nations and talk this thing over . . . and come back next year with some sort of a proposal. They bring back a proposal, and we all look it over and we have to make some changes, so we go home again with it, and then when we finally do agree, in 2, 3, or 4 years, it takes several years to ratify it." Fishing pressures could change dramatically and fish stocks could become severely depleted between the time ICNAF initiated a proposal and the time fishermen had to observe it.[32]

At meetings during the 1960s the commissioners' most important action amended the treaty so that ICNAF could try to enforce its regulations, use more effective management techniques, and act more quickly. In 1963 the United States proposed that the commission adopt international enforcement measures. An amendment to the convention did not go into effect until 1969, and not until 1971 did ICNAF set up a joint system of enforcement. Under that plan inspectors from any ICNAF nation could board the vessels of another ICNAF nation to check for complaince with regulations. In 1964 the United States proposed amendments to make regulations effective within six to nine months if no member objected. That measure took effect in 1969. In 1969 the United States offered amendments which would allow ICNAF to adopt any appropriate measures to achieve the optimum utilization of the fish stocks. That change went into effect in 1970. By 1969 several more fishing nations had joined ICNAF: the Soviet Union, West Germany, Poland, Rumania.[33]

Finally in 1969 conditions in the fisheries had become desperate enough and the international machinery sufficiently malleable for ICNAF to act decisively. Faced with severe shortages of haddock, the commission established annual quotas for haddock for 1970 on Georges Bank and Browns Bank and closed spawning areas to fishing. ICNAF lowered the haddock quota, set quotas on yellowtail flounder on Georges Bank and in southern New England, and prescribed a minimum mesh size for yellowtail in 1971. At the 1972 meeting ICNAF set quotas for most of the important species. For the first time the commission specified national rather than overall quotas and recognized that coastal states had special claims to the resources. The United States and Canada received the largest shares of the total quotas. In 1973 the ICNAF nations agreed to a three-year series of reductions in catch without cutting the quota for American and Canadian fishermen. By the end of that time, the stocks would have recovered, the commission stated optimistically; and new quotas could assure that stocks would not become so badly depleted again. In 1974 the commission adopted a "two-tier" quota system to deal with problems of bycatch.[34]

By 1973, however, virtually all New England fishing interests, their congressional representatives, state fishery administrators, and fishery biologists had lost confidence that ICNAF could successfully regulate the use of the offshore fishery resources. Most believed that ICNAF had demonstrated its ineffectiveness. "As the case of haddock testified—a species which ICNAF has concentrated its greatest effort in managing—the Commission has been incapable of acting in time to prevent the decline of a species. It only reacts after the tragedy has occurred," said Arthur Brownell, commissioner of the Massachusetts Department of Natural Resources, in an echo of many others' comments. According to Frank Grice, the director of the Massachusetts Division of Marine Fisheries, "It is a travesty that this international commission, rather than promoting wise use of the resource has instead lulled the general public, the administration, and Congress into a false sense of security while the fisheries were being overexploited."[35]

Even with the changes in its operating structure, ICNAF's actions only made the unfavorable impressions worse, with good reason. ICNAF moved only under extreme pressure which could be exerted only because American interests were so disenchanted. In 1972 when ICNAF allocated national quotas, the American advisory group had voted to urge the United States to leave ICNAF. The commissioner to ICNAF from the Department of Commerce had blasted ICNAF's ineffectiveness at a commission meeting; and James T. Lynn, Undersecretary of Commerce, had told another meeting, "We in the U.S. are convinced that the fisheries in the northwest Atlantic can survive only if there is a well-nigh revolutionary change within the commission equalling the revolutionary change in fishing, or alternatively, if the commission [is] . . . abandoned in favor of another approach." In 1973 when ICNAF hammered out its most extensive agreement, the United States had threatened again to withdraw from ICNAF. Congressmen had introduced bills to extend the fishery jurisdiction of the United States to 200 miles, and the working sessions of the Law of the Sea conference were producing negotiating texts which favored coastal nation control of fish resources; either approach would have taken fishery management authority away from ICNAF. Only then did the distant-water fishing nations of eastern Europe go along to some extent with American and Canadian proposals for smaller quotas and preference for coastal nations' fishing industries.[36]

Even when pressures forced ICNAF to act, however, the decisions did not go far enough. The quotas often far exceeded the fishing levels biologists thought desirable. For example, biologists stated that the catch of herring on Georges Bank in 1972 could not exceed 90,000 metric tons without reducing the spawning stock, but ICNAF adopted a 150,000 ton quota with stipulations for greater reductions in 1973. Most nations were not willing to accept the sacrifices of the severe cuts in harvests that the scientists recommended. Economic needs impinged on the scientists' assessments of stock conditions by the mid-1970s and made it harder for the scientific committee to present the commission with clear recommendations. Scientists from the socialist eastern European countries occasionally backed assessments which indicated larger stocks in order to support the fishing needs of their countries' expanding fishing fleets.[37]

Once the quotas were prescribed, they had little relation to the amounts of fish harvested. Fishermen, boat owners, congressmen, and others suspected that some of the distant-water fishing vessels, especially those from the Soviet Union, Poland, and East Germany, did not obey the ICNAF regulations and that these countries made no attempt to enforce the rules. The new ICNAF enforcement mechanisms were still ineffective. "We don't have any authority to go out there and actually check on what those vessels are doing," Jacob Dykstra claimed. "We have agreements; we can go aboard the vessel. But if that skipper of a vessel says, 'This is a sovereign part of my nation and you stay off,' we have no way in which we can force our way aboard that vessel."[38]

ICNAF removed these restrictions on inspections at the 1973 meeting, but enforcement still could not be effective. The National Marine Fisheries Service agents could not inspect the large numbers of foreign vessels often enough to be sure that they observed regulations. If a vessel caught too much of restricted species, for instance, the illegal catch could be converted to fish meal before enforcement agents arrived, if they ever did. Christopher Weld of the National Coalition for Marine Conservation claimed that the limited enforcement effort could not even keep track of how many vessels were fishing. In an area of about 250 square miles he reported seeing several hundred fishing vessels although an enforcement team had observed only twelve foreign vessels a few days before.[39]

If the United States inspectors found that a foreign vessel had violated the regulations, the State Department informed the boat's government. The responsibility for following up on violations rested with that country. United States inspectors said they did not know whether or how the distant-water fishing nations handled the violation notices. The National Marine Fisheries Service was essentially giving out "parking tickets," said William Gordon, the deputy director of NMFS in the Northeast.[40]

Even if enforcement could have worked properly, the quota system left loopholes which allowed fleets to catch larger amounts of fish than ICNAF intended. For example, after a country came close to catching its quota in a directed fishery, it could continue to bring in "incidental" catches that could push the total harvests far over the quotas. As Thomas Norris of Old Colony Trawler Corporation in Boston, an ICNAF industry advisor, pointed out, "With large catches of herring and mackerel by the foreign fleets the 10-percent allowance of other restricted species could be more . . . than [the catches in] the directed fisheries of the U.S. fleet." The new quota plan in 1974 took account of bycatch and promised to solve many of these problems.[41]

At any time, many feared, the quotas could be greatly exceeded if new nations sent vessels to the northwest Atlantic to harvest large amounts of fish without joining ICNAF or observing its rules. "ICNAF only consists of 16 nations," warned Spencer Apollonio, commissioner of the Department of Marine Resources in Maine. "There are a lot of other nations which can and do fish."[42]

Others involved in the commission's work did not agree that ICNAF was ineffectual. "ICNAF was a success," argued Robert Edwards, head of the Northeast Fisheries Center of National Marine Fisheries Service and a member of the scientific committee which advised ICNAF. He pointed to its accomplishments in collecting and analyzing scientific information on the status of fish resources. He emphasized that by the mid-1970s ICNAF had reduced quotas on depleted species.[43] ICNAF had indeed served an invaluable function in coordinating scientific data and research on the fisheries of the northwest Atlantic. Despite the views of Edwards and others, however, it had failed to manage the use of the fish resource adequately by the early 1970s. Quotas were reduced; but, principally because enforcement was impossible, lower quotas were no assurance that ICNAF could prevent further depletion. For valid reasons ICNAF had lost the confidence of most of its constituents in the United States by the early 1970s.

Fishermen's and boat owners' objections to ICNAF went much farther than concerns about the ineffectiveness of conservation efforts, however. Many of their criticisms applied not so much to ICNAF as to any fishery management regime. ICNAF forced regulation on New England off-shore fishermen in a significant way for the first time. Restrictions on their fishing infuriated fishermen who did not see why they should suffer for the foreign fleets' deeds and for ICNAF's ineffectiveness. In late 1970 ICNAF prohibited boats from catching more than incidental amounts of haddock as the total catch approached the overall annual quota. The National Marine Fisheries Service, responsible with the Coast Guard's assistance for enforcing the regulations on domestic boats, charged captains who brought in too much haddock and levied fines. "We have received a great many complaints from the fishing industry," Russell T. Norris, regional director of the National Marine Fisheries Service, said. "With all the warning we gave and the releases put out they still didn't believe that the ban would go into effect."[44]

In the next years the protests became stronger. ICNAF's overall quotas were inequitable and too low, the fishing industry claimed; the quotas gave an advantage to large, distant-water vessels because the larger boats could fish in any weather and more persistently. They would leave nothing of the quota for United States fishermen. "The International Commission for Northwest Atlantic Fisheries has put us in a position so we can't make a living," said Gayle Charles, the manager of the Provincetown Cooperative. One spokesman for the New Bedford fishing industry declared, "If quotas proposed for this year are enforced, New Bedford fishing will go down the drain."[45] During at least one ICNAF meeting American industry representatives pushed for higher quotas on haddock than scientists thought were wise.

Different quotas for coastal and distant-water fishing nations did little to ease the resentment against ICNAF. Fishermen in Gloucester said they wanted no quotas on haddock for the United States. Fishermen and boat owners objected to throwing away dead fish and promoting waste in order to stay within the ICNAF catch limits. Mesh regulation alone provided enough restriction, many captains said. Foreign midwater trawling, not American fishing techniques, depleted the stocks, fishermen claimed. The New England industry believed ICNAF was overstepping its responsibilities.

Instead of simply reducing foreign harvests of fish that rightfully belonged to the New England industry, ICNAF was constraining American fishermen. "With ICNAF for a friend, we don't need enemies," said Michael Orlando, the administrator of the Gloucester Fishermen's Welfare and Pension Plan.[46]

The enforcement methods also angered fishermen. The National Marine Fisheries Service fined violators or, on repeated offenses, confiscated their catch. In contrast, fishermen said, NMFS only "slapped the wrists" of foreign violators. In 1975 the Soviet Union and Poland stepped up their boarding of United States vessels to find ICNAF violations. With the combination of foreign and NMFS inspections, fishermen were convinced that they were unfairly forced to observe the rules. "We go along with the regulations," one captain protested, "but it seems as if we're the only guys that have to abide by them." When six British vessels harvested too much haddock, Michael Orlando said, "They ought to hang them. . . . If it happened to our boats, they'd hang us. It looks like they'll get away."[47]

Fishermen became convinced that they did not want effective ICNAF control. They preferred severe restrictions on other countries' fishing with fewer regulations on their own although some admitted that American fishermen probably had to face constraints as well. United States jurisdiction over the fishing grounds would achieve these goals, fishermen were certain.

When congressmen introduced bills for a 200-mile fisheries limit, however, the administration vehemently opposed the move. Wait for the Law of the Sea conference, administration spokesmen said repeatedly. These issues should be settled through international agreement. "Unilateral legislation on our part would almost certainly prompt others to assert extreme claims of their own," Secretary of State Henry Kissinger warned, as had spokesmen from the Law of the Sea delegation. "Our ability to negotiate an acceptable international consensus on the economic zone will be jeopardized. If every state proclaims its own rules of law and seeks to impose them on others, the very basis of international law will be shaken, ultimately to our own detriment."[48]

Fishing industry spokesmen had been pushing the U.S. negotiating team at the Law of the Sea conference to give more weight to fishing industry priorities since 1971 when the preparatory meetings for the third conference began. Events at the Law of the Sea conference had only strengthened the conviction among industry spokesmen that the United States had to act unilaterally.

THE CONFERENCES ON THE LAW OF THE SEA

In 1957 the General Assembly of the United Nations had called for a conference of its members to "examine the law of the sea, taking account not only of the legal but also of the technical, biological, economic and political aspects of the program, and to embody the results of its work in one or more international conventions or such other instruments as it may deem appropriate."[49] The Law of the Sea conferences in 1958 and 1960 had produced several decisions of importance to the fishing industry.

The central issue facing the 1958 meetings was the breadth of territorial seas. The United States sought to keep territorial seas as narrow as possible to protect transit of straits for military and merchant vessels, but when the conference could not agree, the United States suggested extension of the territorial sea to six miles and of jurisdiction over fisheries to another six miles beyond the territorial sea. Although the proposal received a majority of the votes, it failed to receive two-thirds of the votes, the number needed to adopt an official convention.[50]

A second conference on the Law of the Sea convened in 1960 to resolve the width of the territorial sea. A renewed proposal for a six-mile territorial sea and six more miles of fishery jurisdiction failed by one vote to receive the two-thirds majority needed.[51]

East coast fishing interests had not participated in either conference although a State Department official who was an authority on northwest Atlantic fisheries and representatives from the Fish and Wildlife Service, the National Canners Association, and the National Shrimp Congress did advise the United States negotiators. In 1958 and 1960 New England groundfish interests believed that extension of fishery jurisdiction would hurt them because they fished within twelve miles of Canada. They had nothing to gain from wider fishing limits because few foreign vessels fished close to the New England coast. The domestic negotiating team was willing to ignore the industry views to limit the width of territorial seas. According to the chief United States negotiator in 1958, Arthur Dean, "Many a delegate . . . praised the United States for its creative imagination and good will in making the proposal despite the economic detriment to its fishing interests." In 1960 Canada and the United States

had proposed extension of fishery jurisdiction to twelve miles with allowances for fishing rights for ten years. "The sacrifice," Dean stated, "was
offered in the hope of achieving agreement at the Conference on a
territorial sea limited to 6 miles." Security interests, he insisted, had not
overridden all consideration of American fishing needs.[52]

The conference did adopt other conventions which had the potential to
affect the fisheries. The Convention on the Continental Shelf gave coastal
nations sovereignty over the exploration and exploitation of the natural
resources of the continental shelf. Natural resources meant the "mineral
and other non-living resources of the seabed and subsoil together with
living organisms . . . which, at the harvestable stage, either are immobile
on or under the seabed or are unable to move except in constant physical
contact with the seabed or the subsoil." The Convention on Fishing and
Conservation of the Living Resources of the High Seas supported the
right of all countries to fish on the high seas but declared that they had an
obligation to cooperate in multilateral conservation measures. "A coastal
state," the convention stated, "has a special interest in the maintenance
of the productivity of the living resources in any area . . . adjacent to its
territorial sea." The coastal nation could adopt unilateral conservation
measures if international negotiations failed to reach agreement within
six months, but these measures could not discriminate against foreign
fishermen.[53]

The United States Senate ratified both conventions in 1960. The
Convention on the Continental Shelf became effective in 1964 when the
required number of countries had become parties to it. Congress passed
legislation in 1964 to implement the treaty. The Convention on Fishing
and Conservation of the Living Resources of the High Seas entered into
force in 1966, but the administration did not propose implementing
legislation until 1973.[54]

Neither convention touched the New England industry before 1973, in
part because the treaties codified accepted practice and in part because
many countries did not become parties to the agreements. Until new
species were added to the list of resources of the continental shelf in 1971
and 1973, the Convention on the Continental Shelf was widely accepted.
Although only fifty-one nations had ratified the convention by 1973, these
included many of the nations fishing in the northwest Atlantic. The
convention codified the usual international practice, and, therefore, no
behavior changed. In contrast, only thirty-three nations had ratified the
Convention on Fishing and Conservation by 1973. Of the nations fishing
off the New England coast, only Portugal, Spain, and Great Britain had
become parties to the treaty. Therefore, American assertion of the

coastal state's rights under the convention would have constituted uni-lateral action which the State Department deplored. The United States never used the Convention on Fishing and Conservation to try to ease the problems with ICNAF or to handle fishing disputes off the mid-Atlantic coast.

By 1971 when the preparatory sessions for the third conference began, the concerns of the American fishing industry and the condition of the fish resource were quite different than in 1958 and 1960 before the foreign fleets arrived. Nevertheless, the United States position on fisheries juris-diction resembled the 1960 statement. Between the close of the 1960 conference and 1971 a twelve-mile fisheries zone had become accepted international practice. Outside that twelve-mile fisheries limit, the Amer-ican negotiators suggested, international organizations such as ICNAF should govern the use of fish resources. In March 1972, however, at the beginning of a second round of preparatory sessions, Donald McKernan, special assistant to the Secretary of State for fisheries and wildlife, announced a new position, the "species approach," which called for national management of coastal fish stocks and anadromous species, such as salmon, which spawned in fresh water but spent their adult lives in salt water. The coastal nation would have preferential rights to the use of these resources throughout their migratory range but would allocate unutilized resources to other nations. International organizations would manage the use of migratory species such as tuna. As the Law of the Sea conference convened in 1974 in Caracas, Venezuela, the United States delegation offered yet another revision of its position on fisheries jurisdic-tion. "We are prepared to accept, and indeed we would welcome," said John Stevenson, the chief of the delegation, "general agreement on a 12-mile outer limit for the territorial sea and a 200-mile outer limit for the economic zone provided it is part of an acceptable comprehensive pack-age, including satisfactory regime within and beyond the economic zone and provision for unimpeded transit of straits used for international navigation." The coastal state would control the use of coastal and anadromous fish stocks with responsibility for conservation and full uti-lization of resources, as in the earlier United States position. The coastal nation would manage the use of highly migratory species within its economic zone in accordance with international regulations.[55]

The shifts in the American fishery position reflected the political environment at the conference. The United States had no chance of getting agreement on a fisheries zone of only twelve miles. Underde-veloped countries, especially Latin American nations, favored strong coastal state control, and several had already extended their jurisdiction over fisheries to 200 miles. "What we have learned about the concerns of other states has led us to reconsider our own initial position on fisheries in response, in particular, to the economic and social needs of the coastal states," Donald McKernan said. According to John Stevenson, "The developing coastal countries . . . just don't have that much confidence in regional and international organizations" for fishery management. In 1974 when the United States position shifted again, Stevenson said, "In the course of listening to and reading the statements made during the last two weeks, I have been struck by the very large measure of agreement. . . . Most delegations that have spoken have endorsed or indicated a willingness to accept, under certain conditions and as part of a package settlement, a maximum limit of 12 miles for the territorial sea and of 200 miles for an economic zone." Therefore, he said, the United States had reconsidered its own position.[56]

Other governments' views on fisheries jurisdiction and the compromises necessary to get agreement on other issues under debate were crucial in causing the United States to shift its stance on fisheries. Each change in the United States' position, however, also reflected the opinion of the fishing industry. Fishing interests in the United States had achieved sufficient political stature to prevent the State Department from easily sacrificing their needs in order to achieve other goals.

In June 1971 the National Federation of Fishermen held meetings to formulate a position on fishery jurisdiction for the Law of the Sea conference. The organization proposed a three-species scheme, virtually identical to the position the United States took at the Law of the Sea conference the next year. First, a coastal nation would have "ownership" of the fish and shellfish resources of its continental shelf. If those resources were underutilized, the coastal nation would make provisions for other nations to use the stocks. Second, the country where anadromous fish spawned would "own" them, the National Federation of Fishermen stated, but would have to manage the stock with agreement from nations which harvested the fish in their own territorial waters at other stages of the fish's life. Third, international organizations would manage the use of highly migratory species such as tuna; no nation would own these stocks. The New England Fisheries Steering Committee suggested a similar approach, but their call for coastal nation management was weaker than the National Federation of Fishermen's proposal for "ownership" of the coastal and anadromous species.[57]

During the Law of the Sea preparatory meetings in summer 1971, fishing spokesmen felt the United States delegation ignored their recommendations. As industry advisors to the delegation, they found, they were briefed about the negotiations but had no input. They were angry at the official United States statement on fisheries management. Fishing spokesmen and some groups in Congress, especially the House Committee on Merchant Marine and Fisheries, pressured the State Department to make fishermen part of the Law of the Sea delegation and to change the official United States negotiating position.[58]

By the beginning of the 1972 preparatory sessions, the fishing industry had won on both points. The new United States species approach sounded much like the proposals of the National Federation of Fishermen and other fishing organizations. The State Department agreed to include two fishing spokesmen as members of the delegation. Dykstra of the Point Judith Fishermen's Cooperative Association represented the interests of coastal fishermen; August Felando of the American Tuna Boat Association spoke for the distant-water fishermen in the tuna and shrimp fleets. Dykstra noted that as a delegate he could participate in the negotiating sessions and had access to reports that could affect the fishing industry. His principal purpose, he said, was to make sure that nothing hurt coastal fishing interests.[59]

By 1974, when the United States decided to support 200-mile fisheries zones, many congressmen were backing legislation to extend American fisheries jurisdiction to 200 miles. Congressmen called State Department and Law of the Sea negotiators to justify their stands in one hearing after another before the Committee on Merchant Marine and Fisheries in the House and the Committee on Commerce in the Senate. A United States Law of the Sea position opposing 200-mile fisheries jurisdiction would have seemed absurd with such strong support for a 200-mile limit in the Congress. The negotiators' major objective was not to stick to one negotiating position but rather to keep Congress from passing legislation for a 200-mile zone of fishery jurisdiction before they reached accord on other issues at the Law of the Sea conference.

In one session after another, however, the Conference on the Law of the Sea could not reach agreement. The sessions ended without consensus in 1974 and 1975, and the conferees planned to meet again in 1976. John Stevenson, head of the American delegation to the conference, and Thomas Clingan, chief of the fisheries negotiations for the United States, resigned after the 1975 sessions. John Norton Moore, chairman of the National Security Council Interagency Task Force on the Law of the Sea, spoke pessimistically for the first time about the conference's prospects: "It is now clear that the negotiations cannot be completed before mid-1976 at the earliest, and at this time it is not clear whether or not a treaty can be completed during 1976." He would reconsider his recommendations concerning United States fisheries legislation, he said. Congress heard this as a go-ahead for the extension of fishery jurisdiction even though Moore later retracted his offer to cooperate in drafting legislation and returned—at Secretary of State Kissinger's order, congressmen said—to his earlier position that Congress should pass no legislation before the conclusion of the Conference on the Law of the Sea.[60]

Several senators and congressmen had observed the Law of the Sea sessions at Caracas and Geneva and were sure that the conference could not reach a conclusion soon. Congressman Robert Leggett, chairman of the fisheries subcommittee of the House Committee on Merchant Marine and Fisheries, spoke for a majority when he said, "The Law of the Sea Conference is a worthy, necessary and desirable effort. . . . But it is very likely years away from conclusion when one considers we have not yet achieved agreement on a draft treaty, let alone obtained the requisite number of signatures, the sequential ratification and the various individual legislative actions necessary to implement any resulting international law agreements." For too many years, he and others declared, Congress had heeded the requests of Law of the Sea negotiators to wait for the outcome of the next sessions.[61]

State Department officials continued to insist that ICNAF agreements could fill the need for restraints on fishing in the northwest Atlantic until the Conference on the Law of the Sea concluded. As ICNAF failed to constrain fishing enough, however, fewer legislators were persuaded by that argument. While the Law of the Sea conference dragged on, more of them became convinced that the United States had to take unilateral action to control foreign fishing until the Law of the Sea conference ended.

PRECEDENTS FOR UNILATERAL ACTION

While the State Department emphasized the importance of multilateral negotiation on fisheries problems, the United States had frequently made unilateral claims over the fisheries of the northwest Atlantic. In most cases, the behavior had been grounded in accepted international practice.

In 1964 fishing interests from Alaska and Massachusetts led the push to prohibit foreign fishing in territorial waters in order to keep Russian vessels a few miles farther from the coast. The 1958 Conference on the Law of the Sea had recognized a coastal nation's control over fishing in its territorial seas in the Convention on the Territorial Seas and the Contiguous Zone. However, the United States had no legislation which prohibited foreign fishing in the territorial seas or which prescribed penalties. "A naked prohibition is not much use as a deterrent to foreign fishing," wrote Captain C. R. Kear on behalf of the Secretary of the Navy. In the opinion of Senator E. L. Bartlett of Alaska, "In effect the Coast Guard can only say to the master of the offending ship: 'Please go away.'" The law passed in 1964 allowed the United States to confiscate the fish and the boat and to fine or imprison any person who fished in United States territorial waters without authorization. Although the State Department may not have allowed the Coast Guard to enforce the law very strictly, there were fewer complaints about foreign fishing vessels working within three miles of the coast.[62]

Fishing interests from Alaska, the Pacific Northwest, and some parts of New England lobbied for extension of American fishery jurisdiction to twelve miles in 1966 in order to push foreign fishermen farther away. The State Department ended its traditional opposition to extension of fishery jurisdiction and went along with the legislation because the twelve-mile fisheries rule had become accepted international practice. The State Department emphasized, however, that the legislation should allow traditional foreign fishing to continue and should make clear that the action did not affect the width of the territorial sea or traditional freedom of overflight and navigation. The law passed in late 1966 took account of all the points the State Department raised.[63]

A twelve-mile fishery zone was not what the fishing interests would have wanted if they could have had their way. "We feel that both for the protection of the fishing industry and the preservation of the national interest, a limit of 200 miles is the most desirable," said Howard Nickerson, director of the Harbor Development Commission in New Bedford. If not 200 miles of fishery jurisdiction, then the industry would like to see extension of fishery jurisdiction to at least fifty miles or to the 100-fathom depth curve, Nickerson said. Spokesmen from the West Coast expressed the same sentiments. Jacob Dykstra of Point Judith called for extension of fishery jurisdiction far beyond twelve miles. "The proposed extent of the fishery zone is completely inadequate," he said. "A fishery zone of this extent would be ineffective to protect fishery stocks, most of which range the entire coastal shelf. Halfway measures and fractional advances are no answer to this problem." Dykstra supported the legislation because it was all he could hope for, but, he wrote, "Our greatest fear in twelve-mile limit legislation has been that the Congress, upon passage of such law, might feel that the subject of fishery jurisdiction was then established for a long time to come."[64]

Neither the law prohibiting foreign fishing in territorial waters nor the twelve-mile fishing limit had an effect on the problems of foreign fishing. Neither measure reduced foreign fishing pressures on the resource because the fish ranged across the fishery jurisdiction boundary. Fishing pressures outside the territorial waters or the twelve-mile limit were quite sufficient to deplete the fish stocks as fast as if the foreigners had fished in the inshore waters also. The twelve-mile limit legislation may have been more important for political reasons than for its usefulness in addressing problems of foreign fishing. Perhaps, as Dykstra had feared, the legislation relieved pressures for a 200-mile limit, but the pressures were very weak anyway. Most important, the legislation established precedents for congressional intervention in the problems of foreign fishing on the East Coast.

In 1973, Congress acted for the first time to protect fishing from foreign pressures in opposition to the State Department's interests. Fishing groups and state fishery administrators pressed Congress to pass a law which would add the lobster to the list of creatures of the continental shelf. That move would prohibit lobstering by foreigners under the Convention on the Continental Shelf. The previous year the fisheries officials of twelve Atlantic coast states had petitioned Robert White, the chief of the National Oceanic and Atmospheric Administration (NOAA), to declare the lobster a creature of the continental shelf. White had refused to do so but had said he would seek to protect the lobster resource through multilateral agreements. The NOAA position reflected the State Department view that agreements with other countries fishing on Georges Bank could solve problems of foreigners' incidental lobster catch, the only harvest the State Department acknowledged existed or would be important in the future.[65]

State fishery officials were furious. They were attempting, with cooperation of the National Marine Fisheries Service, to manage the use of the depleted inshore lobster resource. The NOAA decision placed the officials in the untenable political position of imposing severe restrictions on American lobstermen fishing inshore while foreign boats could take all they wanted of the offshore resource, which New England fishermen believed mingled with the inshore stock. Governor Francis Sargent of Massachusetts announced that his state would protect offshore lobsters by enforcing its own 200-mile limit, passed in 1971.

State fishery officials and offshore lobstermen were certain, moreover, that if the foreign fleets decided to direct effort toward the lobster stock, international negotiations would take years to slow the fishing activity, and by then the stock would be destroyed. They believed that regulations or legislation had to be in place to prevent that from happening. When White turned down their request, they turned to Congress.[66]

Congressmen recognized that by 1973 New England fishing interests had watched ineffectual efforts at multilateral settlement of foreign fishing problems for too long to be put off. As Congressman William Cohen of Maine said, "The point of declaring the lobsters to be a creature of the shelf is . . . to give them [the fishermen] a sense of confidence that we are really doing something to protect their interests." He told the State Department spokesman, Donald McKernan, "You see the patience of the members here being frayed quite thin . . . they are reflecting the impatience of the fishermen."[67]

In order to prevent a veto, the Senate attached the lobster bill to legislation to implement agreements on shrimping off the coast of Brazil, which both the State Department and shrimp interests who opposed the lobster bill wanted to see pass. The lobster therefore officially became a creature of the continental shelf.

The legislation may have prevented some foreign fishermen from lobstering on Georges Bank but probably had no effect on incidental catches. Enforcement of the law was particularly mild. Under State Department orders, the Coast Guard and National Marine Fisheries Service officials used none of the sanctions that the legislation authorized against foreign trawlers who violated the prohibition. Many months after enactment of the law, the State Department announced the beginning of "tough, unprecedented enforcement." Shortly afterwards, however, after the Coast Guard observed a Canadian boat fishing directly for lobster, the State Department noted, "We had an obligation to sit down and talk with the Canadians before commencing a strict enforcement program."[68]

The legislation was important politically even if it did not conserve the resource. For the first time Congress defied State Department desires and took action on a fishery problem without negotiations with other nations. That made consideration somewhat easier of the much stronger unilateral action to extend fisheries jurisdiction to 200 miles. The lobster legislation may also have fueled the drive for a 200-mile limit among fishing interests because passage of the lobster law demonstrated that Congress allied with the industry against the State Department and against NOAA. Congress reinforced the industry's feeling by passing a concurrent resolution which defined a policy "that our fishing industry be afforded all support necessary to have it strengthened, and all steps taken to provide adequate protection for our coastal fisheries against excessive foreign fishing. . . Congress is fully prepared to act immediately to provide interim measures to conserve overfished stocks and to protect our domestic fishing industry."[69] The support from Congress encouraged the fishing industry to work for the extension of fishing jurisdiction.

THE FISHERY CONSERVATION AND MANAGEMENT ACT

As the lobster legislation passed in late 1973, Congress began the first consideration of bills to extend fishery jurisdiction to 200 miles. In response to opposition from the administration, the House Committee on Merchant Marine and Fisheries and the Senate Committee on Commerce continued to study and revise legislation in 1974 and 1975 while prospects for an early end to the Conference on the Law of the Sea dwindled and while ICNAF's regulations and the multilateral fishery agreements failed to solve the problems of foreign fishing and stock depletion. Support for extension of fishery jurisdiction grew. Among commercial and sport fishing groups, only distant-water tuna and shrimp interests opposed the bills. Large numbers of state and local officials backed the fishermen in pushing for the legislation. Newly formed marine conservation groups supported the bills along with the nationwide organizations of the environmental movement such as the Sierra Club, Friends of the Earth, and the National Wildlife Federation.

One hundred thirty-five members introduced or co-sponsored 200-mile limit bills in the House in January 1975. Robert Leggett, chairman of the House subcommittee overseeing the legislation, described the position of Congress to the Law of the Sea delegates as their 1975 meetings ended. "Look, we have got pressures in the country," he reported saying. "We have got our shores utterly being swept by foreign fishing vessels. Even middle America is concerned in Kansas. I noticed the editorials around the country. . . . we have got to move."[70]

The 200-mile limit bills had evolved considerably from 1973 through 1975. Many of the early bills had used the language of the laws which prohibited foreign fishing in United States territorial waters and extended fishery jurisdiction to twelve miles. As William Mustard of the National Federation of Fishermen said, those bills were "of the 200-mile fence variety." Coastal fishermen would have been happy to see such legislation enacted because the bills got rid of foreign fishermen. Other bills asserted jurisdiction over coastal and anadromous species and called for the negotiation of treaties for the use of those resources by other nations. The National Federation of Fishermen endorsed this approach, saying that it took account of many of the provisions of the United States draft treaty articles at the Conference on the Law of the Sea.[71]

The bill debated in early 1976 was far more elaborate than these earlier ones. It stated that foreign nations could not fish within 200 miles of the coast or for anadromous or continental shelf species beyond 200 miles except under special conditions. Provisions for foreign fishing within 200 miles of the coast involved government management of the activities of domestic and foreign fishermen. Foreigners could harvest that part of the "optimum yield" of a fishery that American fishermen lacked the capacity to catch. The United States would issue a permit to foreigners which allowed a level of fishing consistent with a management plan for the harvest of a species or group of species. Before foreign fishermen could receive a permit, their country would have to sign a "governing international fishery agreement" with the United States in which the foreign nation recognized the exclusive fishery management authority of the United States and agreed to follow regulations, to cooperate with enforcement, to pay fees, and to catch no more fish than its allocation.[72]

These conditions linked foreign fishing to an extensive system of regulation of American fishermen. Fishing interests had not sought government management of the industry as they pushed for a 200-mile fisheries zone, although spokesmen said they were willing to consider a management system if foreigners were severely restricted. "It is our conviction that the fisheries of the United States are in need of more effective management and that it is vitally necessary that legislation be enacted to accomplish this," Jacob Dykstra stated as early as 1973. However, such action was definitely of secondary importance, and understanding of how a management system should work was far too primitive to contemplate setting up a program quickly. Extensive detailed management provisions in some bills "are included in haste, it seems," Dykstra said later, "because some of their proponents feel that now, when the coastal fishermen are so desperate for extended jurisdiction, is the time to saddle them with all sorts of untried schemes to restrict their operations. . . . We heartily endorse the concept that comprehensive domestic fisheries management legislation will have high priority once extended fisheries jurisdiction is a reality."[73] Others agreed with Dykstra. Pass legislation to exclude foreigners first, fishery spokesmen repeated; then draft bills for domestic fishery management.

Although most industry spokesmen declared that they thought domestic fishery management might be necessary, a National Marine Fisheries Service survey showed that they did not like the proposals they saw. They opposed every specific suggestion about how management might work.[74] Fishing spokesmen were caught in a bind. They played up the devastation of the fish resources and emphasized the conservation aspects of excluding foreigners in order to attract the backing of environmental groups and congressmen sensitive to environmental issues. They would have jeopardized that support if they had openly opposed controls on domestic fishermen, but their fishery constituents did not want management. If the spokesmen could just persuade Congress to pass legislation to exclude foreigners first, they could fight bills to manage American fishermen.

Fishing industry leaders failed to postpone the design of a management system. The combined forces in favor of management and conservation measures were strong enough to make such provisions critical for passage of any bill to reduce the number of foreigners in coastal waters.

As congressmen authored the first 200-mile limit bills and debated making the lobster a creature of the continental shelf in 1973, the National Marine Fisheries Service (NMFS) and its parent agency NOAA introduced a bill to manage domestic fishermen. The legislation would solve several problems, Robert White, administrator of NOAA, said. It would help to coordinate state management programs. Such coordination was necessary "if we are ever to break out of the present confusion due to conflicts between regulations of different jurisdictions into an approach which is biologically, economically, and socially sound," White said. The bill also would provide "the Federal Government with the authority necessary to discharge its obligations under our international fisheries agreements," White argued, and would implement the 1958 Convention on Fishing and Conservation of the Living Resources of the High Seas. Without such legislation, the United States had no authority to enforce the provisions of bilateral or multilateral negotiations on its own fishermen except in the ICNAF area. Such international agreements could solve the problem of foreign fishing, the State Department had declared, but not without authority to enforce regulation of American fishermen.[75]

The NOAA/NMFS bill did not get out of committee because of disagreement about the way management should work and because of opposition from fishing interests and congressmen to controls on domestic fishermen without restrictions on foreigners. In the next few years, however, NOAA continued to voice the administration's opposition to unilateral extension of fishery jurisdiction. As Congressman Gerry Studds of Massachusetts pointed out, "The only glimmer of enthusiasm on the part of the administration has to do with the possibility of management provisions" in the legislation to extend fisheries jurisdiction.[76] Domestic fishery management provisions, supporters of a 200-mile limit realized, would certainly reduce NOAA's opposition to extension of fishery jurisdiction.

Provisions for fishery conservation and management also undermined some of the State and Defense Departments' arguments and, therefore, weakened the grounds for opposition from the administration and from congressmen on committees concerned with foreign affairs and the armed forces. International law, the State Department spokesmen said, showed that unilateral extension of fishery jurisdiction to 200 miles was illegal. The International Court of Justice had ruled against Iceland's efforts to keep fishing vessels from Great Britain out of a fifty-mile zone of fishery jurisdiction, and the court would surely not support the United States in a dispute with a foreign nation over rights inside an American fishery zone. In opposition to this State Department view, Professor Louis Henkin, an expert in international law from Columbia University, pointed out conditions under which extension of fishery jurisdiction would be acceptable. "An impartial tribunal might well hold that, unlike assertions of exclusive fishing rights, bona-fide conservation measures applied to all (including fishing by the coastal state) is now within the authority of the coastal state under customary law," Henkin said. "A conservation regulation applicable to all fishing (including our own), moreover, accords with the policies pursued by the United States since the Truman Proclamation of 1945; a large, exclusive fishing zone, on the other hand, would be wholly contrary to the policies, and the view of international law, which the United States has consistently and repeatedly asserted." None of the nations that would be affected by extension of United States fisheries jurisdiction had objected to the principles of the Truman Proclamation[77] or rejected the conservation provisions of the Convention on Fishing and Conservation of the Living Resources of the High Seas, Henkin asserted. They probably would not do so now, but in any case, challenges to a "conservation measure applicable to all" would probably not be sustained under international law.[78]

Management and conservation clauses also made the 200-mile fisheries jurisdiction bills more consistent with the growing consensus on coastal state control over fisheries at the Conference on the Law of the Sea. By the end of the 1975 Geneva session of the Conference, the negotiating texts on fisheries affirmed "sovereign rights" of coastal nations over fisheries to 200 miles, but a coastal state had a duty to conserve the fish resources. This meant that a nation had an obligation to determine allowable catch and adopt measures "to maintain or restore populations of harvested species at levels which can produce the maximum sustainable yield, as qualified by relevant environmental and economic factors"; to ensure "that the maintenance of the living resources . . . is not endangered by overexploitation"; and "to take into consideration the effects on species associated with or dependent upon harvested species." The coastal state had first claim to the fish resources, but it also had to determine the capacity of its industry to harvest the resources in its zone and to give other states the opportunity to harvest the share of allowable catch which its own fishermen could not use.[79] The State and Defense Departments warned that unilateral extension of fishery jurisdiction would destroy the possibility for agreement at the Conference on the Law of the Sea and would lead to claims by other countries that would harm United States interests. However, these predictions seemed less plausible and the objections less reasonable, congressmen argued, when legislation took the same form as the consensus coming out of the conference.

Other groups favored the extension of fishery jurisdiction to 200 miles but also wanted provisions for fishery management. They believed that fishery management could lead to more rational use of fish resources and a healthier, more stable fishing industry. The state offices of marine fisheries were one group that favored management of domestic fisheries. Management of the use of fish and shellfish resources within three miles of the coast had already become an important role for state fishery departments. In Maine, officials had been working with lobstermen for years to adopt measures that would conserve inshore lobsters. As Congress debated the 200-mile limit, Massachusetts and Maine fisheries officials sought ways to protect shrimp from the fishing pressures of inshore draggers. In 1973 the state legislature gave greater authority to manage the state's inshore fisheries to Spencer Apollonio, commissioner of the Maine department of fisheries. "The fisheries value of the Maine Coast could be doubled without too much trouble" with proper management, Apollonio declared.[80]

Officials from eleven Atlantic coast states had met since early 1972 under the auspices of the State-Federal Fisheries Management Program established by NMFS. The purpose of the program was to make uniform fishery management easier by encouraging cooperation among states. While the state fishery administrators failed to achieve their first goal, to agree on an effective uniform lobster management program, their efforts called attention to the need for management authority outside the three-mile limit of state fishery jurisdiction where fishermen drew on the same stocks of fish as in the near-shore waters.[81]

State fishery officials made strong pleas for a fishery management program to accompany the restrictions on foreigners. "It would be ironic and immoral," Apollonio declared, "if, as the economic value of those resources reaches record highs, as the world's needs for protein sharply increase, and as the fisherman attains technologically efficient and eco-

nomical methods of harvesting the sea, we should continue to tolerate
. . . inefficient, costly, and wasteful use of those high seas resources. . . .
It is a fact that a properly managed renewable resource can realize a
maximum sustainable yield in significant excess of the present landings
for the long-term benefit of all." Frank Grice, director of the Division of
Marine Fisheries in Massachusetts, declared, "What we must have is
management control."[82]

The directors of the states' offices of marine fisheries and the NMFS
staff often had degrees in fishery biology, fishery economics, or
oceanography. They had received their training from another group who
spoke for fishery management but usually remained noncommittal on
extension of fishery jurisdiction—academic biologists and economists
who specialized in fisheries research. Dr. Donald Horton, a fishery
biologist and director of the Research Institute of the Gulf of Maine,
stated, "I am quite sure that I would not be in favor of extending the
national jurisdiction for any other purpose than for the protection and
management of fishery resources." Professor Giulio Pontecorvo, an economist who had written numerous books and articles on fishery management, advised Congress on the issues they confronted in establishing a
system of fishery management. Dr. Francis Christy, an economist with
Resources for the Future, worked with NOAA on fishery affairs and
wrote extensively on the benefits of fishery management. His writings
made the economic and biological issues in setting up a system of fishery
management comprehensible to those who were not experts. Professor
James Crutchfield at the University of Washington also wrote on the need
for fishery management and advised policy makers.[83]

Academics advised congressmen and officials at NOAA as they
drafted successive versions of the legislation. They were important because congressmen, congressional committee staff, and agency officials
shared their views and wanted their input, rather than because they
lobbied in Washington. They provided information and offered arguments that were useful to those who supported fishery management.
Congressional committee staff became convinced that a fishery management system that included American fishermen ought to be part of the
legislation. NMFS arguments persuaded them; then they drew an
academic research to support their position. The report of the House
Committee on Merchant Marine and Fisheries on the 200-mile limit bill
used four paragraphs from a study by two University of Rhode Island
economists to explain the problems that arose in fisheries without management and to state that control of fishing effort was "critical to U.S.
fisheries."[84]

Confronted with the necessity for fishery management provisions to assure passage of a 200-mile limit bill, fishing interests sought to influence the form of the management system. Early bills proposed programs controlled by NOAA or Congress with input from fishery advisory groups from the Atlantic, Gulf, and Pacific coasts. Spokesmen for the fishing industry made many suggestions about how management should work, but their greatest concern was to limit the power of NMFS and NOAA and to guarantee representation on any management body for the groups affected by regulation—the fishermen, boat owners, and processors. The spokesmen criticized NOAA and NMFS. William Mustard of the National Federation of Fishermen declared, "It is ironic to note that a bureaucratic agency which has done virtually nothing to promote the best fisheries interests of the Nation, which apparently has no real practical knowledge of what is in the best interests of the several States, is now proposing to save the fishermen and the resources it has watched disappear." Lucy Sloan, also of National Federation of Fishermen, emphasized, "What we think is necessary for the protection of the domestic industry is a system of checks and balances on how the Administrator [of NOAA] can promulgate regulations."[85]

Fishing interests sought more control over management in other ways and also tried to weaken the management authority in the bills. For example, Sloan called for less detailed management provisions: "Many of the management provisions could be provided for in the process of promulgating regulations, a process in which industry should have significantly more input than this bill reflects."[86] Such an arrangement would mean that the industry could try to stop fishery management after they had the 200-mile limit. It would also mean that management procedures would be subject to more legal interpretation and challenge than ones clearly spelled out in law.

The House Committee on Merchant Marine and Fisheries reported out the 200-mile limit bill in August 1975, and the Senate Committee on Commerce followed in October. Congress passed the Fishery Conservation and Management Act (FCMA) in March 1976; President Ford signed it into law in April.

The domestic fishery management program was central to the act. The law set up eight regional fishery management councils to oversee the use of fishery resources in different parts of the country. The New England Fishery Management Council (the Council) would control the use of the fish resources off New England outside the three miles of state jurisdiction, an area covering Georges Bank, the Gulf of Maine, and southern New England waters. The Council's members would include the director of each state's marine fisheries agency, the regional director of the National Marine Fisheries Service, and eleven others "knowledgeable or experienced with regard to the management, conservation, or recreational or commercial harvest, of the fishery resources" of the region. Non-voting members would come from the State Department, the Coast Guard, the Fish and Wildlife Service, and the Atlantic States Marine Fisheries Commission.[87]

The law directed the Council to prepare a management plan for each fishery in the region and to submit it to the Secretary of Commerce. In preparing a plan the Council decided on the optimum yield of a fish resource, which, the law stated, "means the amount of fish—(A) which will provide the greatest overall benefit to the Nation, with particular reference to food production and recreational opportunities; and (B) which is prescribed as such on the basis of the maximum sustainable yield from such fishery, as modified by any relevant economic, social, or ecological factor." The Council, after determining the size of the optimum yield, regulated fishing activity so that the catch did not exceed optimum yield. The law authorized the Council to designate zones where fishermen could fish; to specify limits on catch in terms of weight, size of fish, species, and other factors; to prohibit or require certain kinds of equipment; to require permits for fishing; to set up a system of limited access to the fisheries; and to prescribe any other measures necessary for conservation and management.[88]

"National standards" for fishery conservation and management were to guide the Council's decisions. Measures prescribed by the Council should prevent overfishing while achieving the optimum yield from each fishery on a continuing basis. The Council should adopt measures based on the best scientific information available. The Council should manage an individual fish stock or interrelated stocks as a unit throughout their range. Conservation and management decisions should not discriminate among residents of different states; and allocation of fishing privileges should be fair and equitable, promote conservation, and assure that no individual or group acquired an excessive share of privileges. The conservation and management efforts should promote efficiency in use of fishery resources; should take into account variations among fisheries, fishery resources, and catches; and should minimize costs and avoid unnecessary duplication.[89]

The FCMA incorporated some of the suggestions of fishing interests and left others out. Most significantly, the law did provide for substantial industry representation on the regional councils. Eleven of the seventeen voting members on the New England Fishery Management Council could come from the industry. While that did not guarantee that industry rather than environmentalists, consumer advocates, or fishery researchers would get those seats, and while sectors of the industry could disagree on how management should work, the provision still made industry control of management likely, as their spokesmen had wanted.

THE LEGACY OF THE CAMPAIGN FOR THE 200-MILE LIMIT[90]

When the Fishery Conservation and Management Act passed in early 1976 with great acclaim from congressmen and from coastal fishing interests, it ushered in a new era in fishery policy. For the first time, the United States asserted control over foreign fishing off its coasts and put a system of domestic fishery management in place. The fishery management program promised extensive government regulation of the industry. The decisions of the New England Fishery Management Council could mean that the government would dictate how thousands of fishermen and boat owners fished, would tell fishermen when they could work, and would name the people allowed to work as fishermen. Unlike many other kinds of industry regulation, agricultural programs to encourage farmers to leave some land out of production, for example, or airline rate setting, the legislation did not provide for price setting or subsidies to assure that fishermen, boat owners, and processors would earn an adequate living under the restrictions. The new law included no way for government to pay fishermen if the regulators told them they could not work. Quite unlike the provisions of most other types of regulation, most of the regulators were from the start members of the industry who would be directly affected by restrictions they designed. Fishery management could become indulgent self-regulation unless groups with other interests, environmentalists or consumers, for example, became involved.

The legacy of the many years of work to limit foreign fishing and to extend fisheries jurisdiction to 200 miles included much more than the law itself. The experience had molded views among industry spokesmen, fishermen, and officials at NMFS and NOAA that promised to affect the industry and fishery policy in the new era.

Fishermen and their spokesmen disliked and distrusted NMFS and NOAA, the agencies responsible for working with the Council in implementing and enforcing management plans. Fishermen had formed their opinions in part under ICNAF management. NMFS scientists made the fish stock assessments that demonstrated the need for lower ICNAF quotas. While fishermen wanted conservation, they did not want it at their own expense. Many in the fishing industry had believed the United

States purpose in ICNAF was to constrain foreign fishing. In contrast, Richard Hennemuth, a biologist who worked with ICNAF for many years, argued that the scientific assessments were "not the tool of U.S. industry" and that the assessments did not imply that the United States fishermen should be able to harvest as much as they wanted. The fishermen hated the biologists, said another NMFS biologist closely involved in the ICNAF work, because "we gave the fish to the Russians." The enforcement agents under ICNAF also came from NMFS. They boarded the New England boats, checked the catch at the docks, and initiated procedures which took the fishermen into court and fined them, all of which fishermen greatly resented.[91]

The spokesmen for fishermen disliked NMFS and NOAA for other reasons as well. While they reflected the views of their constituents on the penalties for fishermen under ICNAF, the spokesmen also found the biologists' dire predictions about the condition of the fish stocks useful in their push for extension of fishery jurisdiction. Their animosity came in large part from their feelings that at every turn in their efforts to control the level of foreign fishing, NMFS opposed industry interests or, at best, gave no support. NMFS had not helped to influence the State Department to take a more aggressive stance in ICNAF negotiations or to assure that foreign nations bore the brunt of quota reductions. Instead, the agency had watched the problems worsen, fishing spokesmen felt. They were angry, too, that NMFS and NOAA had sought management authority over American fishermen but stuck to the administration's line opposing restrictions on foreign fishing off the coast. As Congress considered management provisions, fishing spokesmen again fought NMFS and NOAA, this time for control of management. William Mustard of National Federation of Fishermen said, "Both [agencies] . . . are self-serving mechanisms which, under the present set-up, only serve to perpetuate themselves." The fishing industry had no advocate in the executive branch of the government, he claimed. NMFS sought not only to control the management process but also to determine the kind of management, fishing spokesmen said. "Limited entry is neither the only way nor even the best way to manage a fishery, despite what the NMFS National Fisheries Plan says," Mustard protested.[92]

As fishing industry leaders criticized NMFS and NOAA, they pointed repeatedly at "the academics and the bureaucrats" who threatened the fishing industry's welfare. Their statements in turn struck a responsive chord in many fishermen and boat owners. "Academics" usually meant fishery biologists, many of whom worked in National Marine Fisheries Service laboratories on studies of fish behavior and on the stock assessments that would be critical ingredients of the fishery management plans. Less commonly, the term also referred to fishery economists, usually those affiliated with NMFS or NOAA, who favored limited entry programs for fishery management. "Bureaucrats" meant the NOAA and NMFS staff in Washington and in the regional offices in Gloucester who would work closely with the Council. The bureaucrats, the fishing spokesmen felt, wanted to expand their own jobs and responsibilities without benefit to the industry.

Such feelings in the fishermen and their representatives, justified or not, could not aid the transition to fishery management. Many of the fishery spokesmen were to serve as members of the Council and would need to work constructively with the biologists' stock assessments and with administrators from NMFS and NOAA.

For their part, NMFS officials in Washington were accustomed to controlling fishery management because they had served as commissioners or as influential advisors to ICNAF. Decisions about the United States position at ICNAF had been made in Washington by the State Department and by NMFS. NMFS officials had fought hard to cement their management authority in the new legislation. Although they lost that battle, they continued to believe that the authority was rightfully theirs and that they were more qualified to make decisions than the councils. Officials at the State Department had kept the authority to make final decisions about foreign fishing. If a management plan showed that American fishermen could not harvest the optimum yield, the State Department remained convinced that decisions about allocation of the unutilized resource should be made according to State Department priorities. Conflict over fishery management among the councils, the National Marine Fisheries Service, and the State Department was inevitable.

The industry also had expectations about the meaning of the new legislation with implications for the way the management system would work. Fishermen, boat owners, and processors underestimated the importance of the fishery management program. Throughout the campaign for the 200-mile limit, they paid most attention to the restrictions on foreign fishing, on which discussion had focused for years. Detailed management provisions went into the bills late. The restrictions on foreigners were also easier to understand than lengthy debates on the subtleties of a fishery management program, and those in the industry had little time to study the news from Washington. Fishery news sources, furthermore, understated the management aspects of the legislation. Many in the industry who were fully aware of the management provisions

in the law believed that once the foreigners v
management program would not affect their work
so plentiful. They thought the program might beg
years later as the industry grew, but such a distan
cause for concern.

The industry and NMFS agreed that ICNAF m
The reasons for the failure had to do with the deter
with ineffective enforcement; and the foreigners' t
of these problems, many in the industry believed.
mas offered a rich opportunity for learning abou
styles of fishery management, few of the group
lessons. ICNAF's problems, however, may have l
management strategy as with the foreign-domes
understand this on the part of the industry, their s
officials meant domestic fishery management wou
ICNAF battles. The National Marine Fisheries
writing interim fishery management plans while th
tions, used ICNAF's approach as a blueprint.

As Congress passed the 200-mile limit legislat
groundfish industry saw a brighter future than
foreigners were excluded, those in the industry fel
the maintenance of the fish stocks. In contrast to
land fishermen, they pointed out, used larger m
for midwater trawling, and did not have the cap
damage to the stocks. Recovery of the groundfis
ble, and, with that, the industry's prosperity se
larger numbers than ever before, fishermen and t
build and buy new boats, and young people de
promising career. The 200-mile limit, fisherme
processors felt, had solved the most important
faced, and they looked optimistically toward the

6

Implementing Fishery Management

*I*n 1977 THE BRANCALEONES, one of Gloucester's pre-eminent fishing families, decided to purchase a third offshore trawler. Another Brancaleone would have his opportunity as a skipper. The Brancaleones' two boats provided some of the best sites in the Gloucester fleet. "One of the finest captains in Gloucester," another skipper said of Tom Brancaleone. "If you've got a chance to go on the [Brancaleones'] 'Joseph and Lucia,' you're crazy not to take it," a crewman stated.[1]

In fall 1977 Fred Leber, formerly an attorney for the Securities and Exchange Commission, took delivery of his new offshore trawler, the "Hattie Rose," in Gloucester. He and his wife had not wanted to live in Washington any longer, Leber said, and he had not been satisfied with his job. At the same time, he said, "The [fishing] industry looked very prosperous and growing all the time." At first, Leber had problems with the boat operation because he did not know enough about fishing or about how to hire a good captain and crew. He eventually found a good captain, but even then, he admitted, he had "never dreamed that it would be as hard as it is."[2]

The Brancaleone and Leber decisions were but two examples of developments in the groundfish industry. Hundreds of fishermen in Gloucester, Portland, and smaller Maine and Massachusetts ports decided to purchase new boats. Captains complained of a lack of experienced, reliable crew even though many young men now turned to fishing; captains said even more new fishermen could find sites. The passage of the 200-mile limit encouraged the activity. As Leber put it, "The 200-mile limit passage was crucial [in deciding to buy a boat]; otherwise, I wouldn't have had the nerve to get into the fishing industry."[3]

Few fishermen or boat owners talked freely about their optimism or their prosperity. Widespread public knowledge of boat owners' profits and fishermen's earnings could reduce leverage with the Fishery Manage-

149

ment Council and NMFS, attract too many others into fishing, and draw the attention of the Internal Revenue Service. In addition, many still felt unsure about the future. The industry would experience a boom in a few years, not right away, said Thomas Norris of Old Colony Trawling Corporation in Boston. According to Howard Nickerson, executive secretary of the New England Fisheries Steering Committee, "The true results [of the 200-mile limit] won't be felt for three to five years, with proper enforcement and management of our fish stocks."[4]

Industry spokesmen, fishermen, and government fisheries officials agreed that industry prospects depended on the implementation of the 200-mile limit legislation. Congress had passed the Fishery Conservation and Management Act (FCMA) in the hope that it would achieve several goals; one aim was to promote a healthy, prosperous fishing industry.

When the FCMA went into effect in March 1977, the New England Fishery Management Council had been functioning for six months. Congress had appropriated funds to enable the Council to regulate the use of the fish resource under the new law. Government officials had joined the Council, as the law specified, and the Secretary of Commerce had appointed eleven other members from the lists of candidates the governors submitted. Among the voting members were the regional director of National Marine Fisheries Service; five state officials, one from each New England state except Vermont; three representatives of commercial fishermen; a spokesman for a Boston company which owned large vessels; a recreational fisherman who published a sport fishing magazine; two managers of fish processing plants; a professor of fishery economics; and a fishing gear salesman. Non-voting members came from the Coast Guard, the Fish and Wildlife Service, the State Department, and the Atlantic States Marine Fisheries Commission. By March the Council had also hired a staff and installed it in offices. The Council had spent the time from September to March working out administrative problems and therefore had depended on NMFS to prepare preliminary fishery management plans for fisheries where foreigners would be allowed to harvest.[5] By March the Council was ready to begin its work of domestic fishery management.

The degree to which New England fishermen, boat owners, and processors would benefit from the 200-mile limit, the New England industry believed, depended on just one part of the Council's job, not on managing United States fishing but on excluding foreigners from the fishing grounds. As the 200-mile limit went into effect, fishermen and their spokesmen watched the enforcement of the law against foreigners, fearing that foreign fishing would continue without constraints. Events during the first months under the law confirmed industry fears that foreign policy priorities could make the 200-mile limit meaningless.

In the first weeks after the law became effective, the Coast Guard, the agency charged with enforcing the law against foreigners, boarded and released five Soviet vessels. In one instance, the Coast Guard officers found no violations. In at least two others, however, the Coast Guard recommended the seizure of the vessels, but the State Department refused to allow it, in one case because "the issuing of a fine would be effective rather than a seizure," according to a State Department spokesman. New England fishermen saw the effectiveness of the 200-mile limit undermined.[6]

The New England Fishery Management Council and leaders of fishery organizations lodged formal protests with congressional leaders about the State Department decisions. In response, Senator Edward Kennedy and Congressman Gerry Studds from Massachusetts criticized the handling of the incidents. "Neither the spirit nor the letter of the law enacting the 200-mile zone gives the State Department the power to overrule the Coast Guard in questions of enforcement," Studds stated. Studds claimed the State Department prohibited the seizures "because someone in the National Security Council didn't know what the hell they were doing." Congressional leaders and fishermen charged that the Carter administration downplayed the fishing violations to avoid jeopardizing Soviet-United States negotiations on strategic arms limitation.[7]

Perhaps because of the scale of the protest, the State Department agreed in April 1977 to the seizure of a Russian trawler that had harvested large amounts of river herring. The trawler had committed "a gross violation" of the regulation limiting harvest of the herring to one percent of all processed fish aboard, according to the Coast Guard's chief of Maritime Law Enforcement for the region. The next day the Coast Guard seized the catch on a Soviet refrigerator ship. The Coast Guard brought the trawler "Taras Shevchenko" and the refrigerator ship "Antanas Snechkus" into Boston. The government filed civil and criminal charges against the "Taras Shevchenko" and its captain, and the Coast Guard issued a civil citation against the "Antanas Snechkus."[8]

In contrast to the frequent protests in the first weeks of the 200-mile limit, few in the New England industry complained about enforcement again until September 1977 when the Department of State interfered with the seizure of a Polish trawler. The New England Fishery Management Council protested, "If the Congress had intended that foreign policy issues were an over-riding concern, it would not have enacted the Fishery Conservation and Management Act."[9]

The Polish trawler case notwithstanding, such incidents were rare after the April 1977 seizures. Coast Guard surveillance and NMFS observers aboard the foreign boats identified few serious violations. Enforcement seemed thorough enough to assure that the Coast Guard or NMFS would stop flagrant violators. The seizures and the citations appeared to have demonstrated that the United States intended to enforce the new law. The Soviet Ministry of Fisheries stated that fishing captains had received further instructions on fishing in American coastal waters.[10]

Although fishermen, boat owners, and processors remained suspicious of all foreign fishing activity, the industry and the Council gradually gained confidence that the government enforced the law against foreigners. They turned their attention to other matters. By early 1979 a Coast Guard report on enforcement and surveillance methods attracted almost no interest at the Council's meeting.

The New England industry was concerned not just about enforcement of the restrictions on foreign fishing; they also feared that management plans would allocate large amounts of fish to foreigners. The law stated that other nations could harvest the share of the optimum yield that American fishermen lacked the capacity to catch. The New England Fishery Management Council reviewed foreign nations' requests for permits and recommended to the Secretary of Commerce that the requests be rejected or accepted. The Secretary acted on applications after consultation with the Secretary of State and the Secretary of the department from which the Coast Guard operated.[11]

Most Council members wanted as few fish as possible to go to the foreigners, but they were convinced that when they recommended that the Secretary of Commerce deny permits or reduce allocations, the Commerce and State Departments did not go along with their suggestion. When the Council did recommend approval of permits for several foreign countries, fishermen were incredulous and angry. "The purpose of the 200-mile limit is conservation, but then what we don't catch goes to the foreigners," protested a Gloucester fisherman's wife. "Some of our boats could go for those fish, but we know we need it next year. We shouldn't give it away." A Portland fisherman told the Council, "Cod eat squid," and underutilized squid were therefore vital for rebuilding the cod resource. The Council, the fisherman continued, ought to "take care of our own rather than them." A Gloucester fisherman asked, "Why take fish out of our mouths to feed them? We should fill *our* stomachs first." Alan Guimond of the Offshore Fish and Lobster Association repeatedly urged the Council to refuse permits to countries that had violated fishing regulations.[12]

The worst conflicts over foreign allocations centered on the preliminary management plan for herring. The problems reflected the tension between foreign policy concerns and the interests of the domestic fishing industry, the strength of fishing industry hostility toward the foreigners, and the importance of vigilance on the part of the fishing industry to assure that the FCMA's restrictions on foreign fishing were observed. NMFS found biological evidence to support a sizable allocation of herring to foreigners on Georges Bank in 1977. New England fishermen, processors, and boat owners, using alternative economic information on the capacity of the domestic industry and pointing to other biological evidence, insisted that foreigners should not receive an allowance of herring. The State of Maine sued the federal government in an effort to change the allocations. Maine lost the suit, but the court required the Secretary of Commerce to provide more information on the calculation of the foreign share of the optimum yield and on how allocation of the fish to foreigners would benefit the United States. The reply from the Secretary of Commerce justified the size of the foreigners' share primarily on diplomatic and political grounds, not the kind of considerations that the FCMA stated could justify allocations to foreigners.[13]

The size of the foreign herring allocation stood, but the vessels that received permits were unable to harvest their share of herring in the time allowed. The nations involved appealed to the Secretary of Commerce for another opportunity to catch the allocation of fish. France threatened retaliation against American shrimpers off French Guiana unless the herring season were extended, and representatives of the shrimp industry appealed to the Commerce and State Departments to approve the changes. The Secretary of Commerce agreed to the foreigners' requests over strong objections from the New England Council and the herring and sardine industries.[14]

The problems with the herring allocation were unique during the first years of the FCMA. Foreign fishermen received no share of the most valuable, badly depleted species. New England fishermen had not expanded their harvest of other species enough to find the foreign allocations a constraint. The goal of the FCMA to control foreign fishing in coastal waters seemed successfully achieved, although the potential remained for conflict between industry interests and State Department foreign policy priorities.

Foreign-domestic fishing conflicts held little of Council or industry attention after the first months of disputes under the FCMA. As the Council and the industry soon realized, foreign fishing presented few problems compared to management of the New England fishing industry.

The fishery management dilemmas absorbed the attention and energy of the Council members. Furthermore, fishermen, boat owners, and processors quickly saw that not only their prosperity but also their way of life depended on how management worked. The groundfish industry became particularly disillusioned as the management restrictions affected them. By the end of the first year of the FCMA, fishermen and others frequently exclaimed, "We were better off with the Russians!" The greatest controversies and the largest share of the Council's work in the first years of the FCMA centered on the management plan which covered most of the groundfish industry.

MANAGEMENT OF THE GROUNDFISH INDUSTRY UNDER THE FCMA[15]

A few months before the 200-mile limit went into effect, William Gordon, regional director of NMFS, offered the Council a groundfish management plan which covered haddock, cod, and yellowtail flounder. The Council should vote the plan into place immediately, Gordon insisted. He pressed them to act quickly because after the United States resigned from the International Commission for the Northwest Atlantic Fisheries (ICNAF) at the end of 1976, no regulations restricted the harvest. His plan, Gordon argued, would protect the groundfishery, devastated by the heavy fishing of the late 1960s and early 1970s. The Council adopted the plan with few revisions and sent it to public hearings by February 1977. The plan was implemented through emergency regulation in mid-March to avoid the long delay of the conventional approval process.[16]

The authors of the groundfish management plan had aimed to meet the provisions of the FCMA, which required a plan to specify the conservation and management measures governing fishing, to describe the industry harvesting the species, to assess the present and future yield and the capacity of United States fishermen to harvest the optimum yield, and to specify the data submitted to the Secretary of Commerce for managing the fishery. The plan had to meet the requirements of the National Environmental Protection Act as well; the plan would be part of a "final environmental impact statement for the implementation of a fishery management plan."[17]

The result was an odd document. The plan specified no goals, although a major implicit purpose emerged from it. That goal was that the management of the fishery resources should aim to rebuild or to stabilize the fish stocks while attempting to avoid "undue economic hardship" for the fishing industry and coastal fishing communities. The law dictated that conservation and management provisions were to prevent overfishing while taking account of economic, social, and ecological factors. The Council agreed on this purpose with very little discussion as they considered the size of optimum yields for the three species in the plan.[18]

The Council could reach agreement partly because the plan only defined some aspects of the goal. The lack of definitions allowed each member to form his own impression of what the goal meant. More specific statements might have stirred opposition and debate. The plan mentioned "undue economic hardship" for the industry and coastal communities and "adverse economic impacts" on the fishing industry but never said what these were. The plan did not explain how these economic losses should be balanced against stock rebuilding aims.

Furthermore, the parts of the goal which the plan did spell out, the biological assessments of stock conditions and the schedule for rebuilding, did not receive sufficient Council discussion and agreement. The biologists' presentation of data to the Council gave the impression of more confidence in the figures than the scientists themselves felt. The biologists knew that stock assessments had a wide margin of error particularly for recent year classes and that the relation between spawning stock size and size of a new year class was virtually unknown.[19] Both types of information were critical, however, in predicting the speed with which a fish stock could grow. Many Council members, like those in the industry, did not believe the biologists' pessimistic stock assessments, but they felt that they had to accept the assessments because the FCMA stated that the plans had to draw on the best scientific information available. Few Council members were committed to the numbers in the plan.

The plan[20] looked cursorily at alternative measures for achieving goals in order to satisfy National Environmental Protection Act requirements, but these were only minor variations of the management measures selected. The plan did not compare alternative ways to achieve the aims or show that the route chosen was the best for reaching the goals. The plan did not demonstrate that the measures selected would achieve the purposes. Such analyses would have been nearly impossible, however, as long as the goals remained so vague.

The management measures offered little basis for optimism about the results of fishery management during the years to follow. The regulations came directly from ICNAF; even the numbers of pounds allowed as bycatch were the same. The ICNAF experience should have suggested good reasons to try other methods because ICNAF had failed to regulate the use of the fish stocks. Perhaps the Council attributed ICNAF's failure to the intractability of the foreigners rather than to flaws in the management approaches themselves. Perhaps NMFS did not have the power to propose new measures when Council members might more readily accept old ones already debated many times. Neither the Council nor NMFS had enough time or knowledge to attempt new approaches.

The flaws in the plan and the speed with which it was implemented reflected another major implicit goal on which all seemed to agree: to put a plan, any plan, in place as fast as possible. Fearing the results of a long period of unrestricted fishing on the depleted groundfish stocks, NMFS officials pressed the Council to adopt a plan without the opportunity to understand or debate the NMFS draft.

Because of these problems with the plan and with the style of Council planning, Council members lacked a clear idea of their goals in implementing the plan when crises arose later. Definition of goals and interpretations of goals could shift with the political situation, even if the general statement of optimum yield remained the same. Furthermore, the Council had no commitment to the measures spelled out in the plan. When fishermen, boat owners, and processors in the groundfish industry challenged the measures, Council members would have difficulty justifying them and might no longer support them. The groundfish management plan was an inauspicious start of a process that promised to be extremely difficult even with the best of plans.

As a result of the plan formulation, when the Council began its second year of operation in September 1977, the Council had in place a set of specific measures that governed the groundfish industry's activity and would mold the crises of the year that followed. Central to the groundfish management plan were quotas and landing restrictions for cod, haddock, and yellowtail flounder. The plan set quotas based on the optimum yield figures for the catch of the different stocks of fish—cod and haddock in the Gulf of Maine and on Georges Bank and yellowtail flounder east and west of 69 degrees west longitude, a line about fifty miles east of Cape Cod. These were the total amounts of fish which fishermen could harvest for 1977 and, in the case of the yellowtail flounder east of 69 degrees, for each three-month quarter. For haddock and one stock of yellowtail flounder optimum yields were so low that the quotas could be taken as bycatch in other directed fisheries. That is, when fishermen sought cod, they would almost always catch haddock as well even if they did not intend to do so. Haddock caught in this way would fill the quota. Therefore, no fisherman could fish intentionally for yellowtail west of 69 degrees or for haddock. The plan specified the allowable bycatch. No vessel could land more than 5510 pounds or 10 percent of the weight of the total catch on board of yellowtail, whichever was greater, in a given trip from the waters west of 69 degrees. No vessel could land more than 5510 pounds of haddock or 10 percent of the total catch on board (with a few exceptions) until 80 percent of the total allowable haddock bycatch was harvested. Although yellowtail east of 69 degrees was a directed fishery, no vessel could land more than 5,000 pounds of yellowtail flounder per man per trip up to a total vessel trip limit of 25,000 pounds. When the harvest plus the estimated prospective bycatch of cod and of yellowtail flounder east of 69 degrees equalled 100 percent of the quota for a species for the year, the directed fishery for the species would end. Then fishermen could not land more than 5510 pounds of each restricted species or 10 percent by weight of all fish on board, whichever was greater. When the total catch and projected bycatch for the remainder of the year for haddock and for yellowtail flounder west of 69 degrees reached 80 percent of the quota for the year, the Secretary of Commerce could reduce the allowed catch below 5510 pounds per trip to keep fishermen from exceeding the quota. This last provision made complete "closure" of the fisheries possible. The Secretary could reduce the allowable bycatch to zero so that no cod, haddock, or yellowtail flounder could be harvested or landed legally.

These regulations on catch formed the core of the management provisions, but the plan also put other restrictions on fishing. Boats harvesting groundfish could not use mesh smaller than a given diameter when fishing in certain areas. During the spawning season, March, April, and May, fishing with bottom trawl gear was prohibited in some areas. The plan recommended minimum sizes for haddock and cod to try to reduce the catch of fish less than two years old; a boat could have 10 percent of total catch weight made up of fish less than the minimum size.

In September 1977, a handful of new members replaced several on the Council who had completed a year of work. The members' interests would determine many of the ways the Council responded to its task of managing the groundfish industry. The Secretary of Commerce appointed eleven of the seventeen voting members of the Council from lists of nominees submitted by the governors. While the eleven could include anyone knowledgeable about the fishery, in New England these members nearly always came from the industry. Of the eleven industry members on the Council in fall 1977, seven depended on groundfish species in their work or represented groups who did. These seven included the head of a Rhode Island fishermen's cooperative, a New Hampshire fisherman, a sport fisherman, a spokesman for a company that owned large trawlers in Boston, the secretary-treasurer of the fishermen's union in New Bedford, the head of a vessel-owning and processing company in Maine, and a spokesman for Rhode Island fishing interests. Some of the industry representatives were the political spokesmen for their groups; others had not been politically involved in groundfish work except to speak occasionally for the concerns of their own businesses. One member, Jacob Dykstra, had been active in national and international fishery politics for over a decade and had helped formulate the management provisions of the FCMA. Others had served as ICNAF advisers.[21]

The implementation of the plan ran into problems very quickly. By July 1977, only four months into the plan, fishermen had caught enough cod in the Gulf of Maine to end the directed fishery for 1977. By the third week of August they had caught enough cod on Georges Bank and off southern New England to close that directed fishery also. The Council met in the first week of September to seek ways to relieve the financial hardships of the restricted fishery. Larger boats could not meet expenses on only 5510 pounds of cod per trip, fishermen told the Council. In response, the Council asked the Secretary of Commerce to make emergency changes in the regulations to allow bycatches that reflected differences in fishing costs and habits. Large boats, over 125 gross tons, could bring in the most cod per day of fishing; and boats 50 to 125 gross tons could harvest more than small boats, those under 50 gross tons. Boats in the large and medium classes would be better off than before. The changes meant the Council also had to ask the Secretary to approve an increase in the optimum yield for 1977 because fishermen would greatly exceed it. Until the Secretary approved these changes in the first week of November, the limit of 5510 pounds per trip remained in place.

Under either plan, the 5510 pounds or the vessel-size trip allowances, the Council faced serious problems of fishery management which became apparent during Council debate and as NMFS implemented the regulations. The law and the plan dictated the eventual rebuilding of fish resources, but fishery management was not even stabilizing the fish stocks. According to all biologists' estimates of appropriate harvest levels, fishermen were still overfishing the resources.

The Council's management led to overfishing for several reasons. The quota system encouraged fishermen to catch fish as fast as possible in order to get their share before someone else did. When they exhausted the quota and faced restrictions, fishermen protested the expected financial losses. As the September crisis showed, their protests persuaded the Council and Washington fishery officials to increase the quotas and to ease the restrictions so that the total catch rose far above the original optimum yield.

Even if the Council and the Secretary of Commerce had not raised optimum yield, the resources would have been overfished. NMFS could not enforce the management measures. The small number of NMFS officers could not patrol the unloading of every boat each day. The new regulations specified catch allowances in pounds per day of fishing, but NMFS could not monitor the number of days each boat had been gone in order to determine whether the landings were within the required limits.

Fishermen learned quickly that they could land more fish than the regulations allowed without being caught. According to a Gloucester fisherman's wife who helped represent Gloucester interests at the Council meetings, only 20 percent of Gloucester skippers were obeying the regulations as of October 1977. Many boats began to unload at night when most enforcement officers were off duty. Some boats landed at least the illegal surplus of their catch in ports with less enforcement before proceeding to their home ports. Processors handled illegal catches as "mixed" fish or renamed the cod or haddock landings "pollock," a more plentiful groundfish of lower value. Once the fish left the boat, no enforcement officer could tell for certain whether the catches had exceeded the limits or who had landed the fish.[22]

The enforcement efforts made fishermen angry and uneasy; but, they found, on the few occasions when officers cited fishermen for violations, the fines might never be levied. The administrative procedures for processing the violations took months. Then legal challenges to the procedures could take many more months. NMFS and Council warnings that larger catches in 1977 would mean a smaller quota the next year had little effect on the violators. They profited considerably from the excess catches but suffered no immediate consequences which might deter them.

Fishermen also found loopholes in the regulations that allowed them to catch more than the Council had presumably intended. For example, under the emergency regulations boat owners realized they could catch three days' allowance of fish in one day of fishing if they left the dock at 11:59 p.m. one day, fished the next day, and returned to port at 12:01 a.m. the third day.

Fishermen easily harvested more than the allowed bycatch. If they obeyed the law, as many still did in 1977, they had to throw the surplus catch overboard although it was already dead. In an attempt to prevent such waste, to encourage fishermen to try harder not to catch very young fish, and to get an idea of the mortality rates in the youngest year classes, the Council asked the Secretary of Commerce to adopt a "no discards" rule that meant that all groundfish caught had to be landed. As the Coast

Guard representative on the Council pointed out, such a rule was unenforceable because the Coast Guard did not have the capacity and technology for the necessary surveillance at sea. The Secretary of Commerce rejected the request.

A major reason many fishermen caught more than the allowable bycatch was that the fish really were not bycatch. Fishermen continued to direct their efforts toward groundfish rather than toward other species. Their complaints at Council meetings reflected the fact that they were calculating their losses based on fishing principally for cod. "Our main line is cod," the owner of a large boat told the Council. "We can't survive on so little." He needed between 50,000 and 60,000 pounds of fish per trip, he said. Small boats needed the 5510 pounds "to work to," one fishermen's spokesman said to the Council. Rather than switch to other fisheries as they might have done with a fall in the prices for groundfish, fishermen pressed the Council for more leeway in what was really still a directed fishery.

Although a major goal of fishery management was to rebuild the fish resource, most Council members worried much more about the disruption the management procedures caused fishermen. Their views on some conditions that led to overfishing, such as gaps in enforcement, had more to do with fishermen's complaints than with harm to the fish stocks. Consequently, most of the Council's attention went to addressing fishermen's protests.

The Council heard many protests because groundfishermen throughout New England opposed the management measures. Many fishermen, partly accepting the scientists' analyses of stock conditions, agreed that the industry needed controls for a while, but the controls they favored were minimal restrictions such as regulation of mesh and hook size. A Chatham fisherman expressed this view: "Economic influences, such as supply and demand, pretty much told the fishermen which way to go to try and get their next trip. . . . A balance of groundfish stocks can still be roughly maintained in this manner" with mesh and hook regulation.[23] "If we use big mesh now," a New Bedford fisherman claimed, "all the fish we would catch would be marketable, and we wouldn't catch more than the quota."

Many other fishermen believed that even such minor measures were unnecessary. The fishing grounds were "overstocked right now because 300 foreigners are not there," a Gloucester captain insisted. The scientists' figures were a "bunch of baloney," he stated. Another Gloucester captain told the Council he had spent forty-nine years fishing, thirty-five as a captain, "trying to figure out what fish do all the time." As a result, he said, he was convinced "all the conservation needed was to get rid of the [foreign] midwater trawls."

Fishermen opposed both the 5510 pounds rule and the vessel class allowances on several grounds. They correctly believed that the Council's measures threatened their livelihoods. The Council could not avoid doing so, for while each Council member was well informed about his own small sector of the industry, no one either on the Council or off knew how all parts of the industry operated or to what extent they depended on groundfish. Data existed only for the landings of the large boats in the major ports, and therefore did not reflect the behavior of most of the industry. As a result, the Council could not avoid making decisions that affected groups inequitably and even put some people out of business. Council members were most likely to make sure that their own groups did not suffer if only because they knew what regulations would hurt them.

After low prices during a summer glut of fish and much higher prices with restricted catches in September, fishermen said NMFS should have warned them that they would be "shut off for the rest of the year." Could the catch be "smoothed out," one fisherman asked, so that prices and incomes would be more stable and perhaps higher overall? When the Council did nothing to try to solve the problems resulting from gluts each time management restrictions were eased, a Gloucester captain protested, "That's not conservation or nothing . . . we'll have a few big trips and then no more haddock."[24]

Just as frequently as they complained of threats to income, however, fishermen protested management for other reasons. They argued that the management measures and their implementation were inequitable. In fishing, where so many competed intensely to bring in the biggest catches or to earn the highest income, such conditions were particularly unbearable. A spokesman from Gloucester emphasized the importance of this: "The Council should give a quota and regulations, but let them be *fair*." None of the Council's measures were fair, however.

Fishermen were not equal in the race to catch the quotas while the directed fishery lasted. Smaller boats could not fish during bad weather and could not travel far to reach the fish. Fishermen foresaw that big boats could take the entire quota in the first few months of 1978 before the cod came inshore and winter weather moderated. Among smaller boats, Massachusetts fishermen would get a chance at the cod before Maine fishermen because the fish appeared along the Massachusetts coast earlier in the year. Typical of smaller boats' protests, a Chatham fisherman said, "Because of the dogfish" which ate cod off their hooks "and the weather, we didn't catch much for half the year. We didn't catch our share of the quota." The spokesman for the Massachusetts inshore draggers explained that inshore fishermen "can't catch cod early in the year. We need the full year to make an average year pay."

Catch allowances after the directed fishery ended were inequitable, too. The 5510 pounds rule gave an advantage to smaller boats because 5510 pounds of cod provided a profitable trip for one day for a small boat. For a large boat, the revenues from 5510 pounds of cod covered only a share of costs after several days' fishing. Vessel class allowances disturbed the small boat fishermen. The breakdown by boat size was "unfair because it gives most income to a few boats only—the big ones," a Point Judith fisherman told the Council. "It's unfair to have the large vessels take the most fish," reiterated the spokesman for the Cape Cod Commercial Fishermen's Coalition. Within each vessel class some boats had advantages. Boats which were large for their vessel class were worse off than the smaller vessels in the next larger vessel group that received a higher allowance of fish per day. As a result, captains disputed the Council's decisions about divisions between vessel classes. "Larger boats have no more expenses than I have," one Gloucester captain protested, "so they should not get more fish." Basing catch allocations on a boat's gross tonnage was unfair, Gloucester people stated; the Council should instead consider differences in costs and whether a boat fished offshore.[25]

Although fishermen were angry about the catch allowances, uneven enforcement of the regulations probably aroused the greatest rage about inequities in fishery management. Fishermen who obeyed the regulations were furious that others were getting away with harvesting too much fish. "It's a fact that people may kill each other on the the wharf!" a Gloucester fisherman's wife warned in October. Another fisherman pushed for penalties for the violators. "We're talking about a pie. Why should you divide a pie equally when one has his belly full today?" "They're trying to support their families," a captain said in support of the violators, "and you're acting like they're criminals, like they robbed a bank." Two months later when for a short period NMFS levied heavy fines for violations, non-violators were jubilant. "You laughed at me," said one Gloucester captain. "Now I'm laughing at you."[26] The violators raged over the size of the fines, but they were also furious because they had been caught while others had not and because some ports had weaker enforcement than their own.

As the Council and the industry were gradually learning, no management measure and no enforcement procedures treated everyone equally, but they continued to look for more equitable solutions. As a result of the fall 1977 experience, Dan Arnold of the Massachusetts Inshore Draggermen's Association (MIDA) and Jay Lanzillo of Cape Cod Commercial Fishermen's Coalition drafted a management plan for the Council which "would recognize all the New England fisheries needs."[27] MIDA and the Coalition supported "the goal of the New England Regional Fishery Management Council to design a groundfish management plan which is equitable to all those involved in the New England fishery."[28] Gloucester fishermen supported a per man per trip catch allowance which they said would provide for a reasonable catch and an equitable "share" for every fisherman.

Fishermen's hatred of management came from more than the threat of financial troubles and the inequitable treatment. Small boat fishermen resented any government intervention in their work on ideological grounds. As a Chatham fisherman stated, fishermen "hope a different type of thinking will emerge before a great stronghold of free enterprise is buried under federal control." "This government is supposed to be a democracy, not communist," a Gloucester fisherman protested.[29]

Fishermen's anger and suspicion at government regulation intensified in the months after the Council requested vessel class trip allowances. The Secretary of Commerce, Juanita Kreps, did not respond until the beginning of November to the Council's September request for new bycatch allowances, and then she approved parts of the request with several arbitrary changes which made the Council's work more difficult. No one on the Council or in the industry could figure out who had made the changes or why, but both Council members and fishermen came away from meetings with NMFS and NOAA directors convinced that NMFS officials in the regional office and in Washington were trying to undermine the Council and take over fishery management. Dan Arnold said, "To this observer, the constant stream of regulations coming from Washington seem to have one common purpose: CONTROL OF THE FISHERMEN. Future plans these people have, such as individual boat quotas, stock certificates, limited entry, etc. will merely tighten the bureaucratic grip on us all."[30] Fishermen believed that the Council with its large proportion of industry representation promised them some say over measures that would affect their work and incomes. The National Marine Fisheries Service, in contrast, they felt, would remove fishery management from any industry influence in order to build its own power.

Fishermen were correct in believing that the Council would be more sensitive than NMFS to their protests. During the fall 1977 management crises, most of the Council members tried to avoid causing hardship to the industry even if that might mean loss of fish stocks. New implicit management goals were evolving, quite different from those the management plan had suggested. The Council aimed to avoid hurting fishermen, boat owners, or dealers either financially or through disruption of life style and to preserve enough of the fish resources so that fishermen would not suffer because of lack of fish later. At the same time, they wanted to make sure that measures to relieve economic and social problems would not give NMFS and NOAA grounds for interfering in the management process. Ideally, many would have liked to return to some of the conservation and stock rebuilding goals of the FCMA, but the sacrifices were unbearable for the Council because of fishermen's discontent. Opinion in the industry had a strong influence on Council members' decisions for a number of reasons.

Council members felt great concern about the economic hardships and the social disruption they might cause. They did not want to deprive fishermen and their families of employment and income or to destroy a way of life and a style of work. They sympathized acutely with the problems of those in the industry and with their alarm over management. Quite a few agonized over their choices because of the harm they might cause.

Council members identified with the fishermen's troubles in part because they themselves faced hardships either from other fishery management efforts or from groundfish decisions. In Council deliberations they often described their own expected losses, and some pushed hard for measures that would protect their own businesses and those of others like them.

Political considerations made the Council members responsive, too. Some were the leaders of fishery organizations; if they alienated their constituents because of their actions on the Council, they could lose their jobs as heads of those groups. In turn, if they lost leadership positions, governors would not reappoint them to the Council. Even Council members who were not the leaders of particular groups would endanger their positions on the Council by incurring the opposition of the fishing interest groups from their own states. The appointment process was highly political and became more so as the stakes in the management process became clearer in the first management crises. Those who wanted seats on the Council and their supporters lobbied the state fisheries offices which forwarded nominee suggestions to the governors' offices. Fishing interest groups wrote letters and lobbied the governors' offices on behalf of candidates they favored. They lined up their congressmen to pressure the Secretary of Commerce to appoint the people they favored from the governors' lists of nominees. If a candidate could not rally strong support, his chances of appointment were slim. If enough significant fishing interest groups opposed a candidate, he would probably not even make the governor's list.[31]

For a Council member the loss of his seat meant considerable loss of personal prestige and renown not just in local fishery affairs but also in national and international fishery politics. It also meant loss of control over what could happen to the industry. Furthermore, a former Council member's own interests might be ignored once he was no longer on the Council because new members might come from other sectors of the industry. Some members who resigned discovered that lack of representation on the Council presented them with problems in staying informed about what the Council, Congress, and the State Department were doing and in getting attention for their own views. They learned what others in the industry were discovering, as one observer somewhat overstated it, "You don't have one of your guys [on the Council] and you don't have anything."[32]

The state fishery officials had Council seats automatically, but they were sensitive to fishermen's dissatisfaction, too. They were political appointees of the governors; and while the governors were not always sensitive to fishing interests, both the governors and the state legislators wanted to appoint fishery officials the industry favored.[33] Fishery officials often expected that they would continue to work with the fishing industry in NMFS jobs, as Council staff, or in fishing businesses even if they left their state government posts, so that good relations with the industry were important.

Interest groups that might have favored rebuilding the fish resources with greater sacrifices from the fishing industry did not present their views at meetings and offered no support to replace what the Council would lose from the industry. Representatives of environmental groups attended few Council proceedings. As one environmental spokeswoman explained, too many other pressing problems required their attention for them to afford a few days each month for attendance at Council meetings. Furthermore, the leaders of environmental groups wanted the fishing industry as an ally in fighting the leasing of Georges Bank as tracts for oil drilling. The environmentalists would not alienate the industry by opposing decisions that led to overfishing when oil drilling threatened the fish resources with much greater disaster. No representative of consumer interests came to the Council meetings although Council decisions seemed certain to lead to less fish and to higher fish prices for millions of consumers. No consumer groups seemed to realize the implications of fishery management.[34] Council members occasionally tried to persuade some groups, who understood the constraints of the management process and the requirements that the Council pay attention to biologists' analyses, to attend the meetings where fishermen would exert especially strong opposing pressures. As one member told the New England Fisheries Steering Committee in urging many to attend the Council meetings, "Fishermen are getting very emotional about this." He hoped to add a less volatile element to the audience in support of the difficult job the Council faced in September 1977.[35]

Certain conditions of decision-making intensified the effects of sympathy and political pressure. The Council members had almost no information on which to base decisions that were certain to have profound effects on income distribution and social institutions. No economic data could show how costs, revenues, and profit positions would change in any sectors of the industry with different management decisions. No one knew how fishermen and their communities might suffer from disruption in some institutions and in styles of work. When hundreds of angry fishermen converged on meetings to describe the financial and social problems the Council was causing, they provided the best information available. Biological analyses of the condition of the fish resources did exist, but Council members were often skeptical about their accuracy, and they weighed the economic and social information, however exaggerated in the process of political protest, particularly heavily.

The Council members had to make their most important decisions in public meetings often attended by large numbers of fishermen, boat owners, and processors. That, too, intensified the pressures they felt from the industry. Any member was immediately accountable for his action, and fishermen often impressed this upon the Council members in rebuttals and accusations in answer to Council members' comments. The Council members' tension showed when they sought escape to resolve debates or to reach tentative agreement in hurried breakfast and dinner caucuses when fishermen were not present or were not aware of what was happening. The members could then put forward a briefer, more unified discussion at the formal meeting that protected individuals from fishermen's anger. Such recourse was rarely available, however, in part because the style alienated fishing industry representatives and also because Council members often had too many disagreements to resolve in short informal discussions.[36]

The strains of the management process on the Council members showed in later months. Some members resigned, and others declined to be considered for renomination when their terms expired. "How would *you* like to be up there?" asked one Council member after a particularly frustrating and unproductive meeting of the groundfish committee. Observers might find the Council meetings interesting, another said, "But for us, it's *hell*!"

The continuing problems with the restricted fishery through fall 1977 were not the end of the difficult period. In December 1977 the emergency regulations that had increased the optimum yield expired. Therefore, the fishery reverted to the old optimum yield which fishermen had already exceeded. Under the provisions of the plan the director of NMFS closed the whole fishery so that fishermen could not legally land any haddock, cod, or yellowtail flounder. Since fishermen could not avoid catching these species when fishing for other groundfish or flounder, they had to stop fishing altogether. Fishermen, boat owners, and dealers had never experienced such an order. Indeed a measure that ordered people to stop working but offered them no compensation was extremely unusual for workers in any industry. When farmers withheld fields from production voluntarily, the government paid them for doing so or allowed them to participate in favorable price support programs. Most workers who were laid off received unemployment compensation for which few fishermen were eligible. The government was preventing fishermen from working, not offering incentives not to work, but offering nothing in return.

The closure came during the last week of the year when few fishermen worked because of winter weather and holidays, but the closure still outraged both Council members and fishermen. NMFS and higher fishery officials in NOAA had imposed the closure without consulting the Council, which would have opposed it on several grounds, said Edward Mac-Leod, the Council chairman. Fishermen harvested so few fish in the last week of the year that closure served no conservation purpose. "This isn't conservation, it's a slap in the face," MacLeod said. "It's incredible to close a fishery for a week for nothing."[37] Fishermen in general were used to working hard and believed in free enterprise. The government order telling them that they could not do their jobs seemed the ultimate offense even though few would have worked that week. The Council recognized that the needless order caused intense anger at the management system that would make their jobs much more difficult.

The closure heightened the tensions among fishermen that had been growing through the fall. In Gloucester approximately seventy-five fishermen brawled on Fishermen's Wharf after several small boats went fishing despite the closure and NMFS law enforcement did not promise fast enough punishment to satisfy the skippers of larger boats which had to remain tied up.[38]

The closure also increased the alienation between NMFS and NOAA on one side and the Council and the industry on the other. Again NMFS seemed uninformed about the character of the fishing industry and seemed motivated principally by the desire to take over management from the Council. For many on the Council and in the industry the December closure was an alarming indication of what NMFS might do at other times of year when the loss of fishing might be more costly and more lengthy. NMFS as scoundrel offered one benefit, however; the Council could shield themselves for a time from the wrath of the industry because fishermen supported the Council against NMFS.

The events of September through December 1977 contained all the elements of management problems the Council would face in 1978. However, the controversy and difficulty in managing the groundfish industry increased tremendously after the first months. As the Council discussed revisions in the groundfish management plan for 1978, they tried to correct some of the conditions that had caused problems in 1977. They divided the annual quotas into quarterly shares in response to fishermen's pleas to "spread it out more." The new provisions substituted vessel classes for the 5,510 pounds rule and converted the cod fishery from directed to bycatch fishery when a smaller percent of the total catch had been harvested.

The changes solved few problems. On January 1 the closure ended, and boats went fishing again. The race for the fish was more intense than during the spring and summer of 1977 because fishermen understood better that they had to catch fish before others did or lose their opportunity when the fishery closed again. Fishing pressures were also more intense because new fishermen and new boats steadily entered the industry. No one knew exactly how many newcomers had arrived during the last four months of 1977, but according to one report, new boats entered the fishery at the astounding rate of about one every four days.[39]

By the beginning of March the directed fishery for cod ended. This time fishermen had learned how to look for loopholes that would allow them to bring in larger catches of cod, haddock, and yellowtail than the bycatch regulations allowed. Many more fishermen decided that they would profit more by breaking the law than by observing the regulations. Therefore, the restrictions, while grating on the fishermen, had little effect on fishing levels.

Beginning in late February, the Council tried desperately to negotiate with NMFS and NOAA officials to prevent a total closure of the haddock and later the cod fisheries.[40] They succeeded in putting off the closures for awhile, but the Secretary of Commerce closed the cod and haddock fisheries from March 19 until a new quarter with a new allocation of optimum yield began April 1. The spring closure particularly hurt small-scale fishermen who had not been able to fish during the winter months; it especially threatened Maine fishermen for whom the cod became available only in late March. Large boats, in contrast, could take advantage of a loophole in the closure rules; they left for the fishing grounds just before the midnight deadline when the closure took effect and landed catches during the closure as prices rose.

Protests from the industry were more intense than ever before. Hundreds of fishermen attended the Council's March meeting. Gloucester fishermen demanded the resignation of the director of NOAA. Busloads of Chatham, Massachusetts, fishermen arrived to register their objections. As their representatives spoke, they waved signs which read "The Fishing Industry, 1620–1978, May It Rest in Peace" and "In Cod We Trust." Maine inshore fishermen propounded their views. Television crews kept the Council members lit up under bright lights, and newspaper reporters moved through the audience interviewing irate fishermen.

As the industry learned, closure was the worst of all the results of fishery management. It threatened their incomes much more than restricted fishing; it was inequitable; it left them without work. Closure offended fishermen more than any other measure because it showed them so clearly that government had taken control of one of the most important aspects of their lives.

The Council members realized even more acutely than in December that closure put them in the worst possible political position. They had to take blame they felt they did not deserve. They had to bear the protests of more fishermen than at any other time because fishermen who could not work had time to attend the Council meeting to express their anger. By the end of March the Council had another major implicit management goal; they would attempt to avoid another closure at any cost.

In April fishing reopened. During April the Secretary of Commerce approved several more changes in the groundfish plan that the Council and the industry thought might deal with some of the problems they had confronted.

The new regulations restricted the catching of cod at all times rather than after fishermen had taken a percent of the quarterly quota. The Council planned to reduce trip limits as necessary during the quarter to prevent another total closure. Another change put trip limits on a weekly rather than a daily basis, as fishermen had requested. Also, newly defined vessel classes received allocations of each quarter's quota based on the shares they had taken since 1970. Dan Arnold and Jay Lanzillo had designed the vessel allocation plan to ensure that small boats had an opportunity to fish even when large boats could beat them to the quota. At the same time, they wanted "to preserve the possibility to be big achievers" within their own group, said Frank Mirarchi, the president of Massachusetts Inshore Draggermen's Association. According to Lanzillo, the plan left room for competition, and "Competition is what makes fishermen go fishing."

By the middle of May, however, even earlier than in the previous quarter, the Council faced the familiar dilemmas again. They could reduce the landing limits in order to prevent another closure, but to do so they would have to cut the catch allowances so much that they would inflict "economic closure." Fishermen were permitted to continue to fish but had to reduce their catch so much that they would not be able to cover operating costs and would therefore have to stop fishing.

The causes of the problems had become familiar, too: an early race for the fish, loopholes, and illegal catches. Also, the number of boats licensed for groundfishing had risen from about 1100 in 1977 to close to 1600, the NMFS regional director told the Council.[41]

The Council looked for ways to avoid making the decision to reduce catch allowances. They raised administrative questions, criticized the biological analyses, attempted to shift the decision-making responsibility to some other group. With only two weeks on the current catch allowances, one Council member said, NMFS could not possibly project the harvests for the rest of the quarter; therefore, the Council should not change the limits yet. Another Council member agreed. He wanted to avoid inflicting still another change in the regulations on the fishermen, as the new NOAA assistant administrator for fisheries, Terry Leitzell, had recommended. "I can't keep up with all the changes. . . . I have three staff people working on this full time, but I can't make heads or tails of it," said the Council member. Fishermen would have even greater difficulty because they had no staff. "The fishermen can't get away from the fish," the same Council member continued. "The [biologists'] numbers are wrong or something." "What if we create social and economic havoc and save the fish," put in another, "and then we find the biologists made a mistake. The price to pay doesn't make sense." Other members of the Council suggested they should meet with Leitzell and his staff before making a decision even though the Council had spent substantial energy since fall 1976 fighting the efforts of NMFS and NOAA to control the management process. The Secretary of Commerce had not implemented all the new provisions the Council had proposed for the groundfish plan, a Council member argued. "Until we put the plan into effect, I am opposed to monkeying." The Council adopted a motion to put off changes in trip limitations and to meet with Leitzell and his staff "since there appears to be no solution to the problem of groundfish catch limitations other than a total open, total closure situation."[42]

In previous crises, the Council had believed that changes in the plan might solve the problems. While the goals had remained implicit and changeable and the piecemeal measures had not solved the problems, the Council had still adopted new measures to try to achieve some goals. In May, however, the Council finally had no ideas about ways they could deal with the management difficulties. Their planning disintegrated into gimmickry as they looked for escape from the awful choices they needed to make.

Escape proved difficult. Leitzell announced that weekly catch limits for cod and haddock would be sharply reduced by July 2. "If these guys are going to go by the book, they'll starve to death," declared the head of the Atlantic Fishermen's Union in Gloucester.[43] Fishermen were outraged at the low catch levels. They rallied their congressmen to pressure NMFS to raise the trip limitations. Once again, fishermen moved en masse to the Council meetings to protest, although everyone knew that as long as there was no total closure, fishermen and boat owners could do very well by taking advantage of loopholes and by landing illegal catches. Beginning in late July, however, some vessel classes had taken their entire annual quota of some fish stocks despite emergency increases in optimum yields. In the next weeks, more vessel classes faced closures. Boat owners could expect total closure in all areas from September through December.

Confronted with low catch limits and the prospect of closures, the Council agreed to ask the Secretary of Commerce to approve a new start to the fishing year as soon as possible under a fresh annual quota with all the management provisions in place which the Council had requested earlier.[44] Only a new year with its additional allocation of fish would provide the chance for the new management regulations to work, the Council argued. The Secretary agreed to the proposal in late September; a new fishing year began October 1. The new year spared the Council and the industry from closure for the rest of 1978. The respite could only be temporary, however, because the new management provisions to which the Secretary agreed differed in only trivial ways from the ones that had caused the Council and the industry so much trouble during 1978. The "new year" represented the ultimate gimmickry.

ELEMENTS OF A NEW TRY AT GROUNDFISH MANAGEMENT

As groundfish management degenerated during summer 1978, the staff and the Scientific and Statistical (S and S) Committee of the Council pressed the Council to begin work on a better plan. "We have regulations now but not objectives," Spencer Apollonio, executive director of the Council's staff, said. "We have no plan either. We have a partial set of regulations with no clear rationale." Other Council staff reiterated: "The staff wants a distinction between objectives and management instruments." The Council should think about instruments after they had objectives, staff members said. "The staff can't do analysis of consequences without objectives from the Council," Apollonio impressed upon the members. The S and S Committee, made up of biologists, economists, and anthropologists knowledgeable about the New England fisheries, asked for even more: "While we recognize the pressing need to formulate short-run management strategy for groundfish, we would like to emphasize that we cannot appropriately advise the Council on management strategy and techniques until the Council decides on long-term management objectives for the *entire* New England fishery [emphasis added]."[45] Pressure came from Washington as well with the message that only if the Council began to develop a plan would NOAA listen to requests to put off closures. Terry Leitzell approved an increase in the optimum yield for the fisheries threatened with immediate closure in order to give the Council more time to state their management objectives and adopt a new plan. Only under the extreme pressures of impending closures did the Council move to define goals.

At special meetings in July 1978 the Council settled on several goals. The overall objective, the Council decided, "shall be to generate over the period of the plan the greatest possible joint economic and social net benefits from the harvesting and utilization of the groundfish resource, ensuring that by the end of the period the relevant groundfish stocks shall be in conditions which will produce enhanced and relatively stable yields from the groundfish fishery in future years." The Council had a number of sub-objectives: "[1] Prevention of abrupt changes in the relative shares of domestic user-groups in the resources. . . . [2] Freedom of decision-making and choice for individual participants in the fishery should be maintained to the greatest possible extent. . . . [3] Inducement of diversification in the groundfish fishery towards increased utilization of species other than cod, haddock and yellowtail. . . . [4] Minimization of management regulations, subject to attainment of the overall objective. . . . [5] Minimization of enforcement costs, subject to attainment of the overall objective. . . . [6] Provision for accurate and consistent economic, social and biological data required to monitor effectively and assess the performance of the fishery relative to the overall objective."[46]

The staff sought to refine the statement of the overall objective. What were "economic and social net benefits"? Who should benefit? What were "conditions which will produce enhanced and relatively stable yields"? The Council agreed, "Benefits to the users would include incomes to harvesters and processors as well as values to consumers. . . . benefits include the values to the user-groups associated with the size of the fish stocks at the end of the planning period. Costs to users involve harvesting and processing costs, as well as management and enforcement costs." Social benefits and costs "are implied," the Council decided, in the sub-objectives of prevention of abrupt changes in the relative shares of domestic user-groups, freedom of decision-making, and minimization of enforcement costs. The Council agreed that the biological constraint on the overall objective meant "(1) an acceptable probability of achieving the biological stock conditions by the end of the period, and (2) a minimum spawning stock level for each species which ensures an acceptable probability of continued recruitment." Achievement of the objective would require a multiple-year planning period because one year's harvest levels affected options for later years.[47]

The goals represented a significant improvement over the plan of March 1977. The goals were explicit; the Council discussed and agreed upon them, and the Council and the staff could refer back to them in later decisions. The new goals represented the Council's aims better than the original implicit goal to rebuild or stabilize the fish resource without causing undue economic hardship because the overall objective emphasized economic and social benefits rather than fish stocks.

The statement of goals left many issues unresolved and many terms undefined, however. For example, what were "values to consumers"? What did "values . . . associated with the size of the fish stocks at the end of the planning period" mean? What was an "acceptable probability" of achieving biological stock conditions? If the Council did not spell out the definitions before they evaluated management measures and instead allowed the answers to emerge implicitly in the management process as they rewrote regulations, they could again lose sight of goals.

The effort to define the goals raised as many questions as it answered. Most important, perhaps, an evaluation of benefits and costs from different groups' perspectives would suggest contradictory directions for management. Management measures which maximized consumers' net benefits would probably differ from those which maximized net benefits for fishermen. How would the Council trade off consumers' benefits against fishermen's or processors'? In the Council's political setting, mention of consumer interests seemed only lip service to the FCMA's mandate. However, calculation of benefits and costs to different "user-groups" in the fishery would also yield very different results, and inequitable effects of fishery management measures had caused the Council some of its worst problems. How would the plan define user-groups, and how would the Council decide to allocate net benefits among them?

The Council's experience had suggested many important social costs and benefits. Definition of these seemed particularly inadequate for the evaluation of management measures. For example, management efforts had caused brothers to fight each other in Gloucester where the Sicilian fishing community centered on family decision-making and family boat ownership. The statement of objectives did not show whether the Council had decided that issues such as the damage to traditional institutions did not matter, or had neglected to specify them.

Once the Council defined social costs, dilemmas would remain. How could a social cost be valued? How could social costs be compared with economic ones? Which social costs should be considered for which user-groups?

The Council's vague definition of objectives was understandable. They had had considerable difficulty specifying goals at all. Going farther would prove even harder because the members who represented groups with different interests would clash. More specific definitions would also draw the opposition of interest groups who observed the activity of the Council because the Council could not satisfy everyone.

Even a group working in an apolitical setting would have had trouble making goals more specific, however. Such work required a stronger ideological framework and value judgments, guided by that ideology, about the importance of some styles of fishing compared with others. It required considerable knowledge of the fisheries, especially of the social and economic character of the many groups that harvested groundfish. No one had that knowledge; only massive new data collection and frequent socioeconomic studies could provide the Council with adequate understanding for good planning. Indeed, those who understood most about the industry, some of them on the Council, only became more impressed with the complexity of the issues as the Council confronted crises and tried to formulate a stronger plan. Planning for the use of the fisheries constituted an enormous, immensely complicated intervention in the structure of an industry, in the level and distribution of income in the industry, and in the nature of communities dependent on the industry.

The complexity of the task seemed even more troubling as the staff prodded the Council to move from listing goals to discussing alternative management measures. By April 1979 the Council still had not decided on management measures. "I never dreamed we would still not have a plan," said one former Council member. Part of the explanation for the delay was that the Council and its Groundfish Oversight Committee spent enormous amounts of time handling the same recurring crises in the new fishing year.

Another reason for the delay was that regardless of the agreement on goals, some members no longer believed, if they ever had, that the Council should manage the fisheries at all. According to Dan Arnold, a member of the Council as of fall 1978, "On the one hand there is a group of Council members looking for schemes to make Fisheries Management the least onerous to fishermen; and on the other hand a group of Council members that regard Fisheries Management as a series of arbitrary regulations that consider the needs of industry as secondary or even not at all."[48] Neither of the groups Arnold saw, if they could be categorized so clearly, believed in managing the fisheries. Some of the members, particularly ones in Arnold's second group, pressed hard for very narrow group interests or pursued primarily personal or bureaucratic aims. Another group which Arnold did not describe remained committed to fishery management that would try to achieve the goals the Council had specified. Arnold's first group might be called on as allies if the pro-management members could provide enough direction because both groups agreed that management measures should not cause great hardship.

Another partial explanation for the delay in deciding on management measures was that learning within the Council and the fishing industry took place unevenly. Some members who had joined the Council after the earliest crises supported measures that others had long before considered and abandoned as fruitless. Differences in the development of understanding of fishery management between the industry and the Council were more extreme. Most fishermen missed all meetings except the ones held during crises, and they made the same arguments every time they came. The audience of fishermen evolved continually; each newcomer had to learn how the Council operated and what it could do about management problems before his comments became constructive. Few fishermen progressed with the Council in learning about the effects of different management efforts. Proposals that fishermen insisted upon often would cause troubles the Council had already lived through. For example, in 1978 and 1979 Gloucester fishermen pushed for a simple plan to allocate several thousand pounds of fish per man per trip year round. As Council members pointed out, such a plan would place smaller boats at a great disadvantage in the race for the quota during much of the year, because they could not work during bad weather or because the fish were too far from shore, just as the regulations on quarterly allocations with trip limits had put small boats at a disadvantage in early 1978. Moreover, the allocations Gloucester fishermen wanted for each trip were so high that early closures would be inevitable, the Council members stated again. The Council had to address the same points repeatedly as new members and interest groups raised them.

Another especially important reason that the Council's progress stalled was that the members could not figure out what to do. The task was so difficult intellectually and politically that Council discussions began to sound like reruns of debates from the two years before.

For those on the Council who aimed to manage the fisheries and to minimize the problems for fishermen, three major alternative management measures were possible: mesh regulation, quotas, and limited entry.[49] Each approach presented difficult management dilemmas.

Fishermen pushed for mesh regulation and similar measures, such as hook size rules, as the best means of controlling fishing effort. They favored this approach because it would not affect business or fishing decisions; it would be equitable; it was easy to enforce; and it reduced the mortality of young fish that could escape through the larger holes or would not take the bait on the larger hooks. Unless mesh size were regulated, fishermen would use small mesh, however, because they believed they would catch more fish that way. The Council did not seriously consider mesh regulation by itself as an adequate control on fishing mortality during 1978 or early 1979; mesh regulations were included in combination with other measures. Biologists' analyses and experience with mesh regulation showed that mesh alone could not keep harvests near optimum yield.[50] Mesh was a satisfactory way to increase yield from a fish resource by allowing more small fish to mature, but with enough fishing pressure on the resource, the stocks would still be overfished and harvests would decline. While mesh regulation might have achieved the Council's goal of maximizing social and economic benefits in the very short run, it could not result in satisfactory stock conditions, however defined, over longer periods. Furthermore, the Council knew that the Secretary of Commerce would not approve such a plan in 1979.

The second major alternative for management, quotas, was the one the Council had already tried. Everyone on the Council and in the industry agreed that the quota system was not working although opinion varied about why this was so. According to one sizable group, quotas were not working because optimum yield was too low; the biologists' analyses were incorrect. Dan Arnold spoke for this point of view: "It was apparent to many of us that it [the Massachusetts Inshore Draggermen's Association plan for vessel class allocations] wouldn't work because of inadequate quotas. Nor will *any other plan* work with inadequate quotas. No allocation method that does not reflect current abundance of fish and the needs of the industry (producers, processors, and consumers) will work."[51] As many on the Council agreed, the biological assessments may have been incorrect. However, as the staff and some Council members pointed out several times during 1978, even doubling the optimum yield would not solve the quota problems; severe catch restrictions and closures would still be necessary to keep from exceeding optimum yield.

When the Council members set quotas, they had thought that they could make rules that would prevent overfishing, financial hardship, and social disruption. By the time they confronted choices about management measures for the new plan, few still believed that. At the heart of the difficulty, as many correctly came to believe, quotas did nothing to discourage the hundreds of newcomers flooding the groundfish industry.

As the numbers in the industry grew, each boat would get fewer fish if the quotas were enforced. Therefore, some boats would have a hard time meeting expenses and would go out of business. Fishing levels far exceeded the quotas, however; and the political and social pressures to overfish rose as more people bought boats. As Spencer Apollonio recalled, "The present problems became inevitable once the initial step had been made to set quotas. At the time, nobody knew better. No one anticipated that fishing expansion would be so rapid that we would substantially exceed those quotas. Once that happened, all the other things, like season allocations, became unavoidable."[52] Profits and wages in the groundfish industry were exceptionally high in 1977 and 1978, especially for the offshore industry. The entry of many new boats into the industry was inevitable and probably would have doomed any quota system sooner or later; only the speed with which it happened was surprising.

If large numbers of new boats were the root of the Council's difficulties with quotas, the staff and some Council members suggested, the Council should consider measures to restrict entry into fishing. Limiting entry could take many forms. For example, the Department of Commerce could levy such high annual fees for the right to fish that large numbers of fishermen could no longer afford to stay in the industry and others could not enter. The Council could decide to allocate to each boat owner the right to a share of fish based on the size of his past catches; anyone not already in the fishery would receive no share of fish. The Council could issue licenses to fishermen in the industry, allow only licensed fishermen to harvest fish, and set quotas temporarily to constrain fishing effort until enough fishermen left the industry to make other regulations unnecessary.

Whatever the form of limited entry, the Council's purpose would be to reduce the number of boats and fishermen to the level where fishing activity would provide everyone with reasonable income and freedom of decision-making but would not lead to severe overfishing. Ideally, the number of fishermen would exert appropriate fishing effort automatically, and the Council would not need to regulate effort through catch limitations or other measures.[53]

Limited entry in any form could be particularly problematic if instituted with little information about the industry. The Council had very little data on the fishery but would have to make decisions with enormous effects on income distribution. For example, the Council would have to decide who should be part of the industry. Would they include people who fished but worked at other jobs most of the time? Who were dilettantes, and who were serious fishermen? How should they enable inshore fishermen to continue to move among many fisheries to maintain their incomes? Because the industry was already overcapitalized, the Council would have to think about how and when to retire some members of the industry or whether to institute catch restrictions until fish stocks grew or fishermen left the industry. They would have to decide whether fishing rights could be transferred and if so to whom. Could large corporations buy the rights, or should owner-operators be the only ones entitled to do so? Should sons of fishermen have special claims to fishing rights? These were only a few of the complicated issues that the Council would have to confront.

In Apollonio's opinion, "Limited entry will turn out to be as difficult a management concept as optimum yield." Experience with limited entry programs in Alaska and the Pacific Northwest suggested that he was right although such programs still offered much more promise than quotas.[54]

The Council could not begin debate over some of the decisions they might have to make for a program to limit entry, however. No management proposal aroused so much anger and so much opposition from the fishing industry and from many members of the Council as any suggestion of limiting entry. The opposition was so strong that the Council could not discuss alternative forms for a program; they argued only about whether they should even consider limiting entry.

The staff and others pointed out that those already in the industry would do well financially under such a system. Their profits would be assured by keeping newcomers out. Offshore fishermen who specialized in groundfishing would benefit most. That constituency was small, however, especially when groundfish was narrowly defined as cod, haddock, and yellowtail. Suggestions for limited entry programs came from the NMFS spokesman and from the Council members who owned several large boats.

Very few of the larger boat fishermen favored limited entry, however. One Gloucester fisherman's wife who saw its advantages also foresaw the pressure against it. "People will say, 'You have your boat so now you don't want more.'" Gloucester offshore fishermen particularly valued the freedom to buy a new boat so that they could hope to make more money or other members of their families could become skippers.

Few offshore fishermen in any ports expressed views on limited entry. In Gloucester, fishermen were uninformed about it. However, as they became angrier about the quotas and about NMFS enforcement, their opposition grew to any government program.[55]

Small boat fishermen far outnumbered offshore fishermen in the groundfish industry. A number of inshore fishermen were open to considering limited entry, and some said they favored it. "If anybody can go into fishing, then I ought to be able to go plumbing," one groundfish fisherman argued. "Hundreds of skiffs will hit the water [during the summer]," he continued. "There are long lines at the fish pier waiting to unload. . . . It may be only a few fish in a boat, but it adds up. It lowers the price."[56] Except for an occasional comment from a lobsterman on limited entry in the lobster industry, however, inshore fishermen who felt willing to consider limited entry did not speak up at the Council meetings, fishermen's forums, or other places where limited entry was under discussion.

The majority of small boat fishermen adamantly opposed limited entry. Unlike the large boat group, many had thought about such programs, and their spokesmen enumerated the reasons for opposition. Some of their arguments, not always consistent with each other, were based on financial concerns; all reflected strong normative views about the character of the fishing industry, the nature of their work, and the government's role.[57]

Inshore fishermen survived financially, opponents to limiting entry stressed, by moving from one species to another as price and the availability of fish changed. If fishermen were shut out of groundfish or if they could harvest only a small amount of groundfish, they might not be able to stay in business. "Most of us are 'jacks of all trades', and are apt to jump into whatever either pays the most or interests us the most at the moment," editorialized *Maine Commercial Fisheries*. "So we find lobstermen who are seasonal carpenters, groundfishermen switching to scalloping, and so on. . . . Then what happens to, say the 'lobster specialist', if either natural cycles, economics, or whatever puts him between a rock and a hard place?" "To keep the wolf away from the door we have to switch from scallops to fin fish to lobsters," said one Maine fisherman.

Proponents of limited entry argued that such programs would allow greater freedom for fishermen because catch regulations would no longer be necessary. Fishermen countered that the limited entry schemes would mean less freedom. People would find themselves "locked in" one fishery and excluded from others. "To limit entry in one fishery always affects other fisheries," Council member Jacob Dykstra warned. Limited entry programs would spread to other fisheries and end freedom there, too. "Because of low stocks or low prices, the guy in the 'closed shop' of one fishery could find himself outside looking in if he tried to switch to another fishery," said Lucy Sloan of the National Federation of Fishermen.

The cost of a permit to fish would rise so high that individuals could not afford to buy one, fishermen warned. Large corporations, the only groups that could pay for such expensive permits, would buy out fishermen until the remaining boat owners could not compete. That would spell the demise of the entrepreneurial, independent fisherman. Fishing was attractive to many inshore fishermen particularly because it provided these job characteristics, and they wanted it to stay that way.

Fishermen warned that some people talked about extracting "economic rent" from fishermen. That meant that the government would decide how much a fisherman deserved to earn in a year. "I'm not sure I would like to have a situation wherein my income was essentially decided by a civil servant who may be making less money than I am," said Jim O'Malley, one of the most outspoken critics of limited entry. Government controlled prices would follow in a limited entry program, others warned.

Fishermen made many other arguments as well that were not the major reasons they opposed limited entry but served to gather allies. Costs of running limited entry programs had been particularly high, they said. More regulations and more regulators would become necessary as everyone tried to find a way around the rules of the limited entry program, Dykstra stated. The government would get into banning improvements in harvesting technology, O'Malley warned. Limiting entry had not reduced catches where fishery managers had implemented such programs, Dykstra said; fishing effort remained too high to conserve the resource.

The Council might have discussed many of the points the fishermen raised as they considered how limited entry might work. Many of the legitimate problems fishermen saw might have been handled with an appropriate program design. The Council might not have resolved other issues but might have decided that such costs were tolerable considering the problems of alternative management styles.

Behind all the fishermen's arguments, however, were objections that were undebatable. Strong convictions about the right to fish and about government intervention provided the intense energy behind their opposition. Large numbers of small-scale fishermen believed that anyone should be able to fish: "Fish are a common resource, and it's unfair to lock people out." "I don't think you should tell someone whether or not he can go fishing." "Limited entry is a form of communism. . . . If my son decides to become a fisherman—no one should stop him." "Anybody can be President. I guess anybody ought to be able to go fishing."

They held very strong opinions about government's role in directing fishermen's lives. "Not very many of us have a college education, yet we have managed to successfully run our businesses," Dan Arnold said. "Now we are beset by people with 4, 5, 6, or more years of college education in various disciplines (biology, economics, social sciences, law) who are busy telling us how we can better manage our affairs than we have in the past. Do we need them, or *do they need us?*" At another time, Arnold criticized "NMFS' need to *manage people* not fish."[58] Fishing ought to remain a stronghold of "free enterprise," fishermen said. As O'Malley emphasized, limited entry meant a bureaucrat would tell fishermen what they could do as well as how much they could make.

A year after the Council had decided on goals, they had made little progress on the rest of a plan. While the management problems they had confronted with quotas made the beginning of debate on the variety of limited entry possibilities very reasonable, political opposition made such a dialogue virtually impossible. Instead, the Council began to talk about a plan based on mesh regulation supplemented by closed seasons and closed areas. The Council and the industry evidently would have to live through the failure of mesh regulation with more declines in the size of the fish stock before they would consider limiting entry.

Prospects for the health of the groundfish industry were bleak. Fishermen bought new boats, and more newcomers looked for sites in response to high profits and wages; but by 1980 profits had fallen enough that boat owners were vulnerable to changes in costs or revenues. Rising fuel costs in addition to the rising costs of catching fish as more people entered the fishery made it hard for some to do well on many trips. Fishermen in New Bedford tied up their boats to protest low prices because of a glut of groundfish, and newspaper reporters once again wrote stories about hard times in the fisheries. Industry spokesmen testified before congressional committees and lobbied their congressmen for passage of a bill to subsidize certain operating costs and expand boat construction programs.[59] Almost no one in the industry, however, was saying that the fall in prices would not have been so extreme or so painful and the rise in fuel costs would not have been so critical if so many hundreds of newcomers had not joined the fishery since 1976.

Other pressing issues called the attention of the Council and the industry. Furor among boat owners over a NMFS logbook that would require them to keep extensive catch records that might be used to prosecute fishermen for rule violations took much of the Council's and industry spokesmen's time and energy. Again, NMFS actions seemed bewildering and destructive. The Council and NMFS needed better catch data to monitor the condition of the fish stocks, but they could not hope to get good information with methods that might lead to punishment. The anger and opposition which the NMFS logbook proposal aroused among fishermen only served to make management more difficult. A treaty between the United States and Canada, necessary because of overlapping 200-mile zones and traditional fishing in the other country's waters, allocated shares of the fish resources to each country and set up a new management council that would take over some of the responsibilities of the New England Fishery Management Council. The Council, fishermen, boat owners, and processors organized to preserve the Council's authority and to oppose the allocation of fish resources to Canadians that they felt they needed for themselves. All these problems interfered with the Council's deliberation on a new groundfish plan. Political opposition to limited entry did not abate, and decisions to accept some forms of limited entry were as far away as ever.

7 The Failure of Government Efforts

IN SPRING AND SUMMER 1980 groundfish prices fell, as they did every year when the weather allowed boats to spend more time fishing and landings rose. This time, however, the decline put many boat owners and fishermen in serious difficulty. "With the price of fish," a crewman stated in spring 1980, "it isn't worth fishing. By the time we pay our expenses . . . our checks are shot." "How are we supposed to maintain our homes and families on $100 for nine days of fishing?" asked a fisherman's wife. Again in spring 1981, the fall in prices caused severe problems. "All I can say is, if I have three or four trips like my last one, I'll be out of business," said Gaetano Brancaleone, a Gloucester skipper. "This is one of the worst years I can remember," said Joseph Piscitello, another Gloucester captain. "If this keeps up, you'll see a lot of boats tie up," said a third skipper. "I don't see any way for them to make it."[1]

The industry offered a number of explanations for the trouble. "Since May of 1977, our expenses have tripled," said Rosemarie Tocco, the wife of a Gloucester fisherman. Most important, fishermen stated, fuel prices had risen considerably; interest rates on vessel mortgages and the cost of insurance, food, equipment, and services had gone up also. The increase in costs made the industry vulnerable to falling prices. The main reason for the decline in prices, many stated, was that Canadian imports were flooding the market. "In New England," said Lucy Sloan, executive director of the National Federation of Fishermen, "I'd say it [Canadian fish] is one of the major difficulties." Canadian fish could undersell the New England fish, Mrs. Tocco stated, because "Canadian fishing boats, fish companies and fish cutters are all subsidized by the Canadian government." Only a few offered alternative explanations for the fall in prices. The main cause, one captain stated, was the number of new vessels which brought in more fish. As landings rose, prices fell. Restrictions on catch imposed by the Fishery Management Council could not be enforced,

183

stated NMFS officials, who estimated that at least 75 percent of landings came from areas ordered closed to fishing. The illegal fishing also helped push landings up and prices down.[2]

In line with the prevailing diagnoses of the problems, industry leaders planned petitions to the International Trade Commission for higher tariffs on groundfish. In response to industry pressure from New England and other parts of the country, Congress passed a bill in Decenber 1980 which offered low-interest loans to fishermen who were in danger of defaulting on vessel mortgages, extended loan guarantees for construction of shore facilities and purchase and repair of used fishing vessels, and provided funds for local fishery promotion projects.[3]

The groundfish industry's experience since the arrival of the foreign fleets in the early 1960s and the attempts at fishery management offered insight for making new policy for the fishing industry, but that new policy would not mean higher tariffs and more subsidies.[4] The quotas, mesh regulation, and closed areas instituted by ICNAF and the Fishery Management Council could not control fishing pressures effectively. Because management failed to constrain fishing effort, the groundfish industry had grown considerably by summer 1981. Heavy fishing caused gluts, but the large landings would not last indefinitely because as the overfishing continued, the stock would become more depleted. Depletion would make fishing costs rise so that many boats would lose money with fluctuations in price.

Limiting the number of boats and fishermen offered hope of adequate incomes and a rebuilt fish resource. Limiting entry would be extremely complicated, but with considerable debate, analysis, and experimentation by the industry under the New England Fishery Management Council's leadership, that direction would offer more hope than other management measures for preventing heavier fishing with the accompanying resource depletion, higher harvesting costs, lower incomes, and greater vulnerability to price changes.

The groundfish industry showed no evidence of having learned from the mistakes of the past. The new efforts could not solve the industry's troubles because they did not address the causes of the problems. Even if the programs were implemented more effectively than in the past, subsidies to lower costs could not help the industry for long without limits on entry. New programs like those Congress passed in 1980 might raise profits enough to attract more newcomers into fishing. The additional pressures on the resource would cause more depletion, raise costs, and push profits down again. Higher tariffs might raise prices and profits for a while, but the heavier fishing that would result would leave the industry as badly off as before. State and local funding for expansion of piers and improvement of harbors and dock facilities, which indirectly lower fishing costs, would serve at most to shift the concentration of fishing communities along the coast. Like the federal programs, these efforts could not assure the prosperity of the industry without limits on entry.

While the groundfish industry's recent experience holds lessons for new fishery policy, the industry's longer history of efforts to get assistance, the results of the programs, and the reasons for their failure have more general implications both for fisheries policy and for government intervention in other distressed industries. The federal government has traditionally helped distressed industries through pricing policy, tariffs, subsidies, and regulation. For instance, the government has protected farmers with price supports. Tariffs have sheltered the textile and apparel industries for decades despite strong pressures for free trade. The merchant marine and shipbuilding industries benefited from a range of expensive subsidies. Regulatory agencies and Congress have made changes in rules to aid the troubled savings and loan associations.[5] This tradition and the difficulties of large industries such as autos and steel which affect millions of people mean that government will probably continue to assist troubled industries. The story of government's failure to turn the groundfish industry's fortunes around or to assure its prosperity offers a case study of government efforts to revitalize an industry. The industry's experience shows what can go wrong and suggests some way to make future intervention more effective.

Analysis of the groundfish industry's experience suggests several reasons why the government efforts failed to help. First, industry spokesmen, legislators, and agency officials had trouble unraveling the complex reasons for problems, so that programs were based on incorrect assessments of the industry's difficulties. Second, industry representatives and government policy makers could not necessarily find good solutions to the problems. Inappropriate programs in some cases promised to make the problems even worse. Finally, many programs did not work as intended because of difficulties in implementation.

TROUBLES IN IDENTIFYING THE CAUSES OF PROBLEMS

Programs were designed for the wrong problems for several reasons. First, Congress and the federal fishery agencies relied heavily on the industry's assessment of the problems; but those in the industry often were wrong about the causes of their own problems.

From the late 1940s through the mid-1960s, for instance, industry spokesmen argued that large quantities of imported groundfish drove prices so low that New England boats could not break even, fishermen earned very low wages, and dealers realized no profits. Imports sold at low prices because production costs in other north Atlantic countries were much lower than in New England. A more complete explanation for the problems of the groundfish industry would not only have pointed to these cost disadvantages but would also have demonstrated that demand for groundfish had fallen considerably after World War II. Government purchased less fish after the war; and meat, rationed during the war, again competed with fish for the consumer's dollars. Demand fell again in the mid-1950s with the introduction of fish sticks made entirely of imported fish. However, the groundfish industry had expected the prosperity of the war years to continue. They had invested in large numbers of new and converted boats, and new fishermen had filled the additional jobs. Because boats and fishermen could not leave the industry as quickly as they had entered in response to the fall in revenues, many were stuck in the industry. Other boat owners and fishermen were determined to stay despite very low incomes.

This assessment of the groundfish industry's problems suggests that government might have relieved the hardship in the industry by stimulating demand for groundfish during the 1950s and early 1960s. If demand had not fallen as much, more boat owners and dealers in the groundfish industry might have broken even, and more fishermen might have earned attractive wages for a time. Alternatively, the government might have helped vessel owners and fishermen get out of fishing by purchasing boats and providing retraining for fishermen. As boats and fishermen left the industry and landings declined, costs of fishing would have fallen, and prices would have gone up. Those who remained in the industry would have been better off.

The federal government did not take either of these approaches in its attempts to solve the fishing industry's problems. Such programs did not fit the industry's definition of the major causes of their problems. The industry's diagnosis of the problems led instead to efforts to raise tariffs on groundfish and to programs lowering costs to foreign levels.

Although the industry's diagnosis of the problems was very clear, their explanation of parts of the problems was inconsistent with this diagnosis and was wrong. During the 1950s and 1960s, for instance, industry spokesmen stated that one reason for their troubles was that younger workers who would increase productivity were not choosing to become fishermen. Training programs set up to attract young men failed to do so, however, because wages were extremely low, especially on the vessels where newcomers could find positions. Groundfish industry representatives were calling the difficulty attracting new workers a cause of their troubles, but, instead, it was a symptom.

In the 1960s and 1970s, industry spokesmen did no better at explaining new problems. Heavy fishing depleted groundfish stocks and increased the costs of harvesting. The industry was correct that foreign fishing activity contributed to the overfishing of the groundfish resource, but they did not believe that Canadian and American fleets added to the fishing pressures. An accurate analysis of the causes of fish stock depletion would have stated that free access to the fish resources made overfishing inevitable if consumer demand for fish were high enough. Although excluding the foreigners would help to solve the problem, New England fishermen could overfish the resource, too.

In the 1970s, however, other influential groups, such as fishery agency staff, environmentalists, and State Department officials, put forth competing views about the causes of the problems. In designing the 1976 legislation that dealt with overfishing, Congress incorporated alternative views of causes of the problems, proposing fishery management programs which could restrict the free access that contributed to overfishing. The industry did not agree that their own fishing depleted the resource, and their opposition to fishery management helped thwart the program.

In each of these cases, industry put forth the simplest, most obvious reasons for problems, missing less apparent explanations. The industry adopted these simple explanations partly because they did no research on their problems. Most often the spokesmen were union leaders or businessmen who took time off from their usual duties to testify and lobby. The handful of boat owners, labor leaders, and processors who led the campaigns for government aid could not hope to do more than offer off-the-cuff explanations.

Sometimes the best explanations for the problems of the fisheries were counterintuitive and, therefore, particularly hard to understand. The limits to industry growth imposed by the biological characteristics of the resource and by environmental conditions on the fishing grounds did not seem reasonable or logical to most in the industry, as they debated the problems of foreign fishing and the merits of a domestic fishery management system.

The industry made mistakes in explaining their problems partly because of the lack of research and the complexity of the problems, but their errors also involved politics. The industry's willingness to believe certain explanations reflected the best ways to build a constituency and to influence congressmen and agency officials. Industry leaders did not consider and reject better explanations for their problems to find the ones that met their political needs. Instead, their understanding of politics probably unconsciously molded their definition of the problems and the solutions.

The explanations helped industry leaders find support from fishermen, processors, and boat owners. Simple reasons for problems were important because most of those in the industry were not inclined to analyze the causes of problems. Further, the explanations were helpful for rallying industry support because the reasons for the problems led to solutions that were also simple and straightforward. If imports were the problem, tariffs were the cure; if foreign fishing were the problem, excluding foreigners from the fishing grounds was the solution. Finally, the explanations were useful in gathering a constituency because they placed the causes of the problems and the solutions outside the industry. The causes suggested that the industry was the victim of outsiders, foreigners. The solutions did not require fishermen, boat owners, and processors to adjust to new economic conditions or to help themselves without assistance. Rather, the solutions implied, government should enable those in the industry to continue their business as before.

The simpler explanations were also useful in the industry's search for support from Congress and from federal agencies. If imports were the problem, then the traditional ways government helped troubled industry, with tariffs and quotas, were the right ways to help again. Only after the Eisenhower administration denied the industry's request for trade restrictions could the industry justify looking for less conventional assistance from Congress. The industry might have been less successful in looking for subsidies, loans, and other kinds of help later if tariffs had not seemed the obvious solution originally.

The explanations suggested that certain solutions—tariffs, programs to lower costs, or excluding foreign fishermen from coastal waters—would cure all the problems. Therefore, the Tariff Commission, other federal agencies, or Congress could believe that no one would be back for more help later if they provided assistance now.

Finally, the explanations were useful in getting sympathy from Congress because they placed the source of the problems outside the domestic industry and the rest of the American economy. As the explanations implied, the problem was not that American consumers no longer wanted to eat the fish the New England industry produced at the prices necessary for the industry to break even, nor that New England fishermen contributed to the depletion of the fish resource. In both cases the industry was the victim of foreigners' activity. On one hand, the administration could respond that the interests of other nations should take priority, that high tariffs on fish would make north Atlantic countries vulnerable to communism, for instance, and that unilateral extension of fishery jurisdiction would threaten agreement at the United Nations Conference on the Law of the Sea. On the other hand, many congressmen were sensitive to improving the income of American producers. No one's constituents could be blamed for troubles, and none would be clearly hurt if the solutions were implemented.

The industry's difficulties in understanding the causes of their problems were a major reason that programs did not alway address the problems. However, as the discussion above suggests, political expediency was probably important in determining the explanation which the industry presented. Indeed, in some cases the industry's representatives did understand the nature of difficulties but obscured the causes in their lobbying of congressmen and agency officials. The spokesmen's tendency to slant the description of the problems when they understood suggests that even if they had understood all the problems, they still might not have presented the correct explanation to congressmen or agency officials.

This tendency only made the problems harder to solve. For example, as industry representatives talked about their difficulties during the 1950s and 1960s, they suggested that the entire New England industry suffered although they knew that the problems were in the offshore groundfish industry from which they themselves came. Partly as a result, Congress aimed only one of the many pieces of fishery legislation at the groundfishery. The programs helped groups that did not need assistance and usually touched the groundfish industry very little.

Both vessel owners and union leaders believed that union-management disputes contributed to the disproportionate decline of the industry in Boston compared to other ports. While this explanation was probably valid only for redfish harvesting operations, no industry representatives mentioned vessel owner-union conflicts as a cause of the Boston industry's decline. Government programs had little chance to stem the flight of the redfish sector of the groundfish industry from Boston as long as such problems remained.

The explanations for groundfish industry problems were often wrong because the industry had trouble understanding the major problems and intentionally obscured the character of other difficulties. The industry had strong political incentives to describe the causes of problems and their solutions in these ways. Explanations were also incorrect because the causes of the problems changed. Industry spokesmen, elected officials and administrators who listened to them, and government-supported researchers did analyze the problems and might eventually have suggested better explanations, but neither industry nor government could keep up with the changes in the problems to adjust their thinking, the direction of political activity, and policy.

By the mid-1960s when the most thorough studies of cost differences between the United States and Canadian fisheries were complete, the foreign fleets were working on Georges Bank. The perception of the causes of problems evolved slowly. The "foreign competition" which congressmen and the industry talked about came to mean superior foreign fish-catching ability as well as inexpensive imports; but not until the 1970s did industry representatives or government officials completely redefine the causes of the difficulties; and even then some spokesmen talked about imports as a basic industry problem.

Industry spokesmen and government officials had trouble reorienting their thinking about the causes of fishery problems for several reasons. For one, good evidence supporting a new point of view was hard to find. In the early 1960s even the scientists working with the International Commission for the Northwest Atlantic Fisheries had difficulty determining what was happening to the fish stocks because they did not receive complete landings data quickly enough.

Probably more important, however, the leaders who communicated the causes of problems to Congress and to administrators had considerable stake in the old definitions. This made perception of new information more difficult. They had built political constituencies around the old assessment of the problems. They had spent years persuading government to respond to those problems. Their work had resulted in several programs to lower fishing costs that symbolized their success and were a credit to their effectiveness in getting government assistance. Some of their constituents had benefited from the loan programs, mortgage insurance for boats, and boat construction subsidies. With a new definition of the problems few of the programs made sense. As the assessment of the problems evolved among industry spokesmen, the diagnoses changed in ways that preserved the legitimacy of the old aid programs as long as possible.

DIFFICULTIES IN FINDING A GOOD SOLUTION

Not only did the industry and policy makers have trouble understanding the causes of the problems, but they also had a very hard time finding solutions that would improve or at least maintain the industry's condition. One reason good solutions were hard to find was that both the industry's assessment and much of the research on fishery problems leaped from looking at the causes of problems to making recommendations without enough analysis of the character of the industry. Even when assessment of problems was incorrect, more careful study of the way the industry would respond to the programs would have suggested that some of the solutions would not work.

The vessel subsidy programs reflected a leap from an incomplete assessment of the problem to an inadequate solution. Industry spokesmen and fishery researchers agreed that other north Atlantic countries produced fish more cheaply than New England because foreign costs were much lower. Foreign boats, for example, might cost half as much as New England vessels. Therefore, the industry and government officials concluded, subsidizing boat costs would help New England fishermen compete with foreigners. Although boat construction subsidies made the owners who received them more prosperous for a while, such payments could not make long-term improvements in the industry's position. As the new boats harvested more fish, the average costs of production from the fishery would rise as catching fish became more difficult. The increase in costs would partly offset the additional revenues of the new vessels from more efficient harvesting, but the owners of old boats and the fishermen who worked on them would suffer as the harvesting costs rose.

The vessel subsidy example suggests that one reason the industry and government officials did not understand the impact programs would have was that the implications were particularly hard to figure out. In most industries, reductions in the cost of inputs improve a firm's financial position and increase production. In the fishing industry such reductions in costs do not last long, and attempts to produce a larger catch eventually lead instead to smaller harvests because of fishery depletion.

On other occasions, however, the errors in predicting responses to programs had nothing to do with the nature of a renewable resource to which anyone had access. These mistakes showed lack of thought about how any industry would behave. For example, no one publicly questioned whether nearly bankrupt boat owners and processors could act on government recommendations to invest in equipment and to change fish handling practices in ways that might indirectly reduce insurance costs or increase consumer demand. Boat owners and processors rarely could afford to make the investments. No one challenged the implicit assumption behind the loan program and the vessel subsidies that if boat owners could get financing they would make repairs and build new boats. However, most boat owners and fishermen were not earning enough to put up their share of the payment for a new vessel. In addition, their prospective income stream was too small to make the investment worthwhile.

The legislative process did not include careful analysis of how proposed solutions would work. Proponents offered approaches which addressed the general problems they described and which they thought would pass. Opponents criticized programs, but their arguments were never based on analysis of the industry and its responses. Instead, they warned, for instance, that extension of fishery jurisdiction would lead to foreign interference with naval operations or that giving the fishing industry special loans and subsidies would set a dangerous precedent for the federal government's role in the fortunes of troubled industries. A careful analysis of how solutions would work seemed to meet no one's needs.

If sympathetic congressmen had uncovered the complexities of solutions, they might have created difficulties. Examining the solutions more critically would have meant that bills might not pass and that congressmen would have to consider other ways to help the industry. Other measures might not be as popular with the industry or might be harder to get through Congress. Furthermore, individual congressmen would not have to take the blame if the programs did not work, and new political pressures to do something better for the industry could be handled later.

Another major reason that effective solutions were hard to find was that industry spokesmen appealed to congressmen's other concerns to get support for the programs they wanted. Then, to deal with those concerns, congressmen and agency officials pushed programs in directions they would not have taken if determined only by analysis of the industry's problems.

Fishing spokesmen emphasized superior foreign fishing technology and the decline of the United States as a fish producer as they pushed for boat subsidy programs to upgrade the American fishing fleet. Once the subsidy program was in place, however, congressmen wanted to direct the money to vessels which would demonstrate that the United States was a leader among the world's fishing nations. "Seafreeze Atlantic," so ill-suited to the New England groundfishery, was the result.

PROBLEMS IN IMPLEMENTING THE PROGRAMS

Once legislation passed or programs were in place, the efforts rarely had much effect on the New England groundfish industry. Most programs would not have helped the groundfish industry even if properly implemented because they were based on incorrect explanations for the problems or because they were inappropriate solutions. However, the fact that implementation problems nearly always waylaid programs suggested that even if the efforts had been properly conceived, the process of getting programs to do what they were supposed to was very difficult.

Neither legislation nor regulations directed aid toward the groundfish industry except in the first of the vessel subsidy programs. Therefore, although fishermen and boat owners requested loans, researchers applied for grants, and the Department of Defense and the school lunch program purchased fish, little of the activity touched the groundfish industry. Boat owners and fishermen from the most profitable, growing fisheries, and not from the groundfishery, most frequently applied for boat loans and subsidies. Program administrators, seeking to put all their funds to use and hoping to assure that loans were repaid or that subsidized vessels profited, saw the applicants from more prosperous segments of the industry as better risks and gave them the largest proportion of loans and subsidies. Government programs purchased more frozen fish than fresh and, after the mid-1950s, bought large quantities of fish sticks. Much of the frozen fish and all the ingredients for fish sticks were imported.

Another reason that legislation did not work as planned was that funding was inadequate. Funds used for the boat subsidy program were less than half those authorized by the legislation, but even the authorized funding could not begin to achieve the program's goal to replace the groundfish fleet. Purchasing programs to counteract the fall in demand would have needed a larger budget than the total funds allocated to all fishery programs in any year.

Funding was low partly because fisheries programs had low priority in every President's agenda. One fishery agency official claimed that the small commitment of money demonstrated that no one had intended that the fishery programs help the industry. However, programs that could make a difference in the industry's fortunes required more money than most people, even those who favored a higher level of funding, realized.

Finally, programs did not accomplish what policy makers had intended because the programs were exceptionally complicated to implement. The management of the groundfish industry under the Fishery Conservation and Management Act proved extremely difficult. The law had failed to conserve the fish resource or to assure the future prosperity of the industry by 1981 in large part because the stakes in the implementation of the law were very high. Any rules threatened the incomes and the lifestyles of fishermen, boat owners, and processors. Therefore, fishermen found loopholes in the regulations and broke the rules when they realized that the regulations were unenforceable. Those in the industry protested any rule that the Fishery Management Council proposed or put in place. The Council was sensitive to these protests, partly because the members also came from the industry and their businesses were affected, and partly because they had been appointed to represent those who protested. Just as important, the industry's testimony was the Council's only source of information about the effects of the regulations. No one had the social, economic, and biological data or had conducted the analyses to understand how regulations touched different groups in the fishery. Even with the necessary data and good analysis, the job of designing fishery management measures that affected the diverse industry groups equally would have been extremely difficult. As newcomers flooded the industry, the difficulties intensified. With more fishermen, the pressures on the depleted resource became more extreme and the Council's regulations more threatening to incomes.

IMPLICATIONS FOR GOVERNMENT EFFORTS TO AID INDUSTRY IN TROUBLE

This book has looked only at the experience of the New England groundfishery in order to learn what happens when the federal government helps a troubled industry. The fishing industry differs from most other distressed industries in several ways. The industry depends on a renewable natural resource to which almost anyone has access. Unlike the pattern of concentration in most industries, fishing is highly competitive in harvesting and nearly as competitive in processing; thousands of small fishing businesses operate with almost no vertical integration. First and second generation ethnic groups with long traditions of fishing have dominated fish harvesting. These special characteristics should not mean, however, that reasons for government's failure to assure the prosperity of the fishing industry might not also be true of efforts to help other troubled industries.

Research on other troubled industries suggests that the same factors may indeed interfere with the effectiveness of government policy toward other industries. Causes of problems are often extremely hard to identify and to address for a range of intellectual and political reasons. For example, integrated steel manufacturers emphasize the expansion of foreign steel industries and the growth of imports in explaining their difficulties. However, analyses of the steel industry point to other trends which have contributed to the industry's troubles. In contrast to developments in foreign trade, these include factors for which the industry had responsibility in the past and that management and labor can do much to control in the future, such as decisions to invest in new technology or negotiations of new labor contracts. Partly because of the industry's strong, effective lobbying for trade restrictions, federal policies have been skewed toward dealing with problems that have little to do with management decisions; but trade protection is probably not the best way to subsidize the steel industry even if the only goal is to revitalize the industry.[6]

Programs that would solve industry problems are often difficult to find. The merchant marine and the shipbuilding industry have received extensive aid for many years in the form of subsidies, the provision of goods and services at below-market prices, and guaranteed markets. Not only have the programs not succeeded in stemming the industries' decline, but the solutions may have exacerbated problems. Operating subsidies for the merchant marine, for example, were intended to reduce the cost of shipboard labor but had the effects of discouraging operators from introducing new, labor-saving technology and encouraging labor unions to press for higher wages and fringe benefits. Total costs were higher than they would have been without the subsidies. Efforts to help the shipbuilding industry by requiring that all vessels engaged in domestic trade be constructed in United States yards have raised costs considerably for the troubled merchant marine. The government has tried to counteract the higher costs with other subsidies.[7]

The federal government has sought to protect the shoe industry by negotiating orderly marketing agreements with principal manufacturing nations to restrict exports to the United States. The orderly marketing agreements may have made the shoe industry's foreign competition even stiffer because the major foreign manufacturers moved into product lines not covered by the agreements and because uncontrolled exporters expanded their production to serve the markets where other countries had been restricted.[8]

Implementation problems often interfere with programs' success in assisting industries. The 1974 Trade Act expanded trade adjustment assistance programs. One study of assistance to firms suggested that the programs probably could not make troubled firms viable in large part because the loans were not big enough to allow much adjustment and because the process of delivering benefits was so drawn out that firms' financial problems became even worse in the interim and required larger amounts of money. An analysis of assistance to workers who had lost jobs in the shoe industry showed that few workers benefited. Eligibility criteria were so strict that many were excluded; the processing of applications took so long that most workers had to find other ways to adjust before they received assistance; and many workers did not know about the benefits.[9]

If government efforts to help troubled industry often fail for many of the reasons that fisheries programs have not worked, government should take steps to make the assistance more effective. The New England groundfish industry's experience suggests several ways to make government efforts more successful. First, policy makers and industry spokesmen need a better understanding of the causes of their problems than government and industry have had of the fisheries' difficulties. Any industry's diagnosis is likely to be unreliable. Unlike the New England fisheries, the management of some troubled industries have well-established lobbies with a long history of research on their problems, and unions have research departments. Nevertheless, political incentives remain for industry to perceive some problems incorrectly and to disguise the character of other difficulties.

Because the industry's views are likely to be wrong, Congress and the administrative branch need the capacity to investigate the causes of industry problems before the troubles become crises that force Congress to base policy on the industry's analysis alone. The Office of Technology Assessment of the Congress, the General Accounting Office, and some offices in the Department of Commerce, for example, could carry out studies to provide a foundation for making policy. They have done so to a more limited extent in the past. However, their capacity for analysis is not enough; an agency must be able to operate independently of the industry and to keep the agency's own agenda from influencing the findings. For example, agencies such as the Department of Agriculture and the Maritime Administration, who have close ties with farm interest groups and with the merchant marine, might not provide analyses that were not the industries'. The Bureau of Commercial Fisheries and the National Marine Fisheries Service examined the problems of the fisheries independently from the industry to some extent but with too little understanding of social and political factors, too much faith in economic and biological theories, and too much interest in building the agency's power in place of looking for the best direction for the industry.

The existence of alternative assessments of an industry's problems does not guarantee them attention. In the legislative process, the industry's view of the problem gets more notice than any other. Therefore, Congress, with the help of agencies, needs to institutionalize ways to take account of other analyses of industry problems in the hearings process.

Agreement within an industry on useful legislation makes passage possible and success in implementation more likely. Legislators and agency staff need to look for ways to reconcile government, management, and labor views of the problems and their solutions so that the industry supports a policy direction that is likely to solve problems.

Not only is far better analysis of the causes of the problems necessary but also much more extensive, careful analysis of the industry is needed before a crisis develops in order to predict the responses of the industry to solutions that government implements. The fishing industry's experience suggests that Congress, agency officials, and the industry would find better solutions if they thought more carefully about the way any worker, manager, or entrepreneur in financial difficulty behaves. In other cases, however, a good assessment of how the industry might react to programs requires detailed knowledge of technology and of social norms. Such industry analysis must consider cultural, institutional, and political factors as well as economic ones.

Analysis of how an industry will respond to new solutions can benefit from evaluations of earlier programs, those aimed at the industry as well as similar efforts intended to help other industries. The General Accounting Office, administrative agencies, and researchers outside the government have evaluated many programs. In other cases, Congress or agency officials should study the results of the efforts.

The fishery experience suggests that implementation analysis also should accompany policy analysis to enable Congress and agencies to foresee the obstacles that programs will confront and to suggest ways that programs should be changed to try to avoid interference. Implementation analysis would consider a range of questions. For example, what agency goals will conflict with the aims of the programs? How will that conflict affect the way the agency implements the programs? How large an appropriation will the program receive? Can the proposed program operate effectively at that level of funding? How will groups outside the industry respond to the efforts to help the industry, and how will their behavior affect these efforts? The answers to these questions and others should suggest ways to modify programs to make their implementation easier and should point to strategies useful in implementation.

The implications of the groundfish industry's experience are important not only for major troubled industries asking the federal government for assistance but also for the fishing industry. The failures of fishery management mean that the industry will have serious problems to confront in the future and will continue to seek government help. The effectiveness of the aid they get will depend largely on whether industry, Congress, and administrators can learn from the past.

Notes

Chapter 1   An Industry in Trouble

1. Burton T. Coffey, William B. Walker, and Henry S. Galus, "Sail on Washington Centers on 200-Mile Limit: On to Washington," *National Fisherman* 55, no. 4 (Aug. 1974): 4A, 29A.

2. U.S., Congress, House of Representatives, Hearings before Committee on Merchant Marine and Fisheries, "Fisheries Promotion" in "Fishery Jurisdiction," 93rd Cong., 2d sess., June 11, 1974; Tim Sullivan, "Haddock Skeleton: Symbol of Effort," *Gloucester Daily Times*, June 6, 1974, p. 1.

3. U.S., Department of the Interior, Fish and Wildlife Service, *Fishery Statistics of the United States*, Statistical Digests, nos. 27, 30, 34, 36, 39, 41 (Washington, D.C.: GPO, 1950–1955); U.S., Department of the Interior, Bureau of Commercial Fisheries, *Fishery Statistics of the United States*, Statistical Digests, nos. 43, 44, 49, 51, 53 (Washington, D.C.: GPO, 1956–1960); U.S., Department of Commerce, Bureau of the Census, *Statistical Abstract of the United States* (Washington, D.C.: GPO, 1976), p. 393.

4. *Fishery Statistics of the United States*, 1950–1960.

5. U.S., Department of the Interior, Bureau of Commercial Fisheries, *Fishery Statistics of the United States*, Statistical Digests, nos. 54, 56–61 (Washington, D.C.: GPO, 1961–1967); U.S., Department of Commerce, National Oceanic and Atmospheric Administration, National Marine Fisheries Service, *Fishery Statistics of the United States*, Statistical Digests, nos. 62–67 (Washington, D.C.: GPO, 1968–1973).

6. *Fishery Statistics of the United States*, 1950–1973; Bureau of the Census, *Statistical Abstract, 1976*, p. 393.

7. Edward A. Ackerman, *New England's Fishing Industry* (Chicago, Ill.: University of Chicago Press, 1941), pp. 1–3; Homer Haberland, "Gloucester: Three Centuries a Fishing Port," in Fishing Masters' Association, *Official Yearbook of the Fishing Masters' Association* (Boston, Mass.: The Association, 1946); George Brown Goode, *The Fisheries and Fishery Industries of the United States*

199

(Washington, D.C.: GPO, 1887), vol. 1, sec. 5; Tour Office, Massachusetts State House, Boston, Mass., personal communication, May 1982.

8. Margaret Dewar, Ronald Lake, Mary Lord, Deborah Wishner, Julia Wondolleck, "The Fishing Industry of Chatham and Its Importance to the Town" (Department of Urban Studies and Planning, Massachusetts Institute of Technology, Cambridge, Mass., Aug. 1978).

Chapter 2   Structure and Problems of the Fisheries

1. "The Future of Lobstermen," *Atlantic Fisherman* 26, no. 7 (Aug. 1945): 7; "Popularity of Frozen Foods Will Increase Fish Demand," *Atlantic Fisherman* 26, no. 11 (Dec. 1945): 23.

2. Fred Lardner, "Report from Washington," *Atlantic Fisherman* 26, no. 5 (June 1945): 40.

3. "Changes in New England Fishing Fleet, 1940–44: The Result of an Independent Survey by the Editor of *Atlantic Fisherman,*" *Atlantic Fisherman* 25, no. 7 (Aug. 1944): 21; Fishing Masters' Association, *Official Yearbook of the Fishing Masters' Association* (Boston, Mass.: The Association, 1941).

4. "The Future of Lobstermen," p. 7; "Good Quality Now Will Insure Post-War Market," *Atlantic Fisherman* 24, no. 12 (Jan. 1944): 7; Fred Lardner, "Washington Wants to Increase Fish Production," *Atlantic Fisherman* 26, no. 4 (May 1945): 23.

5. U.S., Department of Commerce, Bureau of the Census, *Historical Statistics of the United States* (Washington, D.C.: GPO, 1975), ser. L236–253, D739–764; "Earnings and Methods of Wage Payment in the Fishing Industry," *Monthly Labor Review* 43, no. 3 (Sept. 1936): 551–557.

6. "Fishing Is Getting Better; Now for a Cold, Windy Winter!" *Business Week*, Nov. 9, 1932, pp 16–17; Jonathan Mitchell, "Fresh Fish," *New Republic* 81 (Nov. 14, 1934): 14; Bertram B. Fowler, "Sharecroppers of the Sea," *Scribner's Magazine* 51, no. 5 (May 1937): 35–39.

7. U.S., Congress, House of Representatives, Hearings before Committee on Banking and Currency, "To Provide Loans through Reconstruction Finance Corporation," 73rd Cong., 2d sess., Feb.–March 1934, p. 116; "Statement Setting Forth Serious Situation Confronting Fishermen, Captains, and Vessel Owners at the Port of Gloucester, Massachusetts," presented by fishermen and captains who traveled to Washington on the Gloucester schooner "Gertrude L. Thebaud," 1933 (files of the Gloucester Fisheries Commission, Gloucester, Mass.); U.S., Congress, House of Representatives, Hearings before Committee on Merchant Marine, Radio, and Fisheries, "Rehabilitation of the Fishing Industry," 73rd Cong., 2d sess., Feb.–Mar. 1934, pp. 5–20.

8. Donald J. White, *The New England Fishing Industry: A Study in Price and Wage Setting* (Cambridge, Mass.: Harvard University Press, 1954), pp. 27–29; Bernard Breedlove, "C.I.O. Fish," *Literary Digest* 124, no. 22 (Dec. 11, 1937),

pp. 20–22; U.S., Department of Commerce, Bureau of the Census, *Sixteenth Census of the United States, 1940: Population*, vol. 3, "The Labor Force," Tables 16, 17.

9. White, *The New England Fishing Industry*, pp. 25–26, 33 ff.

10. "Fishing Troubles," *Time* 40, no. 4 (July 27, 1942): 71; "Changes in New England Fishing Fleet," p. 21; Fishing Masters' Association, *Official Yearbook*, 1941; Marc A. Rose, "Fishing Is a War Job, Too," *Reader's Digest* 42, no. 249 (Jan. 1943): 55; Eldon E. Lindsey, "Wanted, More Fishing Boats," *Christian Science Monitor Weekly Magazine Section*, Mar. 13, 1943, p. 15.

11. Bureau of Census, *Historical Statistics*, ser. L236–253; Federal Trade Commission, "Part VIII: Cost of Production and Distribution of Fish in New England," *Report of the Federal Trade Commission on Distribution Methods and Costs* (Washington, D.C.: GPO, 1945), p. 36; John Gould, "Maine Busy Canning Fish," *New York Times Magazine*, Nov. 22, 1942, p. 28.

12. Rose, "Fishing Is a War Job," p. 55.

13. Federal Trade Commission, "Part VIII," *Report*, pp. 97–100; "Kettle of Fish: OPA Is Caught between the Devil and the Deep Blue Sea," *Business Week*, Dec. 16, 1944, p. 40. One of the reasons that stories of spectacular earnings did not tell the whole tale was that fishermen did not work all the time. In Boston, the union supervised the rotation of crews on vessels because one-third more fishermen sought work than could have places on boats at any one time. Work on a small dragger was seasonal and depended on the migration of fish into inshore areas. During the winter and when fish did not come inshore, fishermen on small boats earned very little.

14. White, *The New England Fishing Industry*, pp. 31, 34, 26.

15. U.S., Department of the Interior, Fish and Wildlife Service, *Fishery Statistics of the United States*, Statistical Digest, no. 27 (Washington, D.C.: GPO, 1950).

16. The agencies that have collected fisheries statistics since the last century, first the Fish and Wildlife Service, then the Bureau of Commercial Fisheries, and recently the National Marine Fisheries Service, have focused on the fact that all fishermen harvest fish rather than on economic and social differences. Their data describe the fish caught far better than the industry that harvested them. As a result, information about what happened to different sectors of the industry from 1945 to 1965 is usually unavailable.

17. Like any typology, the inshore and offshore division oversimplifies the character of the industry. Some medium-sized boats share some features of each group. In ports where both inshore and offshore boats work, those in the industry sometimes see boats' character in a continuum from smallest to largest, with few clear divisions. For some purposes ethnic differences may distinguish fishermen in more meaningful ways than boat size.

18. This section relies heavily on testimony by inshore fishermen at the New England Fishery Management Council meetings, usually in Peabody, Massachusetts; on conversations with inshore fishermen at those meetings and in

Chatham, Massachusetts; and on the notes from interviews with Chatham and Gloucester fishermen by Mary Lord, Julia Wondolleck, and Meta Cushing in 1978 and 1979.

19. *Fishery Statistics of the United States*, 1946, 1950, 1960, 1965; Fishing Masters' Association, *Official Yearbook*, 1950; International Commission for the Northwest Atlantic Fisheries (hereafter ICNAF), "List of Vessels over 50 Gross Tons Fishing in the ICNAF Convention Area in 1959," ICNAF, Dartmouth, Nova Scotia, Canada, Nov. 1960; ICNAF, "List of Fishing Vessels and Summary of Fishing Effort in the ICNAF Convention Area, 1965," ICNAF, Dartmouth, Nova Scotia, Canada, Jan. 1967. The numbers of boats should be considered approximate and probably quite unreliable. Boats less than five tons did not have to be registered, and agents from the fishery bureaus would have had great difficulty distinguishing correctly or consistently between sportfishermen and commercial fishermen or between part-timers and those who fished as much as possible.

20. ICNAF, "List of Fishing Vessels, 1965," and "List of Vessels, 1959"; *Fishery Statistics of the United States*, 1950, 1960, 1965.

21. *Ibid. Fishery Statistics of the United States* gives the number of fishermen working on boats smaller than five tons. The number of fishermen on boats five to sixty gross tons is an estimate assuming between three and four men per boat.

22. Phil Schwind, *Cape Cod Fisherman* (Camden, Me.: International Marine Publishing Co., 1974); Ellery Thompson, *Draggerman's Haul* (New York: Viking Press, 1950), p. 89; "6 to 1, It's Chathams," *Boston Globe*, June 22, 1977, p. 3; Margaret Dewar, Ronald Lake, Mary Lord, Deborah Wishner, Julia Wondolleck, "The Fishing Industry of Chatham and Its Importance to the Town" (Department of Urban Studies and Planning, Massachusetts Institute of Technology, Cambridge, Mass., Aug. 1978), pp. 51, 54.

23. Schwind, *Cape Cod Fisherman*; Harold B. Clifford, *Charlie York: Maine Coast Fisherman* (Camden, Me.: International Marine Publishing Co., 1974); Mary Breslauer, "Ah, the Fisherman's Life—Boom or Bust and Ernie's Cooking," *Vineyard Gazette*, June 21, 1977, pp. 1, 7.

24. Ted Van Winkle, *Fred Boynton: Lobsterman, New Harbor, Maine* (Camden, Me.: International Marine Publishing Co., 1975), pages unnumbered.

25. "Loran," an acronym for "long range aid to navigation," is a navigation aid which shows a captain his exact location using signals received from shore stations.

26. William Ronco, "Case Study of the Chatham Seafood Cooperative" (Center for Community Economic Development, Cambridge, Mass., Feb. 1978); Lord, interviews with Chatham fishermen, 1978–1979.

27. Schwind, *Cape Cod Fisherman;* Van Winkle, *Fred Boynton;* Thompson, *Draggerman's Haul;* Lord and Cushing, interviews with Chatham and Gloucester fishermen, 1978–1979.

28. For a discussion of how these factors affect the distribution of many species, see Edward A. Ackerman, *New England's Fishing Industry* (Chicago, Ill.: University of Chicago Press, 1941), chs. 2, 3.

29. Van Winkle, *Fred Boynton;* "Monhegan Maintains Her Traditional Aura," *National Fisherman* 53, no. 5 (Sept. 1972): 19C; Lord, interviews.

30. *Fishery Statistics of the United States*, 1945–1965; Charles H. Lyles, "Historical Catch Statistics (New England States)," Bureau of Commercial Fisheries, Fish and Wildlife Service, Department of Interior, ser. Current Fisheries Statistics (hereafter CFS) 4145, Apr. 1967; Ronald W. Green, "Erratic Maine Fishing Season Closes Near 1960 Level," *National Fisherman* 42, no. 10 (Feb. 1962): 2; James L. Warren, executive director, Maine Sardine Council, Ellsworth, Me., personal communication, Jan. 1978.

31. Van Winkle, *Fred Boynton;* William B. Walker, "Trap Day," *National Fisherman* 54, no. 13 (Apr. 30, 1974): 50 ff.; Lyles, "Historical Catch Statistics"; *Fishery Statistics of the United States*, 1945–1965; Ackerman, *New England's Fishing Industry*, ch. 5.

32. *Fishery Statistics of the United States*, 1945–1965; Lyles, "Historical Catch Statistics"; Leslie W. Scattergood, "The Northern Shrimp Fishery of Maine," *Commercial Fisheries Review* 14, no. 1 (Jan. 1952): 1–15; Maine Department of Sea and Shore Fisheries, "Harvesters of the Sea: The Story of Maine's Commercial Fisheries," Augusta, Me., 1971, pp. 18–21; Van Winkle, *Fred Boynton*; Robert L. Dow, "Fluctuations in Maine Shrimp Landings," *Commercial Fisheries Review* 25, no. 4 (April 1963): 5–6. The shrimp fishery collapsed again in the mid-1970s.

33. Lyles, "Historical Catch Statistics"; *Fishery Statistics of the United States*, 1945–1965; John J. O'Brien, "New England Whiting Fishery and Marketing of Whiting Products, 1946–61" (Bureau of Commercial Fisheries, Market News Service, Boston, Mass., Dec. 1962); Raymond L. Fritz, "A Review of the Atlantic Coast Whiting Fishery," *Commercial Fisheries Review* 22, no. 11 (Nov. 1960): 1–11; Tom V. Binmore, "Whiting Fishery Boon to Smaller Inshore Boats: Help Needed If Industry to Realize Gains," *National Fisherman* 44, no. 6 (Oct. 1963): 5; Lyman Owen, "Small Draggers Live Off Whiting in Summer," *National Fisherman* 49, no. 4 (Aug. 1968): 2B; "Gloucester Men Plan Action Against Maine Whiting Moves," *National Fisherman* 40, no. 7 (Nov. 1959): 15–16.

34. Albert C. Jensen and Robert K. Brigham, "Line-Trawl Fishery for Cod and Haddock at Chatham, Mass.," *Commercial Fisheries Review* 25, no. 6 (June 1963): 14–19; Ackerman, *New England's Fishing Industry*, ch. 4; "Fishing Vessel and Gear Developments, Equipment Note no. 5—Sink Gill-Net Fishing in New England," *Commercial Fisheries Review* 22, no. 11 (Nov. 1960): 16–19; tabulations of trip data for 1965, Northeast Fisheries Center, National Marine Fisheries Service, Woods Hole, Mass. All tabulations from trip data are landings by boats under fifty gross tons, rather than the sixty gross tons defined in this chapter as the distinction between inshore and offshore boats. How much groundfish inshore fishermen harvested before 1965 is not known because their landings are not distinguished from those of offshore boats.

35. *Fishery Statistics of the United States*, 1965; trip data tabulations, Northeast Fisheries Center; Tom V. Binmore, "Sea Scallops Win Top Spot Through Organization," *National Fisherman* 42, no. 3 (July 1961): 10; "Scallops Gain in

Popularity; Higher Prices Pose Challenge," *National Fisherman* 66, no. 4 (Aug. 1965): 50; Schwind, *Cape Cod Fisherman*, ch. 19.

36. "The Southern New England Fisheries," *National Fisherman* 39, no. 12 (April 1959): 18 ff.; Charles Buffum, "Rhode Island's Trappers . . . and Their Lunch Box Fishery," *National Fisherman* 47, no. 7 (Nov. 1966): 12A ff.; "Simplicity and Skill Keep Stonington Dragger Going," *National Fisherman* 49, no. 4 (Aug. 1968): 3B; Stephen B. Olsen and David K. Stevenson, "Commercial Marine Fish and Fisheries of Rhode Island," Marine Technical Report no. 34 (Kingston, R.I.: University of Rhode Island, Coastal Resources Center, 1975); Dewar *et al.,* "Fishing Industry," pp. 38–39.

37. George W. Snow, "Development of Trash Fishery at New Bedford, Massachusetts," *Commercial Fisheries Review* 12, no. 7 (July 1950): 8 ff.; Robert L. Edwards, "Gloucester's Trawl Fishery for Industrial Fish," *Commercial Fisheries Review* 20, no. 8 (Aug. 1958): 10 ff.; Robert L. Edwards and Fred E. Lux, "New England's Industrial Fishery," *Commercial Fisheries Review* 20, no. 5 (May 1958): 1 ff.; Olsen and Stevenson, "Commercial Marine Fish," part 1; Robert A. Hall and Henry R. McAvoy, "New England Fisheries—Annual Summary, 1963" (Bureau of Commercial Fisheries, Market News Service, Boston, Mass. 1964), p. 40.

38. John Ward, "Quahoggers Are Hard-Working, Independent Lot," *National Fisherman* 48, no. 4 (Aug. 1967): 6B; Lennox F. Bodman, "Fisherman Describes Gear, Methods Used to Harvest Nantucket Scallops," *National Fisherman* 46, no. 3 (July 1965): 42; "Southern New England Fisheries," pp. 18 ff.; Dewar *et al.,* "Fishing Industry," pp. 7 ff.; Lyles, "Historical Catch Statistics."

39. Dan Arnold, executive director, Massachusetts Inshore Draggermen's Association, Marshfield, Mass., personal communication, Oct. 1978; Andreas A. Holmsen, "Remuneration Systems and Ownership Patterns in the Fishing Industry and Their Relation to Investment Decisions," University of Rhode Island, Kingston, R.I., undated, p. 12; Bureau of Census, *Historical Statistics,* ser. D740. No studies of Maine fishermen's incomes exist; they may have been less prosperous than fishermen in Massachusetts and Rhode Island.

40. Arnold, personal communication; U.S., Congress, House of Representatives, Hearings before Committee on Merchant Marine and Fisheries, "Fishing Rights" in "Miscellaneous Fisheries Legislation," 89th Cong., 2d sess., May-June 1966, p. 344; Lord, interviews. The fishermen who remained to offer this information were the ones who did not go out of business during the 1950s and 1960s, so they may have remembered better conditions than a more balanced sample would have.

41. O'Brien, "New England Whiting Fishery" (Market News Service), p. 2. On the other hand, fishermen in the inshore fisheries today seem particularly predisposed to feel that government should not bail anyone out. The absence of appeals for aid could have reflected this sentiment rather than their well-being.

42. This section relies on testimony by offshore fishermen before the New England Fishery Management Council; on conversations with offshore fishermen at those meetings; and on Lord and Cushing, interviews.

43. *Fishery Statistics of the United States*, 1945–1965; Fishing Masters' Association, *Official Yearbook*, 1946, 1950, 1951; ICNAF, "List of Vessels, 1959"; ICNAF, "List of Vessels over 50 Gross Tons Fishing in the ICNAF Convention Area in 1962," ICNAF, Dartmouth, Nova Scotia, Canada, Jan. 1964; ICNAF, "List of Fishing Vessels, 1965."

44. Fishing Masters' Association, *Official Yearbook*, 1950; *Fishery Statistics of the United States*, 1965.

45. Charles R. Hitz, "Catalogue of the Soviet Fishing Fleet," *National Fisherman* 48, no. 13 (Apr. 30, 1968): 9 ff.

46. Ackerman, *New England's Fishing Industry*, ch. 2; Stephen Olsen and Dale Brown, "Petroleum, Fisheries, and the Georges Bank Environment," in *Fishing and Petroleum Interactions on Georges Bank*, vol. 2: *The Characteristics of the Two Industries, Potential Future Trends, and an Assessment of Foreseeable Conflicts*, Energy Program Technical Report no. 77-1 (New England Regional Commission, Boston, Mass., 1977).

47. Frederick L. Gaston and David A. Storey, "The Market for Fresh Fish That Originates from Boston Fish Pier Landings," in Frederick W. Bell and Jared E. Hazleton, eds., *Recent Developments and Research in Fisheries Economics* (Dobbs Ferry, N.Y.: Oceana Publications, 1967).

48. David P. Jackson, "NF Signs On as Supercargo for Trip to Georges Bank," *National Fisherman* 57, no. 5 (Sept. 1976): 15B; Kim Bartlett, *The Finest Kind: The Fishermen of Gloucester* (New York: W.W. Norton, 1977), part 2; Charles Buffum, "Scalloping Is Mechanized But Still Tedious Work," *National Fisherman* 48, no. 4 (Aug. 1967): 4B; "'Henry Underwood' Log Reveals Value of Radar," *Atlantic Fisherman* 33, no. 7 (Aug. 1952): 17; "Use of Loran as Navigational Aid," *Atlantic Fisherman* 31, no. 9 (Oct. 1950): 14–15; James F. Hunt, "Loran Helps Fishermen to Return to an Invisible X on Empty Ocean," *National Fisherman* 47, no. 1 (May 1966): 1C; "Locating Fish with Echo Sounders," *Atlantic Fisherman* 34, no. 3 (April 1953): 14, 28–29.

49. ICNAF, "List of Vessels, 1959"; "Rigging for Scallop Fishing Is Expensive Job," *National Fisherman* 48, no. 10 (Feb. 1968): 16A, 21A; George Ross, vessel loan officer, National Marine Fisheries Service, Gloucester, Mass., personal communication, Sept. 1977; "100′ Steel Scalloper Pat-San-Marie Is Third of Her Type for New Bedford," *National Fisherman* 48, no. 3 (July 1967): 20A; "Stern Trawler Is Converted to Herring Seiner," *National Fisherman* 49, no. 3 (July 1968): 14B.

50. ICNAF, "List of Vessels, 1959"; ICNAF, "List of Fishing Vessels, 1965"; Paul V. Mulkern, "Annual Earnings of Boston Fishermen in 1964," Bureau of Labor Statistics, Regional Report, Boston, Mass., Feb. 1966, p. 2; John J. O'Brien, "Landings and Prices of Fishery Products, Boston Fish Pier, 1956" (Branch of Commercial Fisheries, Market News Service, Fish and Wildlife Service, Boston, Mass.), p. v.

51. John Jessen, anthropologist, New Bedford, Mass., personal communication, fall 1977; David Boeri and James Gibson, *"Tell It Good-Bye, Kiddo": The Decline of the New England Offshore Fishery* (Camden, Me.: International

Marine Publishing, 1976), p. 26; White, *The New England Fishing Industry*, p. 88; James D. Ackert, "Comment" in Bell and Hazleton, *Recent Developments*; James D. Ackert, fishery policy specialist, Gorton Corporation, Gloucester, Mass., personal communication, March 1978; Virgil J. Norton and Morton M. Miller, "An Economic Study of the Boston Large-Trawler Labor Force," circ. 248, Bureau of Commercial Fisheries, Fish and Wildlife Service, Department of the Interior, Washington, D.C., May 1966, pp. 12–13; Lord and Cushing, interviews.

52. Another reason is that in ports in the 1950s and 1960s except New Bedford, a fisherman had only one choice of vessel type. He would have had to move to another port to get a different kind of job. A third reason is that fishermen establish personal contacts and earn reputations which get them more desirable sites on one kind of vessel. If they go to another kind of boat and gear, they may have to take less desirable sites again.

53. Bartlett, *The Finest Kind*; Mulkern, "Annual Earnings," pp. 2–3; Boeri and Gibson, *"Tell It Good-Bye,"* ch. 2; Jackson, "NF Signs On"; S.F. Manning, "Fishermen Weigh Benefits of Stern Trawling," *National Fisherman* 44, no. 11 (March 1964): 8–9.

54. Bartlett, *The Finest Kind*; Mulkern, "Annual Earnings," pp. 2–3; Boeri and Gibson, *"Tell It Good-Bye,"* ch. 2; Jackson, "NF Signs On"; George F. Kelly *et al.,* "Redfish," *Fishery Facts: 1,* National Marine Fisheries Service, Department of Commerce, Oct., 1972; Lord and Cushing, interviews.

55. Buffum, "Scalloping Is Mechanized," pp. 4B, 5B; Marilyn A. Altobello, David A. Storey, and Jon M. Conrad, "The Atlantic Sea Scallop Fishery: A Descriptive and Econometric Analysis," Research Bulletin no. 643, Massachusetts Agricultural Experiment Station, University of Massachusetts (Amherst, Mass., Jan. 1977), p. 19; Binmore, "Sea Scallops," p. 10.

56. Robert Kolbe, "Without Boats and Fish, a Fisherman Just Isn't," *National Fisherman* 54, no. 1 (May 1975): 28A; Bartlett, *The Finest Kind*; John Christie, "Gloucester Fisherman Loses Arm at Sea, Regains Limb in Hospital," *National Fisherman* 53, no. 7 (Nov. 1972): 13A; Norton and Miller, "An Economic Study," pp. 19–21.

57. White, *The New England Fishing Industry*, ch. 5; Norton and Miller, "An Economic Study," pp. 29–30; notes on union agreements in O'Brien *et al.,* "Landings and Prices" (Market News Service), various years; "Fishermen's Income Depends on Auction Outcome," *National Fisherman* 45, no. 4 (Aug. 1964): 26.

58. White, *The New England Fishing Industry*, chs. 4, 5; John J. O'Brien, "New England Fisheries—Annual Summary" (Bureau of Commercial Fisheries, Market News Service, Boston, Mass.), various years; John J. O'Brien, "New England Sea Scallop Fishery and Marketing of Sea Scallop Meats, 1939–60" (Bureau of Commercial Fisheries, Market News Service, Boston, Mass., Nov. 1961), p. 15; *Gloucester Daily Times*, Sept.–Oct. 1966; Charles Buffum, "2-Week New Bedford Strike Ends; Problem of Fuel Cost Is Ironed Out," *National Fisherman* 48, no. 3 (July 1967): 3A, 21A; "N. Bedford Skipper Protests Price

Cutting after Auction," *National Fisherman* 47, no. 12 (April 1967): 23A; Henry S. Galus, "Long Strike Hurts New Bedford," *National Fisherman* 52, no. 1 (May 1971): 20A; E. L. Pintor, "1971 Tie-Up Achieved Little for New Bedford," *National Fisherman* 52, no. 12 (April 1972): 18A, 25A; Henry S. Galus, "Boatowners United No 'Armchair Clique': Roche," *National Fisherman* 53, no. 3 (July 1972): 6C; Solomon Shapiro, "Annual Earnings of Boston Fishermen in 1951," *Monthly Labor Review* 74, no. 6 (June 1952): 668–669; Mulkern, "Annual Earnings," p. 6; Ackert, personal communication; Norton and Miller, "An Economic Study," pp. 21, 31.

59. Frederick W. Bell, "The Economics of the New England Fishing Industry: The Role of Technological Change and Government Aid," Research Report no. 31, Federal Reserve Bank of Boston, Boston, Mass., Feb. 1966, ch. 7; White, *The New England Fishing Industry*, pp. 19–27; "Hub of Knox County's Progressive Fishing Industry—Rockland: Host to the 13th Annual Maine Seafoods Festival," *National Fisherman* 40, no. 3 (July 1959): 21, 23; Federal Trade Commission, "Part VIII," *Report*, p. 8; Edward L. Lynch, Richard M. Doherty, and George P. Draheim, "The Groundfish Industries of New England and Canada," circ. 121, Fish and Wildlife Service, Department of Interior (Washington, D.C., FWS, July 1961), Table V-12, p. 167.

60. Peter K. Prybot, "Old-Line Gloucester Family 'Fishes' on Land and at Sea," *National Fisherman* 55, no. 9 (Jan. 1975): 9B, 16B; Jerry Murphy, "Gloucester's Brancaleones, New Dragger Owners, Are Veterans of Rugged Industry," *National Fisherman* 45, no. 5 (Sept. 1964): 22; Ross, personal communication; Area Redevelopment Administration, Department of Commerce, "A Technical Study of the Scallop and Flounder Industry of New Bedford, Mass.," Area Redevelopment Administration, New Bedford, Mass., 1964, p. 25; U.S., Congress, House of Representatives, Hearings before Committee on Merchant Marine and Fisheries, "Problems of the Fishing Industry," 81st Cong., 1st sess., Feb. 1949, pp. 49–50; Lord and Cushing, interviews.

61. Frank Mazzaglia, director, Gloucester Fisheries Association, Gloucester, Mass., personal communication, Sept. 1977; Norton and Miller, "An Economic Study," p. 34; Richard M. Doherty, G. Paul Draheim, Donald J. White, and Charles L. Vaughn, "Economic Study of Sea Scallop Production in the United States and Canada," *Fishery Industrial Research* 2, no. 3 (Nov. 1964): 60–61; Lord and Cushing, interviews.

62. For some years after World War II boats fished farther south during the worst winter months and landed their catches in New York City or in Virginia ports.

63. *Fishery Statistics of the United States*, 1945–1965; "New Bedford Fish and Shellfish Catch Sets New Record," *Atlantic Fisherman* 32, no. 1 (Feb. 1951): 44; "New Bedford Landings Set Value Record in 1952," *Atlantic Fisherman* 34, no. 1 (Feb. 1953): 26–27; "New Bedford Fourth in Nation in Value of Fish Landed," *Atlantic Fisherman* 35, no. 1 (Feb. 1954): 35; "New Bedford Ranks Third in Value of Fish Landed," *National Fisherman* 37, no. 10 (Feb. 1957): 46.

64. *Fishery Statistics of the United States*, 1945–1965; Jon Lawrence, "Scallop

Fleet, Landings Shrink in New Bedford," *National Fisherman* 47, no. 5 (Sept. 1966): 24B. Most scallop income went to the offshore fleet. In 1965 inshore boats landed no sea scallops in New Bedford. Numbers that distinguish between offshore and inshore are not available for earlier years (trip data tabulations, Northeast Fisheries Center).

65. *Fishery Statistics of the United States*, 1945–1965; trip data tabulations, Northeast Fisheries Center; "Rigging for Scallop Fishing Is Expensive Job."

66. Doherty *et al.*, "Economic Study," pp. 60–62; U.S., Department of Commerce, National Oceanic and Atmospheric Administration, National Marine Fisheries Service, *Scallops 1930–72: Basic Economic Indicators*, CFS no. 6127, June 1973, Table 1–2.

67. Doherty *et al.*, "Economic Study," pp. 60–62; Area Redevelopment Administration, "A Technical Study," pp. 11–13.

68. *Fishery Statistics of the United States*, 1945–1965. Inshore boats caught a share of the total weight of landings: 15 percent in 1947, 17 percent in 1950, only 3 percent in 1965. The inshore share of revenue was 14 percent in 1948, 3 percent in 1965 (trip data tabulations, Northeast Fisheries Center); O'Brien *et al.*, "Landings and Prices," various years.

69. *Ibid.*

70. O'Brien *et al.*, "Landings and Prices" (Market News Service), various years. The inshore fleet shrank as well—from thirty draggers (each less than fifty gross tons) and twenty line trawlers in 1947 to one dragger and seven line trawlers in 1965.

71. Lynch *et al.*, "Groundfish Industries," ch. 5, Tables V–7, V–8, V–10.

72. Norton and Miller, "An Economic Study," pp. 3, 14–18; Mulkern, "Annual Earnings."

73. *Fishery Statistics of the United States*, 1945–1965.

74. *Ibid.* In 1965 inshore boats harvested less than 4 percent of redfish sold in Gloucester. Before 1950 inshore boats probably depended on redfish more, but as stocks in the Gulf of Maine became scarce, boats moved farther offshore to the richer resource on the Nova Scotia banks, in the Gulf of St. Lawrence, and on the Grand Banks, far out of range of smaller boats (trip data tabulations, Northeast Fisheries Center; Kelly *et al.*, "Redfish," pp. 4, 6).

75. *Fishery Statistics of the United States*, 1955–1965.

76. O'Brien, "New England Whiting Fishery" (Market News Service), p. 4; *Fishery Statistics of the United States, 1945–1965*. In 1965, the only year for which data distinguished between inshore and offshore activity in Gloucester, offshore boats brought in 63 percent of the whiting catch (trip data tabulations, Northeast Fisheries Center).

77. *Fishery Statistics of the United States*, 1960–1965; Hall and McAvoy, "New England Fisheries" (Market News Service), p. 16. Almost all of the growth of haddock landings came from offshore boats. Inshore boats brought in only 9 percent of the haddock in 1965 (trip data tabulations, Northeast Fisheries Center).

78. ICNAF, "List of Fishing Vessels, 1965"; U.S. Tariff Commission,

"Groundfish: Fishing and Filleting" (Washington, D.C.: GPO, May 1957), Table 5, pp. 67–69; Lynch *et al.,* "Groundfish Industries," pp. 70–71. The trend in numbers of offshore vessels is approximate because the ICNAF number is for boats registered in Gloucester while the Tariff Commission numbers are for boats which landed fish in Gloucester.

79. U.S. Tariff Commission, "Groundfish," pp. 52–59; Lynch *et al.,* "Groundfish Industries," Table V–18; Salvatore Favazza, chairman, Gloucester Fisheries Commission, to Commission, Sept. 14, 1961 (files of the Commission, Gloucester, Mass.).

80. Hall and McAvoy, "New England Fisheries" (Market News Service), p. 40; *Fishery Statistics of the United States,* 1945–1965; U.S. Tariff Commission, "Groundfish," pp. 52–59, 69–71; Arthur N. Thurston, "Long Distance Ocean Perch Fishery Conducted on Big Scale by Me. Firm," *National Fisherman* 42, no. 4 (Aug. 1961): 24; "Hub of Knox County's Progressive Fishing Industry."

81. The following discussion draws on Lord and Cushing, interviews; Susan Peterson, policy associate, Marine Policy and Ocean Management Program, Woods Hole Oceanographic Institution, Woods Hole, Mass., personal communication, Feb. 1982; James Wilson, professor, Department of Economics, University of Maine, Orono, Me., personal communication, Feb. 1982. Other sources are noted.

82. U.S., Congress, House of Representatives, Hearings before Committee on Merchant Marine and Fisheries, "Fishing Vessel Subsidies," 88th Cong., 1st sess., Aug. 1963, pp. 70 ff.

83. Norton and Miller, "An Economic Study," pp. 33 ff.

84. Fishing Masters' Association, *Official Yearbook,* 1950; ICNAF, "List of Vessels, 1959."

85. U.S., Cong., "Problems of the Fishing Industry."

86. Haddock, cod, redfish, and silver hake (whiting) were the most important commercially; others were harvested as bycatch in fishing for the more valuable species. Cod, too, was landed principally as bycatch from the directed haddock fishery.

87. U.S. Tariff Commission, "Groundfish Fillets (1954): Report to the President on Escape-Clause Investigation no. 25" (Washington, D.C.: GPO, May 1954); U.S. Tariff Commission, "Groundfish Fillets (1956): Report to the President on Escape-Clause Investigation no. 47" (Washington, D.C.: GPO, Oct. 1956); hearings before Senate Committee on Interstate and Foreign Commerce and House Committee on Merchant Marine and Fisheries; statements by senators and congressmen in the *Congressional Record,* 1954–1956.

Chapter 3   Efforts at Revitalization

1. U.S., Congress, House of Representatives, Hearings before Committee on Merchant Marine and Fisheries, "Problems of the Fishing Industry," 81st Cong., 1st sess., Feb. 1949, pp. 14 ff.

2. U.S. Cong., "Problems of the Fishing Industry," pp. 56, 95–99; U.S., Congress, Senate, Hearings before Committee on Interstate and Foreign Commerce, "Fisheries Legislation," 84th Cong., 2d sess., March 1956, p. 164; John H. Fenton, "Future of Fishing Frets Northeast," *New York Times*, Sept. 25, 1951, p. 59. Information that follows on the New Englanders' view is from U.S. Cong., "Problems of the Fishing Industry."

3. U.S. Tariff Commission, "Groundfish Fillets: Report on the Escape-Clause Investigation," Report no. 182 (Washington, D.C.: GPO, 1953), p. 25; Donald J. White, *The New England Fishing Industry: A Study in Price and Wage Setting* (Cambridge, Mass.: Harvard University Press, 1954), pp. 125–126; U.S. Cong., "Problems of the Fishing Industry," p. 46.

4. Tariffs were quite high on salt fish by most standards, 25 percent ad valorem. White, *The New England Fishing Industry*, pp. 125–126; U.S., Congress, House of Representatives, Hearings before Committee on Merchant Marine and Fisheries, "Defining American Fishery," 76th Cong., 3d sess., April 1940.

5. White, *The New England Fishing Industry*, pp. 127 ff.; "Fish Folks Seek Tariff Increase, Smaller Imports," *Gloucester Daily Times*, Jan. 29, 1947, p. 1; "Present Tariff Rates on Fish May be Further Slashed 50%," *Gloucester Daily Times*, May 20, 1959, p. 1; House Resolution no. 147, *Congressional Record*, vol. 95, part 3 (April 4, 1949), p. 3821; "Effect of Foreign Competition on the United States Fishing Industry," House doc. 180, letter from Assistant Secretary of State transmitting a report authorized under House Resolution no. 147 with reference to the domestic fishing industry, 81st Cong., 1st sess., 1949; "Industry Leaving No Stone Unturned in Import Battle," *Gloucester Daily Times*, Feb. 21, 1949, p. 1; U.S., Congress, Senate, Hearings before Committee on Finance, "Trade Agreements Extension Act of 1951," 82d Cong., 1st sess., Feb.-April 1951, pp. 214 ff., 331 ff.

6. Don D. Humphrey, *American Imports* (New York: Twentieth Century Fund, 1955), p. 362n; Howard S. Piquet, *The Trade Agreements Act and the National Interest* (Washington, D.C.: Brookings Institution, 1958), pp. 15–17.

7. U.S. Tariff Commission, "Groundfish Fillets," 1953, pp. 2–19.

8. U.S. Tariff Commission, "Groundfish Fillets (1954): Report to the President on Escape-Clause Investigation no. 25" (Washington, D.C.: GPO, May 1954), pp. 4–5.

9. "Eisenhower Bars Higher Fish Duty," *New York Times*, July 3, 1954, p. 17.

10. "New Product Seen Spurring Fish Use," *New York Times*, Oct. 3, 1953, p. 26; "490 Now Work on Fish Sticks, Gloucester's Big New Product," *Gloucester Daily Times*, Dec. 14, 1953, p. 1.

11. "Fish Stick Production," *National Fisherman* 35, no. 5 (Sept. 1954): 9; U.S., Department of the Interior, Fish and Wildlife Service, *Fishery Statistics of the United States*, Statistical Digest no. 41 (1955); U.S., Department of Commerce, National Oceanic and Atmospheric Administration, National Marine Fisheries Service, *Fisheries of the United States, 1976* (Washington, D.C.: GPO, 1977), p. 64.

12. Fishing Masters' Association, *Official Yearbook of the Fishing Masters' Association* (Boston, Mass.: The Association, 1950, 1951); Fenton, "Future of Fishing"; U.S. Cong., "Fisheries Legislation," pp. 160 ff; James P. Clark, Jr., "Sharp Questions Bring Out Facts," *Gloucester Daily Times*, Oct. 23, 1953, p. 1.

13. U.S. Cong., "Fisheries Legislation," p. 281; James S. Carlson, Massachusetts Fisheries Association, Inc., and Boston Fisheries Cooperative, "Brief Filed with the United States Tariff Commission in Compliance with Section 7 of the Trade Agreements Extension Act," June 1956 (files of International Trade Commission, Washington, D.C.) pp. 3–4; "Fish Commission Airs Differences for Tariff Stand," *Gloucester Daily Times*, April 30, 1956, p. 1.

14. Articles on appeal to Tariff Commission, *Gloucester Daily Times*, April 17, June 17, and Oct. 19, 22, 23, 1953; "Boat Owners Resent Reverses on Tariff," *Gloucester Daily Times*, July 7, 1954, p. 1.

15. "Low Duty on Fish Sticks," *Atlantic Fisherman* 35, no. 3 (April 1954): 8; "Duty on Fish Sticks," *National Fisherman* 35, no. 3 (July 1954): 9; Amendment offered by Senator Leverett Saltonstall, *Congressional Record*, 83rd Cong., 2d sess., vol. 100, part 11 (Aug. 11 and 16, 1954), pp. 14009, 14629. The fish stick industry also succeeded in preventing the reduction of fish stick tariffs during the next few years (articles on fish stick duties, *Gloucester Daily Times*, March 26 and 28, 1955).

16. Secretary of State Dean Acheson in U.S. Cong., "Trade Agreements Extension Act of 1951," pp. 3 ff.; "Boat Owners Resent Reverses on Tariff," p. 6.

17. Piquet, *Trade Agreements Act*, pp. 12–18; Humphrey, *American Imports*, pp. 113–114; Dwight D. Eisenhower, "The Trade Agreements Program—Its Relation to National Well-Being and Security," Department of State Publication no. 6640 (Washington, D.C.: GPO, 1958).

18. "Canada Warns U.S. on Import Curbs," *New York Times*, July 21, 1953, p. 6; "Canada Reassured on Imports to U.S.," *New York Times*, Aug. 13, 1953, p. 28.

19. U.S. Tariff Commission, "Groundfish Fillets (1956): Report to the President on Escape-Clause Investigation no. 47" (Washington, D.C.: GPO, Oct. 1956), pp. 3–4; "Text of Eisenhower Letter on Tariff," *New York Times*, Dec. 11, 1956, p. 35.

20. U.S., Congress, House of Representatives, Report of the Committee on Ways and Means, "Trade Agreements Extension Act of 1955," 84th Cong., 1st sess., Feb. 14, 1955, p. 28; Humphrey, *American Imports*, pp. 371–373; W. H. Laurence, "President Bars Tariff Rise on Fish to Assist 3 Allies," *New York Times,* Dec. 11, 1956, p. 1; "New Policy Seen in Veto on Tariff," *New York Times*, Dec. 16, 1956, sec. 3, p. 1; "Fillets and Tariffs," editorial, *New York Times,* Dec. 13, 1956, p. 36; "President Reaffirms Liberal Trade Policy," *New York Times*, Dec. 16, 1956, sec. 4, p. 7.

21. "President Reaffirms Liberal Trade Policy"; "New Policy Seen in Veto on Tariff"; Laurence, "President Bars Tariff Rise"; U.S., Congress, House of Representatives, Hearings before Committee on Merchant Marine and Fisheries, "New England Fisheries Subsidies," 85th Cong., 2d sess., May-June 1958, pp. 5

ff.; James D. Ackert, fishery policy specialist, Gorton Corporation, Gloucester, Mass., personal communication, March 1978.

22. "Gloucestermen Seek Meeting with President," *National Fisherman* 42, no. 4 (Aug. 1961): 3; "Resolution to Protect the American Fresh Groundfish Producer," adopted by the Gloucester Fisheries Commission, Oct. 14, 1963 (files of the Commission, Gloucester, Mass.); Salvatore Favazza, "Fresh Fish Irradiation (Blessing or Curse?)" (reprint from *The Master Mariner*, 1967, in files of Gloucester Fisheries Commission, Gloucester, Mass.); "Brief of the New England Association for the Preservation of the Groundfish Industry," before U.S. Tariff Commission, Groundfish Fillets Investigation under sec. 221, Trade Expansion Act of 1962, Jan. 28, 1964; U.S. Department of Commerce, National Oceanic and Atmospheric Administration, National Marine Fisheries Service, *Atlantic and Pacific Groundfish 1932–72: Basic Economic Indicators*, Current Fisheries Statistics (hereafter CFS) no. 6271, Table X-2; House of Representatives bill no. 8048, introduced by Representative Bates, April 5, 1967, and referred to Committee on Ways and Means, 90th Cong., 1st sess. (files of the Gloucester Fisheries Commission, Gloucester, Mass.); *Congressional Record*, 1967. The fears about irradiation were premature. Research did not produce commercially useful techniques for irradiating fish until the late 1970s (John Kaylor, supervisor, food research, Gloucester Laboratory, National Marine Fisheries Service, Gloucester, Mass., personal communication, Jan. 1980).

23. U.S., Congress, House of Representatives, Hearings before Committee on Ways and Means, "Foreign Trade and Tariff Proposals," part 7, 90th Cong., 2d sess., June and July 1968, pp. 3387 ff.; "3 Sections of N.E. Fishing Industry Join in Move to Restrict Imports," *National Fisherman* 48, no. 12 (April 1968): 26A.

24. "Gloucester Boatowner Groups Merge to Improve Industry," *National Fisherman* 35, no. 4 (Aug. 1954): 44; U.S., Cong., "New England Fisheries Subsidies," pp. 87 ff.; John J. O'Brien, "Landings and Prices of Fishery Products, Boston Fish Pier, 1956" (Bureau of Commercial Fisheries, Market News Service, Boston, Mass.), p. x; O'Brien, "Landings and Prices of Fishery Products, Boston Fish Pier, 1957" (Bureau of Commercial Fisheries, Market News Service, Boston, Mass.), p. 11; Thomas A. Fulham, president, Suffolk University, Boston, Mass., personal communication, March 1980.

25. White, *The New England Fishing Industry*, p. 145; "Mass. Fish Industry Needs New Outlook Investors Club Told," *Gloucester Daily Times*, Jan. 3, 1955, p. 8.

26. Fulham, personal communication; Francis Sargent, former governor of Massachusetts, Boston, Mass., personal communication, March 1980; Ackert, personal communication. Except where otherwise indicated, information that follows on state efforts draws on interviews with Fulham and Sargent.

27. "Annual Report of the Atlantic States Marine Fisheries Commission to the Congress of the United States and to the Governors and Legislators," Atlantic States Marine Fisheries Commission, Washington, D.C., 1942–1970;

testimony by representatives of Atlantic States Marine Fisheries Commission before House Committee on Merchant Marine and Fisheries and Senate Committee on Interstate and Foreign Commerce, 1950s and 1960s; "Massachusetts Committee to Study Problems of Industry," *Atlantic Fisherman* 35, no. 3 (April 1954): 22.

28. O'Brien, "Landings and Prices, 1956," p. ix; Massachusetts Purchasing Office, Boston, Mass., personal communication, March 1980; Massachusetts Division of Marine Fisheries, Boston, Mass., personal communication, March 1980.

29. U.S. Cong., "New England Fisheries Subsidies," p. 83.

30. U.S., Congress, House of Representatives, Hearings before Committee on Banking and Currency, "To Provide Loans Through Reconstruction Finance Corporation," 73rd Cong., 2d sess., Feb.-March 1934, p. 116; U.S., Congress, House of Representatives, Hearings before Committee on Merchant Marine, Radio, and Fisheries, "Rehabilitation of the Fishing Industry," 73rd Cong., 2d sess., Feb.-March 1934, pp. 5–20; U.S., Congress, Senate, Hearings before Committee on Interstate and Foreign Commerce, "To Encourage the Distribution of Fishery Products," 83rd Cong., 2d sess., April 1954, p. 106; see *Congressional Record* during 1950s and 1960s.

31. White, *The New England Fishing Industry*, p. 120; "Fishing Vessel Owners Asking for Subsidies," *Gloucester Daily Times*, Aug. 5, 1948, p. 1; "Price Support," *Atlantic Fisherman* 31, no. 3 (April 1950): 9; "Resolution Favors Fish Price Support," *Gloucester Daily Times*, July 19, 1954, p. 1.

32. Fulham, personal communication.

33. U.S. Cong., "New England Fisheries Subsidies," p. 55.

34. *Ibid.*, p. 39; U.S., Congress, House of Representatives, Hearings before Committee on Merchant Marine and Fisheries, "Assistance to Depressed Segments of the Fishing Industry," 86th Cong., 1st sess., April and June 1959, pp. 94, 55, 73.

35. Public Law (hereafter referred to as P.L.) 466, Ch. 447, 83rd Cong., 2d sess., 1954.

36. O'Brien, "Landings and Prices, 1956" (Market News Service), pp. xi, xiii, xiv.

37. U.S., Congress, Senate, Hearings before Committee on Commerce, "Fishery Products Protection Act of 1967," 90th Cong., 1st sess., July 1967, pp. 114–115; U.S., Congress, House of Representatives, Hearings before Committee on Merchant Marine and Fisheries, "Fishery Products Protection" in "Fish and Wildlife Legislation," part 3, 90th Cong., 2d sess., Feb. 1968.

38. "Fishery Research Funds Increased by $3½ Million," *National Fisherman* 37, no. 11 (March 1957): 13; U.S., Department of Interior, Fish and Wildlife Service, "Fish and Shellfish Preferences of Household Consumers—1951," Fishery Leaflets, nos. 407, 408, 409, 410; Richard A. Kahn and Walter H. Stolting, "Household Consumer Preferences for Breaded Shrimp and Breaded Fish Sticks," Fishery Leaflets, nos. 424, 425, 426 (U.S., Department of Interior,

Fish and Wildlife Service, 1956); U.S., Department of Commerce, Bureau of Commercial Fisheries, "Fish and Shellfish Consumption in Public Eating and Drinking Places," Special Scientific Report—Fisheries no. 295, March 1959.

39. "New England Market Reseach," *National Fisherman* 38, no. 12 (April 1958): 7; "How Saltonstall-Kennedy Funds Aid Industry," *National Fisherman* 36, no. 4 (Aug. 1955): 44.

40. Ackert, personal communication, March 1978; O'Brien, "Landings and Prices" (Market News Service), 1956," p. ix; "Fishery Research Funds Increased," p. 13; U.S., Congress, House of Representatives, Hearings before Committee on Merchant Marine and Fisheries, "Study of the Operations of the Fish and Wildlife Service," 84th Cong., 1st sess., March 1955, p. 143.

41. James L. McCloskey, public affairs officer, Defense Personnel Support Center, Philadelphia, Pa., personal communication, March 1980; Fulham, personal communication; data compiled by Defense Personnel Support Center, Philadelphia, Pa., March 1980; *Fishery Statistics of the United States*, 1966.

42. William Thornton, School Programs Division, Food and Nutrition Service, Department of Agriculture, Washington, D.C., personal communication, April 1980; Thomas O'Hearn, director, Bureau of Nutrition Education and School Food Services, Massachusetts Department of Education, Boston, Mass., personal communication, May 1980.

43. Warner C. Danforth and Chris A. Theodore, "Hull Insurance and Protection and Indemnity Insurance of Commercial Fishing Vessels," Special Scientific Report—Fisheries no. 241 (Fish and Wildlife Service, Department of Interior, Washington, D.C., Dec. 1957), p. 314; "Massachusetts Boat Owners Seek Insurance Aid," *National Fisherman* 38, no. 8 (Dec. 1957): 25; "Gloucester Vessel Owners Seek Solution to Insurance Problems," *National Fisherman* 37, no. 12 (April 1957): 38; "Massachusetts Committee on Fisheries Discusses Insurance," *Atlantic Fisherman* 35, no. 4 (May 1954): 50.

44. U.S., Congress, House of Representatives, Hearings before Committee on Merchant Marine and Fisheries, "Review of Fish and Wildlife Service," 85th Cong., 2d sess., June 1958, pp. 61–62; "Safety in the Fishing Industry," *New England Business Review*, Oct. 1958, pp. 1–4; John J. Murray, "Safety for the Commercial Fishing Vessel and Crew," *Commercial Fisheries Review* 30, no. 6 (June 1968): 46–52.

45. John J. Murray, retired fishing vessel safety officer for New England, Arlington, Mass., personal communication, May 1980.

46. Darrel A. Nash and Morton M. Miller, "Insurance Coverage for U.S. Commercial Fishing Vessels—A Survey of Current Insurance Costs, Availability and Other Special Problems," File Manuscript no. 74, Economic Research Laboratory, National Marine Fisheries Service, Dec. 1970, Appendix Table A-4; Murray, "Safety for Commercial Fishing Vessel and Crew," pp. 46–47; Edward L. Lynch, Richard M. Doherty, and George P. Draheim, "The Groundfish Industries of New England and Canada," circ. 121 (Fish and Wildlife Service, Dept. of Interior, Washington, D.C., July 1961), pp. 65–66.

47. U.S., Cong., "New England Fisheries Subsidies," p. 55; "Massachusetts Boat Owners Seek Insurance Aid"; U.S., Congress, House of Representatives, Hearings before Committee on Merchant Marine and Fisheries, "Increased Assistance to Commercial Fisheries," 91st Cong., 2d sess., Feb. 1970.

48. U.S., Cong., "Fisheries Legislation," p. 121; U.S., Congress, House of Representatives, Hearings before Committee on Merchant Marine and Fisheries, "Training of Fishing Personnel," 84th Cong., 2d sess., June 1956; "Fisheries College on Atlantic Coast," *Atlantic Fisherman* 33, no. 9 (Oct. 1952): 5.

49. P.L. 1027, ch. 1039, 84th Cong., 2d sess., 1956; "Gloucester Fishing Students Won't Have to Hunt for Jobs," *National Fisherman* 44, no. 12 (April 1964): 34; R. Anthony Barnes, "Meeting the Challenge: Marine Technology Thrives at MVTI," *National Fisherman* 43, no. 10 (Feb. 1963): 24.

50. John J. Murray, "On-the-Job Training Program for Trainee Commercial Fisherman," *Commercial Fisheries Review* 27, no. 4 (April 1965): 9–11; Robert A. Hall and Henry R. McAvoy, "New England Fisheries—Annual Summary, 1963" (Bureau of Commercial Fisheries, Market News Service, Boston, Mass., 1964), p. 19; John J. O'Brien, "New England Fisheries—Annual Summary, 1964" (Bureau of Commercial Fisheries, Market News Service, Boston, Mass., 1965), p. 16; John J. O'Brien and Henry R. McAvoy, "New England Fisheries—Annual Summary, 1965," (Bureau of Commercial Fisheries, Market News Service, Boston, Mass., 1966), p. 15; James D. Ackert, "Comment," in Frederick W. Bell and Jared E. Hazleton, eds., *Recent Developments and Research in Fisheries Economics* (Dobbs Ferry, N.Y.: Oceana Publications, 1967).

51. U.S. Cong., "To Encourage Distribution of Fishery Products," pp. 63–70.

52. U.S. Cong., "Study of the Operations of the Fish and Wildlife Service," p. 2; "Frozen-at-Sea Round Fish Landed at Boston," *Atlantic Fisherman* 33, no. 6 (July 1952): 14–15; "Freezing Fish Aboard Ship," *Atlantic Fisherman* 35, no. 4 (May 1954): 5.

53. U.S., Congress, House of Representatives, Hearings before Committee on Appropriations, "Department of Interior and Related Agencies Appropriations for 1956," 84th Cong., 1st sess., Feb. 1955, and "Department of Interior and Related Agencies Appropriations for 1957," 84th Cong., 2d sess., Jan. 1956; U.S. Cong., "Review of Fish and Wildlife Service"; Sumner M. Rosen, "An Economic Analysis of Freezing Fish at Sea," *Commercial Fisheries Review* 20, no. 11 (Nov. 1958): 1–14. The results of research on freezing fish at sea were reported in detail in *Commercial Fisheries Review* from Feb. 1952 through late 1955.

54. P.L. 1027, ch. 1039; "Commercial Fisheries Research and Development Act of 1964," P.L. 88–309, 88th Cong., 2d sess., 1964; "National Sea Grant College and Program Act of 1966," P.L. 94-461, 94th Cong., 2d sess., 1966; meetings of the New England Fisheries Development Program, Boston, Mass., 1977.

55. U.S. Cong., "Training of Fishing Personnel," pp. 14–15; H. V. R. Palmer, Jr., "The Red Crab Potentially Profitable," *National Fisherman* 55, no. 13 (April 30, 1975): 28–29; Neil K. Williams, "Costs and Benefits of Completed

Fishery Development Projects," Task Force Report no. 10, National Marine Fisheries Service, May 17, 1979.

56. Frederick W. Bell, "The Economics of the New England Fishing Industry," Research Report no. 31, Federal Reserve Bank, Boston, Mass., Feb. 1966, ch. 6; U.S. Cong., "Review of Fish and Wildlife Service," p. 65; Herbert W. Graham, "A Minimum Net-Mesh Size for the New England Haddock Fishery," *Commercial Fisheries Review* 14, no. 12 (Dec. 1952): 1–5.

57. U.S. Cong., "Fisheries Legislation," p. 279.

58. U.S. Cong., "New England Fisheries Subsidies," especially pp. 81, 145; U.S., Congress, Senate, Hearings before Committee on Interstate and Foreign Commerce, "Fisheries Legislation," 85th Cong., 2d sess., July 1958; U.S. Cong., "Assistance to Depressed Segments of the Fishing Industry"; U.S., Congress, Senate, Hearings before Committee on Interstate and Foreign Commerce, "Fishery and Wildlife Legislation," 86th Cong., 1st sess., Aug. 1959.

59. "Fish and Wildlife Act of 1956," P.L. 1024, 84th Cong., 2d sess., 1956, sec. 4.

60. U.S. Cong., "Fisheries Legislation," 1958, pp. 136–137; U.S. Cong., "New England Fisheries Subsidies," pp. 137–138; Edward J. Raymond, director, Financial Assistance Division for Northeast Region, National Marine Fisheries Service, Gloucester, Mass., personal communication, Sept. 1978.

61. U.S., Congress, Senate, Hearings before Committee on Commerce, "Fisheries Legislation—1965," 89th Cong., 1st sess., May 1965, p. 99; U.S., Congress, House of Representatives, Hearings before Committee on Merchant Marine and Fisheries, "Fisheries Loans" in "Miscellaneous Fish and Wildlife Legislation, 1965," 89th Cong., 1st sess., May 1965, pp. 16 ff.

62. 706 loans went to boat owners in the National Marine Fisheries Service's Northeast Region which covers coastal states from Maine through North Carolina. Edward Raymond, director of the Financial Assistance Division for the Northeast, estimates that half the total went to New England owners. Raymond says 75 to 100 loans went to big boats. Records of the Financial Assistance Division in Washington, D.C., show 154 loans to boats in the Boston, Gloucester, New Bedford, and Portland areas, but some of these boats must have fished inshore. Twenty-nine percent of the loans to the four ports went to New Bedford; between 1957 and 1971, 32 percent of the applications for loans from Boston, Gloucester, and New Bedford came from New Bedford. Raymond, personal communication; Fred J. O'Hara, financial assistance specialist, Financial Services Division, National Oceanic and Atmospheric Administration, Washington, D.C., personal communication, Oct. 4, 1978; O'Brien *et al.*, "Landings and Prices" (Market News Service) and "New England Fisheries" (Market News Service), 1957–1971.

63. Frederick W. Bell, "The Upgrading of Fishing Vessels: Some Research and Recommendations," Policy Position Paper no. 1: Financial Assistance, File Manuscript no. 119, Economic Research Laboratory, National Marine Fisheries Service, Nov. 1972.

64. "Mortgage and Loan Insurance," Fishery Leaflet no. 499, Branch of Loans and Grants, Bureau of Commercial Fisheries, Department of Interior, 1960; U.S., Congress, House of Representatives, Hearings before Committee on Merchant Marine and Fisheries, "Fish and Wildlife Legislation," 86th Cong., 2d sess., March and June 1960, pp. 66 ff., 71; National Marine Fisheries Service, *Atlantic and Pacific Groundfish 1932–72*, Table XI-1; Raymond, personal communication. The program could insure mortgages bearing interest of 5 or 6 percent. These rates were in line with the interest on other kinds of investments during most of the 1960s.

65. P.L. 86-516, 86th Cong., 2d sess., 1960, sec. 4.

66. U.S., Congress, House of Representatives, Hearings before Committee on Merchant Marine and Fisheries, "Fishing Vessel Subsidies," 88th Cong., 1st sess., Aug. and Nov. 1963, pp. 146–147, 53.

67. "United States Fishing Fleet Improvement Act," P.L. 88-498, 88th Cong., 2d sess., 1964.

68. U.S., Congress, House of Representatives, Hearings before Committee on Merchant Marine and Fisheries, "U.S. Fishing Fleet Improvement Act," 91st Cong., 1st sess., June 1969, pp. 64, 39.

69. U.S. Cong., "Fishing Vessel Subsidies," p. 14; U.S. Cong., "U.S. Fishing Fleet Improvement Act," p. 10; U.S., Congress, Senate, Hearings before Committee on Commerce, "Fishing Vessel Construction," 88th Cong., 1st sess., May 1963. The total U.S. harvest had fallen from 4.8 billion pounds in 1949 to 4.3 billion pounds in 1969 *(Fishery Statistics of the United States*, 1969).

70. Joseph Slavin, deputy director of Utilization and Development, National Marine Fisheries Service, Washington, D.C., personal communication, May 1980; U.S. Cong., "U.S. Fishing Fleet Improvement Act," p. 18.

71. U.S. Cong., "U.S. Fishing Fleet Improvement Act," p. 18.

72. P.L. 88-498, sec. 9(7); U.S. Cong., "U.S. Fishing Fleet Improvement Act," pp. 39–40; U.S., Congress, "Interior Department and Related Agencies Appropriations," 1966–1969, sections on the budget of the Bureau of Commercial Fisheries.

73. International Commission for the Northwest Atlantic Fisheries (hereinafter ICNAF), "List of Fishing Vessels, 1971, with Summaries of Fishing Effort for 1969, 1970, and 1971," ICNAF, Dartmouth, Nova Scotia, Canada, 1972; *Fishery Statistics of the United States*, 1969.

74. John Frye, "Seafreeze Ships Have Huge Handling Capacities," *National Fisherman* 49, no. 8 (Dec. 1968): 20A–22A.

75. John Frye, "Owners of 294' Factoryship Accept Challenge," *National Fisherman* 49, no. 6 (Oct. 1968): 15C.

76. *Ibid.*; Ackert, personal communication.

77. Ackert, personal communication; Burton T. Coffey, "Seafreeze Atlantic Ship of Fools to Crewman," *National Fisherman* 53, no. 1 (May 1972): 5C.

78. Ackert, personal communication; U.S. Cong., "U.S. Fishing Fleet Improvement Act," p. 18.

79. Ackert, personal communication.

80. *Ibid.*; Coffey, "Seafreeze Atlantic," pp. 4C–7C; Bill Cahill, "Remember the Seafreeze? The Factory Ship May Make a Comeback," *Gloucester Daily Times*, Jan. 4, 1980, p. 16.

81. Ackert, personal communication.

82. U.S., Congress, House of Representatives, Hearings before Committee on Merchant Marine and Fisheries, "Seafreeze Atlantic" in "Fish and Wildlife Miscellaneous—Part 1," 94th Cong., 1st sess., June 5, 1975.

83. *Fishery Statistics of the United States*, 1950; U.S., Department of Commerce, Bureau of the Census, *Historical Statistics of the United States* (Washington, D.C.: GPO, 1975), ser. D 26–28. The following analysis of the industry's success in getting help from the federal government draws from debate on fishery legislation in the *Congressional Record*, hearings before the Senate Committee on Commerce and the House Committee on Merchant Marine and Fisheries, and interviews with several leaders of the industry's efforts to get help during the 1950s and 1960s.

84. *Congressional Record*, vol. 105 (Aug. 26, 1959), 86th Cong., 1st sess., p. 17048.

85. *Congressional Record*, vol. 100 (May 14, 1954), 83rd Cong., 2d sess., p. 6583; *Congressional Record*, vol. 105 (Aug. 26 and Sept. 11, 1959), 86th Cong., 1st sess., pp. 17048, 19058.

86. *Cong. Record*, vol. 100 (May 14, 1954), pp. 6587, 6583.

87. *Cong. Record*, vol. 100 (May 14, 1954), p. 6586.

88. *Congressional Record*, vol. 102 (May 24, 1956), 84th Cong., 2d sess., p. 8938; *Cong. Record*, vol. 105 (Sept. 11, 1959), p. 19058.

89. *Cong. Record*, vol. 105 (Aug. 26, 1959), p. 17038.

90. *Cong. Record*, vol. 100 (May 14, 1954), p. 6583; *Cong. Record*, vol. 105 (Sept. 11, 1959), p. 19055; *Cong. Record*, vol. 102 (May 21, 1956), p. 8542.

91. *Cong. Record*, vol. 105 (Aug. 26, 1959), p. 17038; *Cong. Record*, vol. 102 (May 24, 1956), p. 8941.

92. *Cong. Record*, vol. 102 (July 2, 1956), p. 11625; *Congressional Record*, vol. 109 (Oct. 2, 1963), 88th Cong., 1st sess., pp. 18556, 18557, 18560; *Cong. Record*, vol. 105 (Sept. 11, 1959), p. 19062.

93. *Cong. Record*, vol. 102 (July 2, 1956), p. 11627.

94. *Cong. Record*, vol. 100 (May 14, 1954), p. 6612.

95. *Cong. Record*, vol. 105 (Aug. 26, 1959), p. 17044; *Congressional Record*, vol. 110 (Aug. 14, 1964), 88th Cong., 2d sess., p. 19699.

96. *Cong. Record*, vol 102 (July 2, 1956), p. 11628; *Congressional Record*, vol. 110 (Aug. 14, 1964), p. 19703.

97. *Cong. Record*, vol. 100 (May 14, 1954), p. 6610.

98. *Cong. Record*, vol. 102 (July 7, 1956), p. 12046.

99. Title 50, ch. 2F, part 255, *Federal Register*, 39, no. 97 (May 17, 1974); P.L. 91-469, 91st Cong., 2d sess., 1970, sec. 607; O'Brien, "New England Fisheries—Annual Summary, 1969" (Market News Service), p. 2, "1970," p. 2.

Chapter 4   The Shortcomings of Intervention

1. U.S., Department of the Interior, Fish and Wildlife Service, *Fishery Statistics of the United States*, Statistical Digest, no. 39 (1954); U.S., Department of the Interior, Bureau of Commercial Fisheries, *Fishery Statistics of the United States*, Statistical Digest, no. 59 (1965); U.S., Department of Commerce, Bureau of the Census, *Statistical Abstract of the United States* (Washington, D.C.: GPO, 1957 and 1966); Virgil J. Norton and Morton M. Miller, "An Economic Study of the Boston Large-Trawler Labor Force," circ. 248, Bureau of Commercial Fisheries, Fish and Wildlife Service, Department of the Interior, Washington, D.C., May 1966, p. 14.

2. "Weakness of the U.S. Fisheries Policy Emphasized," *National Fisherman* 53, no. 5 (Sept. 1962): 11; "Saltonstall Urges Fisheries Help," *National Fisherman* 56, no. 1 (May 1965): 2; "Crowther Urges Subsidy Boost," *National Fisherman* 57, no. 12 (April 1967): 3A; "Crowther Sees Little Letup in Fisheries Problems," *National Fisherman* 58, no. 4 (Aug. 1967): 10C.

3. James L. McCloskey, public affairs officer, Defense Personnel Support Center, Philadelphia, Pa., personal communication, March 1980; Edward J. Raymond, director, Financial Assistance Division for Northeast Region, National Marine Fisheries Service, Gloucester, Mass., personal communication, Sept. 1978.

4. "490 Now Work on Fish Sticks, Gloucester's Big New Product," *Gloucester Daily Times*, Dec. 14, 1953, p. 1; Thomas O'Hearn, director, Bureau of Nutrition Education and School Food Services, Massachusetts Department of Education, Boston, Mass., personal communication, May 1980.

5. Thomas Fulham remembered that the Defense Department did buy more New England fish after they announced they would do so (Thomas A. Fulham, president, Suffolk University, Boston, Mass., personal communication, March 1980).

6. U.S., Congress, Senate, Hearings before Committee on Commerce, "Fishery Products Protection Act of 1967," 90th Cong., 1st sess., July 1967, p. 64.

7. U.S. Cong., "Fishery Products Protection Act," pp. 1, 21, 114; Gloucester Fisheries Commission, "Yes 'Wholesome Fish' Legislation But . . . ," 1967 (files of the Commission, Gloucester, Mass.); Louis J. Ronsivalli, director, Gloucester Laboratory, National Marine Fisheries Service, Gloucester, Mass., personal communication, March 1980.

8. *Fishery Statistics of the United States*, 1970–1973.

9. U.S., Congress, House of Representatives, Hearings before Committee on Merchant Marine and Fisheries, "Manpower Shortage in the Fishery Industry," 78th Cong., 2d sess., March and May 1944, pp. 24, 67; Donald J. White, *The New England Fishing Industry: A Study in Price and Wage Setting* (Cambridge, Mass.: Harvard University Press, 1954), p. 25.

10. *Fishery Statistics of the United States*, 1941–46, 1953; Fulham, personal communication.

11. U.S. Tariff Commission, "Groundfish: Fishing and Filleting" (Washington, D.C.: GPO, May 1957), Table 27, p. 82.

12. John A. Fulham's testimony to the U.S. Tariff Commission at its investigation of groundfish fillets, 1951 (files of International Trade Commission, Washington, D.C.), pp. 190–191; White, *The New England Fishing Industry*, p. 25.

13. Richard A. Kahn and Walter H. Stolting, "Consumer Preferences for Breaded Shrimp and Fish Sticks," part 1, "National and Regional Summary," Fishery Leaflet no. 424 (U.S., Department of Interior, Fish and Wildlife Service, July 1955), p. 40. In the mid-1960s as much as 87 percent of the Boston catch may have been consumed in the Northeast; see Frederick L. Gaston and David A. Storey, "The Market for Fresh Fish That Originates from Boston Fish Pier Landings," in Frederick W. Bell and Jared E. Hazleton, eds., *Recent Developments and Research in Fisheries Economics* (Dobbs Ferry, N.Y.: Oceana Publications, 1967), pp. 65–81.

14. "Report of the Secretary of the Interior to the President and the Congress on the Effects of Imports on the United States Groundfish Industry," Washington, D.C., May 1969, p. 41; Frederick W. Bell, "The Pope and the Price of Fish," *American Economic Review* 58, no. 5, part 1 (Dec. 1968): 1346–1350. Many studies have analyzed the demand for groundfish during the 1950s and 1960s, but they do not make conclusions possible about the role of imports. Most analyses depend on equations which suffer from identification problems. Some also leave out important variables, use price and quantity from different market levels, or use quantity as the dependent variable although the single equation form implies that quantity is not influenced by price (Margaret E. Dewar, "Industry in Trouble: Economics and Politics of the New England Fisheries," dissertation, Massachusetts Institute of Technology, Cambridge, Mass., Aug. 1979, pp. 171–178). The best demand study is by Bell in "The Pope and the Price of Fish," but the coefficients which show the effects of imports on ex-vessel groundfish prices are ambiguous, and problems of autocorrelation undermine the conclusions from statistical tests on the coefficients.

15. Fulham, personal communication; Bell, "The Pope and the Price of Fish." Autocorrelation in Bell's equations weakens his conclusion that the papal ruling caused a fall in demand for groundfish.

16. Raymond, personal communication.

17. U.S., Congress, House of Representatives, Hearings before Committee on Merchant Marine and Fisheries, "New England Fisheries Subsidies," 85th Cong., 2d sess., May-June 1958, pp. 137–138.

18. U.S., Congress, House of Representatives, Hearings before Committee on Merchant Marine and Fisheries, "Fishing Vessel Subsidies," 88th Cong., 1st sess., Aug. and Nov. 1963, p. 150; Leah J. Smith and Susan B. Peterson, "The New England Fishing Industry: A Basis for Management," Technical Report no. 77-57, Woods Hole Oceanographic Institution, Woods Hole, Mass., Aug. 1977, p. 44.

19. U.S., Congress, House of Representatives, Hearings before Committee

on Merchant Marine and Fisheries, "Assistance to Depressed Segments of the Fishing Industry," 86th Cong., 1st sess., April and June 1959, p. 49; John J. O'Brien, "New England Fisheries—Annual Summary, 1959" (Bureau of Commercial Fisheries, Market News Service, Boston, Mass.), p. 15.

20. U.S., Congress, House of Representatives, Hearings before Committee on Appropriations, "Department of Interior and Related Agencies Appropriations," for 1961–1965, sections on the budget of the Bureau of Commercial Fisheries.

21. U.S. Cong., "Department of Interior and Related Agencies Appropriations," for 1964–1969, sections on the budget of the Bureau of Commercial Fisheries, "Department of Interior and Related Agencies Appropriations for 1970," part 1, 91st Cong., 1st sess., Feb. 1969, p. 816.

22. U.S. Cong., "Fishing Vessel Subsidies," pp. 70 ff.; International Commission for the Northwest Atlantic Fisheries (hereafter ICNAF), "List of Vessels over 50 Gross Tons Fishing in the ICNAF Convention Area in 1962," ICNAF, Dartmouth, Nova Scotia, Canada, Jan. 1964; Ronald B. Harrison, "Fishermen Begin Feeling Effects of Subsidy," *National Fisherman* 45, no. 8 (Dec. 1965): 4; Raymond, personal communication.

23. U.S., Congress, House of Representatives, Hearings before Committee on Merchant Marine and Fisheries, "Study of the Operations of the Fish and Wildlife Service," 84th Cong., 1st sess., Mar. 1955, p. 2; Raymond, personal communication; Joseph Slavin, deputy director of utilization and development, National Marine Fisheries Service, Washington, D.C., personal communication, May 1980.

24. John J. Murray, retired fishing vessel safety officer for New England, Arlington, Mass., personal communication, May 1980.

25. Edward L. Lynch, Richard M. Doherty, and George P. Draheim, "The Groundfish Industries of New England and Canada," circ. 121, Fish and Wildlife Service, Department of the Interior, Washington, D.C., July 1961, pp. 65–66; Warner C. Danforth and Chris A. Theodore, "Hull Insurance and Protection and Indemnity Insurance of Commercial Fishing Vessels," Special Scientific Report—Fisheries no. 241, Fish and Wildlife Service, Department of Interior, Washingon, D.C., Dec. 1957, pp. 99–103.

26. Paul V. Mulkern, "Annual Earnings of Boston Fishermen in 1964," Bureau of Labor Statistics, Regional Report, Boston, Mass., Feb. 1966, p. 6; James D. Ackert, "Comment," in Bell and Hazleton, *Recent Developments*.

27. Ackert, "Comment," in Bell and Hazleton, *Recent Developments*; Burton T. Coffey, "Seafreeze Atlantic Ship of Fools to Crewman," *National Fisherman* 53, no. 1 (May 1972): 4C.

28. Norton and Miller, *An Economic Study*; Mulkern, "Annual Earnings."

29. U.S., Congress, House of Representatives, Hearings before Committee on Merchant Marine and Fisheries, "Miscellaneous Fish and Wildlife Legislation," 87th Cong., 1st sess., May–July 1961, p. 227; Ernest W. Carlson and Darrel A. Nash, "Administration of the Fisheries Loan Fund with Special Consideration of the 'Delinquency Problem,'" Policy Position Paper no. 3: Financial Assistance,

File Manuscript no. 121, Economic Research Laboratory, National Marine Fisheries Service, Dec. 1972. Estimated percent of defaults in groundfish industry from number of loans granted to New England groundfish boats, 1960–1972, and number in default by 1972 (U.S. Department of Commerce, National Oceanic and Atmospheric Administration, National Marine Fisheries Service, *Atlantic and Pacific Groundfish 1932–72: Basic Economic Indicators*, Current Fisheries Statistics no. 6271, Table XI-1).

30. U.S. Cong., "Fishing Vessel Subsidies," pp. 146–147, 53, 57; "Why Isn't Gloucester Seeking Subsidy?" *Master Mariner*, 1966, p. 28 (reprint from *The Master Mariner*, 1966, in files of Gloucester Fisheries Commission, Gloucester, Mass.); Jerry Murphy, "Gloucester's Brancaleones, New Dragger Owners, Are Veterans of Rugged Industry," *National Fisherman* 45, no. 5 (Sept. 1964): 22–23.

31. U.S. Cong., "Fishing Vessel Subsidies," pp. 71–75; Fulham, personal communication.

32. White, *The New England Fishing Industry*, chs. 3, 5; Federal Trade Commission, "Part VIII: Cost of Production and Distribution of Fish in New England," *Report of the Federal Trade Commission on Distribution Methods and Costs* (Washington, D.C.: GPO, 1945), p. 8; "Hub of Knox County's Progressive Fishing Industry—Rockland: Host to the 13th Annual Maine Seafoods Festival," *National Fisherman* 40, no. 3 (July 1959): 19 ff.

33. Fishing Masters' Association, *Official Yearbook of the Fishing Masters' Association* (Boston, Mass.: The Association, 1950); Fish and Wildlife Service, "Firms Producing Fish Sticks—1955," Washington, D.C., Feb. 1956; O'Brien *et al.*, "Landings and Prices of Fishery Products, Boston Fish Pier," 1950–1958 (Bureau of Commercial Fisheries, Market News Service, Boston, Mass.); O'Brien, "New England Fisheries—Annual Summary," 1959, 1960; ICNAF, "List of Vessels over 50 Gross Tons Fishing in the ICNAF Convention Area in 1959," ICNAF, Dartmouth, Nova Scotia, Canada, Nov. 1960; James D. Ackert, fishery policy specialist, Gorton Corporation, Gloucester, Mass., personal communication, March 1978; Lee White, aide to Governor Richard Lamm of Colorado, Denver, Colo., based on interviews of Gorton Corporation managers about their investment decisions, personal communication, Sept. 20, 1978. The Fulham family was an exception to the trend. They owned fish stick processing plants in Massachusetts and California in 1955, but they also planned the construction of new boats for Boston in the late 1950s.

34. O'Brien, "New England Fisheries—Annual Summary, 1959," p. 19.

35. U.S., Congress, Senate, Hearings before the Committee on Interstate and Foreign Commerce, "Fisheries Legislation," 84th Cong., 2d sess., March 1956, p. 164; Joseph Joyce, staff for market news reports, Market News Service, Boston, Mass., personal communication, Nov. 1978; Ackert, personal communication.

36. U.S. Tariff Commission, "Groundfish," pp. 58–61; White, *The New England Fishing Industry*, pp. 60–67; Mulkern, "Annual Earnings," pp. 4–5; Norton and Miller, "An Economic Study," pp. 11–12, 16.

37. White, *The New England Fishing Industry*, pp. 53, 73–75, 177; Fishing Masters' Association, *Official Yearbook*, 1950; General Foods Corporation, New

York, N.Y., annual reports, 1944–47, 1957; Ackert, personal communication; Jane Sullivan, senior corporation communications specialist, General Foods Corporation, White Plains, N.Y., personal communication, Nov. 10, 1978; Thomas J. Risoli, "Landings and Prices of Fishery Products, Boston Fish Pier, 1959" (Bureau of Commercial Fisheries, Market News Service, Boston, Mass.), p. v; "Hub of Knox County's Progressive Fishing Industry," p. 23.

38. White, *The New England Fishing Industry*, p. 177; "Maine Dragger Fleet Upgraded with Large New Steel Vessel," *The Fish Boat* 12, no. 10 (Oct. 1967): 38; Fishing Masters' Association, *Official Yearbook*, 1950; ICNAF, "List of Vessels, 1959."

39. Fulham, personal communication; Joyce, personal communication, Nov. 1977; Economic Resources Center, "Boats of Gloucester," Gloucester Fisheries Association, Gloucester, Mass., Jan. 1, 1978, with corrections; Smith and Peterson, "The New England Fishing Industry," pp. 28 ff.

40. Subsidy estimated from total number of offshore groundfish boats in New England and from differences in costs for a sample of boats. Lynch *et al.*, *Groundfish Industries*, Tables VI-7 and VI-7b.

41. U.S. Cong., "Fisheries Legislation," pp. 272, 274; U.S. Cong., "New England Fisheries Subsidies," pp. 15, 18.

42. U.S. Tariff Commission, "Groundfish Fillets (1956): Report to the President on Escape-Clause Investigation no. 47" (Washington, D.C.: GPO, Oct. 1956), p. 4.

43. *Fishery Statistics of the United States*, 1956; Dominion Bureau of Statistics, "Newfoundland" and "Nova Scotia," *Fisheries Statistics of Canada*, 1956–1960; Food and Agriculture Organization of the United Nations (hereafter FAO), "International Trade," *Yearbook of Fishery Statistics*, 1960–61, vol. 11 (Rome, Italy: FAO, 1962), Tables 1-C. Transportation costs are for 1960–1962 and are not available for other years (Frederick W. Bell, "The Economics of the New England Fishing Industry," Research Report no. 31, Federal Reserve Bank, Boston, Mass., Feb. 1966, p. 30).

44. FAO, *Yearbook of Fishery Statistics*, 1960–61, vol. 13, Tables 1-C; "Newfoundland" and "Nova Scotia," *Fisheries Statistics of Canada*, 1956–1960; *Fishery Statistics of the United States*, 1956. The cost estimate for the Canadian product is a maximum. It assumes tariffs increased prices by the full amount of the duty, that the above-quota tariff level was in effect, and that transportation costs from Nova Scotia were at their 1960–1962 level (Bell, "The Economics of the New England Fishing Industry," p. 30). Data on transportation costs are not available for other years.

45. *Ibid.*

46. "O'Hara Launches Subsidy Vessels," *National Fisherman* 52, no. 6 (Oct. 1971): 14A–15A; "Maine Dragger Fleet Upgraded with Large New Steel Vessel"; U.S., Congress, House of Representatives, Hearings before Committee on Merchant Marine and Fisheries, "U.S. Fishing Fleet Improvement Act," 91st Cong., 1st sess., June 1969, pp. 39–40; U.S. Cong., "Fishing Vessel Subsidies," p. 146; O'Brien *et al.*, "New England Fisheries—Annual Summary," 1963–1965;

ICNAF, "List of Fishing Vessels, 1971, with Summaries of Fishing Effort for 1969, 1970, and 1971," ICNAF, Dartmouth, Nova Scotia, Canada, 1972; "Fishermen Neglecting 'Big Catch,'" *National Fisherman* 52, no. 1 (May 1971): 6A.

47. ICNAF, "List of Fishing Vessels and Summary of Fishing Effort in the ICNAF Convention Area, 1965," ICNAF, Dartmouth, Nova Scotia, Canada, Jan. 1967; "Fishery Market News Report" (daily) (Bureau of Commercial Fisheries, Market News Service, Boston, Mass., 1966).

48. ICNAF, "List of Fishing Vessels and Summary, 1965"; John J. Murray, "Safety for the Commercial Fishing Vessel and Crew," *Commercial Fisheries Review* 30, no. 6 (June 1968): 46–47; U.S. Cong., "Fishing Vessel Subsidies," pp. 71–72.

49. The number of boats over sixty gross tons which used otter trawls to fish offshore in 1959 and were not based in New Bedford. Some of the boats may have fished for flounder, but, on the other hand, some of the New Bedford boats may have been in the groundfish industry (ICNAF, "List of Vessels, 1959").

50. Generalizations about levels of sustainable yield are probably truer for haddock than for cod, about which less in known. Frederick M. Serchuk, fishery biologist, Northeast Fisheries Center, National Marine Fisheries Service, Woods Hole, Mass., personal communication, Aug. 1978; Richard C. Hennemuth, "Status of the Georges Bank Haddock Fishery," ICNAF Research Document no. 69/90, June 1969; Steve Clark, "Current Status of the Georges Bank (5Ze) Haddock Stock," ICNAF Research Document no. 75/48, June 1975; New England Regional Fishery Management Council, "Atlantic Groundfish," Supplement no. 2 to Final Environmental Impact Statement, draft, May 1978, p. 9; ICNAF, "Research Reports by Member Countries," "United States Research Report, 1965," *Redbook*, part 2 (Dartmouth, Nova Scotia, Canada, Nov. 1966), pp. 109–111.

51. Clark, "Current Status," ICNAF, p. 2; ICNAF, *Redbook*, part 2, 1966, p. 109.

52. New England Regional Fishery Management Council, "Atlantic Groundfish," p. 9; Serchuk, personal communication.

53. Ralph K. Mayo, "A Preliminary Assessment of the Redfish Fishery in ICNAF Subarea 5," ICNAF Research Document no. 75/59, June 1975, pp. 3–6; Ralph K. Mayo, fishery biologist, Northeast Fisheries Center, National Marine Fisheries Service, Woods Hole, Mass., personal communication, Jan. 1978.

Chapter 5   *Foreign Fleets and Questions of Fisheries Control*

1. John. J. O'Brien, "New England Fisheries—Annual Summary, 1960" (Bureau of Commercial Fisheries, Market News Service, Boston, Mass.), p. 11; "Soviet Trawler is Discovered off L.I. near Polaris Submarine on Maneuvers," *New York Times*, April 30, 1960, p. 1; "Soviet Defector in U.S. Warns Moscow Has Nuclear-Raid Plan," *New York Times*, Sept. 15, 1960, p. 1.

2. "Red Fleet Sweeping Georges Bank," *National Fisherman* 42, no. 6 (Oct. 1961): 2; "Russian Vessels Push to Edge of U.S. Waters," *National Fisherman* 42, no. 8 (Dec. 1961): 3.

3. O'Brien, "New England Fisheries" (Market News Service), 1961, pp. 8–9; Robert A. Hall and Henry R. McAvoy, "New England Fisheries—Annual Summary, 1963" (Bureau of Commercial Fisheries, Market News Service, Boston, Mass.), p. 14; Leah J. Smith and Susan B. Peterson, "The New England Fishing Industry: A Basis for Management," Technical Report no. 77–57, Woods Hole Oceanographic Institution, Woods Hole, Mass., Aug. 1977, p. 16; U.S., Congress, House of Representatives, Hearings before Committee on Merchant Marine and Fisheries, "Fishing in U.S. Territorial Waters," 88th Cong., 2d sess., Feb. 1964, p. 50; Tim Sullivan, "The 200-Mile Limit: Three Views," *Gloucester Daily Times*, March 18, 1974, p. 13; U.S., Congress, Senate, Hearings before Committee on Commerce, "Interim Fisheries Zone Extension and Management Act of 1973," 93rd Cong., 2d sess., April–June 1974, p. 918.

4. U.S. Cong., "Fishing in U.S. Territorial Waters," p. 50; U.S. Cong., "Interim Fisheries Zone Extension and Management Act of 1973," p. 840; "Russian Vessels Push to Edge of U.S. Waters," p. 3.

5. Charles R. Hitz, "Catalogue of the Soviet Fishing Fleet," *National Fisherman* 48, no. 13 (April 30, 1968): 9–24; Comptroller General of the United States, "The U.S. Fishing Industry: Present Condition and Future of Marine Fisheries," vol. 2 (Washington, D.C.: GAO, Dec. 23, 1976), pp. 337–349, 360–371; Commander Adrian L. Lonsdale, "'No Contest' on the Fishing Grounds," in U.S. Naval Institute, *Proceedings*, vol. 94 (Annapolis, Md.: The Institute, July 1968), pp. 62–70.

6. U.S. Cong., "Fishing in U.S. Territorial Waters," p. 55; Lena Novello, member of Gloucester Fishermen's Wives Association, Gloucester, Mass., personal communication, Oct. 1978.

7. Smith and Peterson, "The New England Fishing Industry," pp. 16, 17; "Magnuson Fisheries Management and Conservation Act," Report of Senate Committee on Commerce on S.961, Oct. 7, 1975, in U.S., Congress, Senate, Committee on Commerce, " A Legislative History of the Fishery Conservation and Management Act of 1976," p. 669.

8. O'Brien *et al.*, "New England Fisheries—Annual Summary" (Bureau of Commercial Fisheries, Market News Service, Boston, Mass.), 1961–1971; "Soviets Plan Big Fleet Expansion; May Agree to Conservation Moves," *National Fisherman* 47, no. 8 (Dec. 1966): 4A; "Are NW Atlantic Banks Being Overfished?" *National Fisherman* 47, no. 8 (Dec. 1966): 3A; Richard C. Hennemuth, "Status of the Georges Bank Haddock Stock and Effects of Recent High Levels of Fishing Effort," International Commission for the Northwest Atlantic Fisheries (hereafter ICNAF), Research Document no. 68/92; "Haddock, Herring, Yellowtail Suffering from Overfishing," *National Fisherman* 52, no. 2 (June 1971): 1A.

9. "Are NW Atlantic Banks Being Overfished?" p. 3A; Charles Buffum,

"Haddock, Scallops to Be Scarcer on Banks in '67; Control Is Debated," *National Fisherman* 47, no. 10 (Feb. 1967): p. 15A; O'Brien, "New England Fisheries" (Market News Service), 1969 (p. 2), 1970 (p. 2).

10. U.S., Congress, House of Representatives, Hearings before Committee on Merchant Marine and Fisheries, "Fishing Vessel Subsidies," 88th Cong., 1st sess., Aug. 1963, pp. 62, 54.

11. The "bag" is the cod end of the net on a trawler. A "big bag" is a large catch of fish in a single trawl or just a large catch of fish. Meta Cushing, interviews with Gloucester fishermen and their wives, 1978–79; Salvatore Testaverde, fishery biologist, National Marine Fisheries Service, Gloucester, Mass., personal communication, Oct. 1978.

12. U.S. Cong., "Fishing Vessel Subsidies"; U.S., Congress, Senate, Hearings before Committee on Commerce, "Twelve-Mile Fishery Zone," 89th Cong., 2d sess., May 1966; U.S., Congress, House of Representatives, Hearings before Committee on Merchant Marine and Fisheries, "Fishing Rights" in "Miscellaneous Fisheries Legislation, Part 1," 89th Cong., 2d sess., May–June 1966.

13. U.S. Cong., "Fishing in U.S. Territorial Waters," pp. 175–176; O'Brien, "New England Fisheries" (Market News Service), 1969, p. 2; "Discussion of Industry Problems Aired at Gloucester Conference," *The Fish Boat* 18, no. 5 (May 1973): 21 ff.; Salvatore Favazza, "U.P.I.," undated (files of Gloucester Fisheries Commission, Gloucester, Mass.).

14. U.S., Congress, House of Representatives, Hearings before Committee on Merchant Marine and Fisheries, "Fishery Jurisdiction," 93rd Cong., 2d sess., May–Oct. 1974, pp. 511–512, 1; U.S. Cong., "Interim Fisheries Zone Extension and Management Act of 1973," pp. 52–53, 872, 129.

15. ICNAF, "List of Fishing Vessels, 1971, with Summaries of Fishing Effort for 1969, 1970, and 1971," ICNAF, Dartmouth, Nova Scotia, Canada, 1972; ICNAF, "List of Fishing Vessels, 1974," ICNAF, Dartmouth, Nova Scotia, Canada, 1976; John Enos, "Gloucester Skippers Diversify, Boost 1973 Landings Over Top," *National Fisherman* 54, no. 12 (April 1974): 13A; John Enos, "'74 Was Good to Gloucester Despite Inflation, Less Fish," *National Fisherman* 55, no. 13 (April 30, 1975): 71; James D. Ackert, fishery policy specialist, Gorton Corporation, Gloucester, Mass., personal communication, Sept. 1977; tabulations of trip data for 1974 and 1976, National Marine Fisheries Service, Northeast Fisheries Center, Woods Hole, Mass.; Sullivan, "The 200-Mile Limit: Three Views," p. 13; Brooks Townes, "New England Fishing—Back from the Brink?" *National Fisherman* 49, no. 13 (April 30, 1975): 22.

16. Thomas A. Fulham, president, Suffolk University, Boston, Mass., personal communication, March 1980.

17. Sullivan, "The 200-Mile Limit: Three Views," p. 13; Townes, "New England Fishing—Back from the Brink?" p. 22; Peter K. Prybot, "First New Dragger Since '70 Is Fishing Out of Gloucester," *National Fisherman* 56, no. 2 (June 1975): p. 5C; Enos, "'74 Was Good to Gloucester," p. 71.

18. U.S. Cong., "Fishing Rights," p. 344; U.S., Congress, House of Repre-

sentatives, Hearings before Committee on Merchant Marine and Fisheries, "Fisheries Agreements and Negotiations," 90th Cong., 1st sess., Dec. 1967, 2d sess., Feb. 1968, p. 7; U.S. Cong., "Twelve-Mile Fishery Zone," p. 165; U.S. Cong., "Fishing Rights," p. 323. New Bedford did suffer from foreign fishing pressures. Canadians harvested large quantities of scallops on Georges Bank, but the Canadians were not among the foreigners most fishermen complained about.

19. U.S., Congress, House of Representatives, Hearings before Committee on Merchant Marine and Fisheries, "Soviet Fishing Violations" in "Commercial Fisheries," 92nd Cong., 1st sess., May 1971, p. 551; U.S. Cong., "Interim Fisheries Zone Extension and Management Act of 1973," p. 852; numerous articles in *National Fisherman* from 1971–1976 including: "Offshore Gear War Cooled But Not Over," *National Fisherman* 52, no. 3 (July 1971): 4A; Burton T. Coffey, "Offshore Gear War Continues; U.S. Firm Tries to Fight Back," *National Fisherman* 52, no. 4 (Aug. 1971): 3A; Burton T. Coffey, "Overexploitation, Offshore Wars Clouding Lobster Fishing Future," *National Fisherman* 52, no. 13 (April 30, 1972): 92; H. V. R. Palmer, Jr., "Cape Cod Lobsterman Grapples with Offshore Gear Loss Crisis," *National Fisherman* 54, no. 2 (June 1973): 11A; "Offshore Gear Conflicts Simmer," *National Fisherman* 54, no. 10 (Feb. 1974): 17C.

20. U.S., Congress, House of Representatives, Hearings before Committee on Merchant Marine and Fisheries, "Territorial Seas," 93rd Cong., 1st sess., May, June 1973, p. 104 and other comments.

21. Allan J. Ristori, "Save America's Marine Resources; 200 Mile Limit . . . Now!" *National Fisherman* 53, no. 13 (April 30, 1973): 62.

22. Burton T. Coffey, "Changes in Federal Policies Goal of New England Fisheries Group," *National Fisherman* 52, no. 7 (Nov. 1971): 8C.

23. U.S. Cong., "Territorial Seas," p. 108; "NFF Underwrites Plan Organizing U.S. Fishermen," *National Fisherman* 54, no. 2 (June 1973): 12A.

24. John Enos, "Gloucester Fishermen Respond to Unity Move," *National Fisherman* 51, no. 12 (April 1971): 15B; Ackert, personal communication, March 1978.

25. U.S. Cong., "Fishing Rights"; U.S. Cong., "Twelve-Mile Fishery Zone"; Novello, personal communication, fall 1977.

26. The groundfish industry focused efforts on ICNAF, but other sectors of the industry negotiated many other multilateral agreements which this discussion does not evaluate. Rhode Island fishermen pressured the State Department to make bilateral agreements to restrict foreign fishing off the mid-Atlantic states in the late 1960s before this area came under ICNAF jurisdiction. The State Department and offshore lobstermen negotiated gear marking regulations and worked out claims procedures for lobstermen to obtain payments for damages from the foreign countries whose boats destroyed their gear. See U.S. Cong., "Fisheries Agreements and Negotiations"; U.S. Cong., "Soviet Fishing Violations"; James Ostergard, "Facts Behind U.S.-Soviet Pact Told; Aims to Save Atlantic Coast Stocks," *National Fisherman* 48, no. 9 (Jan. 1968): 3A; Brooks Townes, "U.S.

Lobsterman's Loss Aired by Claims Panel," *National Fisherman* 56, no. 2 (June 1975): 2A; Brooks Townes, "Lobstermen Are Irate After Claims Hearings," *National Fisherman* 57, no. 1 (May 1976): 2A.

27. U.S., Congress, Senate, Hearings before Committee on Foreign Relations, "The Fisheries Conventions," 81st Cong., 1st sess., July 14, 1949, pp. 6, 13–14, 48–49, 51.

28. "International Convention for the Northwest Atlantic Fisheries" in U.S., Cong., "The Fisheries Conventions," pp. 8–15; L. R. Day, executive secretary, ICNAF, Dartmouth, Nova Scotia, personal communication, Jan. 30, 1980; Richard C. Hennemuth, director, Woods Hole Laboratory, Northeast Fisheries Center, National Marine Fisheries Service, Woods Hole, Mass., personal communication, Aug. 1980.

29. William C. Herrington, "A Crisis in the Haddock Fishery," circ. 4, Fish and Wildlife Service, 1941; U.S. Cong., "The Fisheries Conventions," p. 86; "Advisory Group on Treaty Favors Minimum Mesh Size," *Atlantic Fisherman* 32, no. 3 (April 1951): 27; Herbert W. Graham, "A Minimum Net-Mesh Size for the New England Haddock Fishery," *Commercial Fisheries Review* 14, no. 12 (Dec. 1952): 1–5; John J. O'Brien, "Landings and Prices of Fishery Products, Boston Fish Pier, 1951" (Fish and Wildlife Service, Market News Service, Boston, Mass.), p. 12; Thomas J. Risoli, "Landings and Prices of Fishery Products, Boston Fish Pier, 1952" (Fish and Wildlife Service, Market News Service, Boston, Mass.), p. vi.

30. O'Brien *et al.*, "Landings and Prices" (Market News Service), 1956–63; Fulham, personal communication; G. Möcklinghoff, "Management and Development of Fisheries in the North Atlantic," *Journal of the Fisheries Research Board of Canada* 30, no. 12, part 2 (Dec. 1973): 2409–2411.

31. ICNAF's research documents and other publications.

32. M. S. Edelman and I. E. Dokuchaev, "Development of National Quotas by the International Commission for the Northwest Atlantic Fisheries," *Journal of the Fisheries Research Board of Canada* 30, no. 12, part 2 (Dec. 1973): 2427–2435; U.S. Cong., "Twelve-Mile Fishery Zone," p. 97; U.S. Cong., "Interim Fisheries Zone Extension and Management Act of 1973," pp. 816–817.

33. U.S. Cong., "Interim Fisheries Zone Extension and Management Act of 1973," pp. 816–817; ICNAF, *Proceedings of the 19th Annual Meeting* (Dartmouth, Nova Scotia, Canada: ICNAF, 1969).

34. "ICNAF Sidesteps Atlantic Fishing Crisis," *National Fisherman* 52, no. 4 (Aug. 1971): 4A; "National Quotas Set for East Coast Species," *National Fisherman* 53, no. 4 (Aug. 1972): 4A; "Fishing Pressure to Ease in East," *National Fisherman* 54, no. 9 (Jan. 1974): 3A; Day, personal communication, pp. 6–7; ICNAF, proceedings of annual and special meetings, Dartmouth, Nova Scotia, Canada, 1968–1974.

35. Burton T. Coffey, "ASMFC Weighs Management, Foreign Fishing," *National Fisherman* 52, no. 8 (Dec. 1971): 11A; U.S. Cong., "Interim Fisheries Zone Extension and Management Act of 1973," p. 31.

36. "National Quotas Set for East Coast Species," p. 5A; Burton T. Coffey,

"Control of Foreign Fishing Sought; Advisors Urge U.S. to Quit ICNAF," *National Fisherman* 53, no. 3 (July 1972): 3A; Burton T. Coffey, "U.S. Beefs Up Stand on Fisheries Control; Ending ICNAF Participation Now Seen as Possibility," *National Fisherman* 54, no. 4 (Aug. 1973): 4A.

37. R. C. Hennemuth, "Management of Sea Herring Fisheries in the Northwest Atlantic," *Journal of the Fisheries Research Board of Canada* 30, no. 12, part 2 (Dec. 1973): 2449; Hennemuth, personal communication.

38. U.S. Cong., "Fishery Jurisdiction," p. 45.

39. U.S. Cong., "Interim Fisheries Zone Extension and Management Act of 1973," p. 912.

40. Brooks Townes, "Fishermen Blast ICNAF Control," *National Fisherman* 55, no. 11 (March 1975): 3A.

41. Burton T. Coffey, "Fishing Agreements Prove of Small Value," *National Fisherman* 54, no. 1 (May 1973): 2A; U.S. Cong., "Interim Fisheries Zone Extension and Management Act of 1973," p. 894; Hennemuth, personal communication.

42. U.S. Cong., "Fishery Jurisdiction," p. 64.

43. Robert L. Edwards, director, Northeast Fisheries Center, National Marine Fisheries Service, discussion with members of Marine Policy Program, Woods Hole Oceanographic Institution, Woods Hole, Mass., Oct. 1979.

44. "Boats Face Fines for Landing Haddock; Outlook Very Bleak," *National Fisherman* 51, no. 9 (Jan. 1971): 3A.

45. "Offshore Problems Debated at R.I. Forum," *National Fisherman* 53, no. 1 (May 1972): 4A; "N. Bedford Fishermen Air Gripes on ICNAF, Nets," *National Fisherman* 52, no. 11 (March 1972): 2A; "National Quotas Set for East Coast Species," p. 4A.

46. Townes, "Fishermen Blast ICNAF Control," p. 3A.

47. *Ibid.*; Brooks Townes, "Soviets Board American Boats to Seek Out ICNAF Violators," *National Fisherman* 56, no. 4 (Aug. 1975): 3A; Tim Sullivan, "6 Britishers Load Up on Haddock," *National Fisherman* 55, no. 8 (Dec. 1974): 22A.

48. U.S., Congress, Senate, Hearings before Committee on Commerce, "Emergency Marine Fisheries Protection Act of 1975," 94th Cong., 1st sess., June, Sept. 1975, p. 184.

49. Arthur H. Dean, "The Geneva Conference on the Law of the Sea: What Was Accomplished," *American Journal of International Law* 52, no. 4 (Oct. 1958): 607.

50. *Ibid.*

51. Arthur H. Dean, "The Second Geneva Conference on the Law of the Sea: The Fight for Freedom of the Seas," *American Journal of International Law* 54, no. 4 (Oct. 1960): 751–789.

52. Dean, "Geneva Conference on the Law of the Sea," p. 615; Dean, "Second Geneva Conference on the Law of the Sea," p. 776.

53. "Convention on the Continental Shelf" in U.S. Cong., "Territorial Seas," pp. 69–71; "Convention on Fishing and Conservation of the Living Re-

sources of the High Seas" in U.S., Congress, House of Representatives, Hearings before Committee on Merchant Marine and Fisheries, "Fisheries Jurisdiction," 94th Cong., 1st sess., March 1975, pp. 139–145, articles 6 and 7; Dean, "The Geneva Conference on the Law of the Sea."

54. "Parties to 1958 Geneva Law of Sea Conventions," in U.S. Cong., "Territorial Seas," pp. 67–68; Public Law (hereafter P.L.) 88-308, 88th Cong., 2d sess., 1964; "High Seas Fisheries Conservation Act of 1973," in U.S. Cong., "Territorial Seas."

55. "Wide Gulf Exists between Nations with Regard to Fisheries Limits," *National Fisherman* 52, no. 10 (Feb. 1972): 3A; Burton T. Coffey, "U.S. Revises Stand on Limits; Fishermen's Interests Reflected," *National Fisherman* 53, no. 2 (June 1972): 3A; Burton T. Coffey, "U.S., Soviets Tentatively Accept 200-Mi. Limitation at Caracas," *National Fisherman* 55, no. 5 (Sept. 1974): 3A; John R. Stevenson and Bernard H. Oxman, "The Third United Nations Conference on the Law of the Sea: the 1974 Caracas Session," *American Journal of International Law* 69, no. 1 (June 1975): 17.

56. Coffey, "U.S. Revises Stand on Limits; Fishermen's Interests Reflected," p. 3A; Coffey, "U.S., Soviets Tentatively Accept 200-Mi. Limitation at Caracas," p. 3A.

57. "Ideas Offered in Struggle for a Sea Policy—NFF Meeting Adopts Position on Coastal Fish," *National Fisherman* 52, no. 5 (Sept. 1971): 4A; "Ideas Offered in Struggle for a Sea Policy—New Control Suggested for Shelf Stocks," *National Fisherman* 52, no. 5 (Sept. 1971): 4A.

58. Burton T. Coffey, "Fishermen Get LOS Recognition," *National Fisherman* 53, no. 1 (May 1972): 3A; "Wide Gulf Exists Between Nations with Regard to Fisheries Limits," p. 3A; Gerard Mangone, *Marine Policy for America: The United States at Sea* (Lexington, Mass.: Lexington Books, 1975), p. 155.

59. Coffey, "Fishermen Get LOS Recognition," p. 3A; Coffey, "U.S. Revises Stand on Limits; Fishermen's Interests Reflected," p. 3A.

60. John R. Stevenson and Bernard H. Oxman, "The Third United Nations Conference on the Law of the Sea: the 1975 Geneva Session," *American Journal of International Law* 65, no. 4 (Oct. 1975): 763 ff.; U.S., Congress, House of Representatives, Hearings before Committee on International Relations, "Potential Impact of the Proposed 200-Mile Fishing Zone on U.S. Foreign Relations," 94th Cong., 1st sess., Sept. 1975, pp. 28–31; U.S. Cong., "A Legislative History of the Fishery Conservation and Management Act of 1976," pp. 828–829.

61. U.S. Cong., "Potential Impact," p. 33.

62. U.S. Cong., "Fishing in U.S. Territorial Waters," pp. 13, 9, 24; Dean, "The Geneva Conference on the Law of the Sea," p. 614; P.L. 88-308, 1964.

63. U.S. Cong., "Fishing Rights," p. 248; U.S. Cong., "Twelve-Mile Fishery Zone"; P.L. 89-658, 89th Cong., 2d sess., 1966.

64. U.S. Cong., "Fishing Rights," pp. 323–324; U.S. Cong., "Twelve-Mile Fishery Zone," pp. 95–101.

65. Burton T. Coffey, "Lobsters Top List in Move toward Regional Manage-

ment," *National Fisherman* 53, no. 6 (Oct. 1972): 3A; U.S. Cong., "Territorial Seas."

66. Burton T. Coffey, "Mass. Declares Lobster Control to 200 Miles," *National Fisherman* 54, no. 2 (June 1973): 2A; U.S. Cong., "Territorial Seas."

67. U.S. Cong., "Territorial Seas," pp. 66, 67.

68. P.L. 93-242, 93rd Cong., 1st sess., 1973; Steve A. Saft, "First Vessel Nabbed Taking Lobsters on Shelf," *National Fisherman* 55, no. 6 (Oct. 1974): 17A; Tim Sullivan, "U.S. Set to Enforce Shelf Law; 200-Mile Limit Due Within Year," *National Fisherman* 55, no. 9 (Jan. 1975): 28A; U.S. Cong., "Fisheries Jurisdiction," p. 113.

69. "Eastland Resolution" in U.S. Cong., "Legislative History of the Fishery Conservation and Management Act of 1976," p. 908.

70. U.S. Cong., "Potential Impact," pp. 28–29.

71. U.S. Cong., "Fisheries Jurisdiction," pp. 7–46, 234–235; U.S. Cong., "Interim Fisheries Zone Extension and Management Act of 1973," pp. 5–22.

72. "Fishery Conservation and Management Act of 1976," P.L. 94-265, 94th Cong., 2d sess., 1976, Title 2; U.S. Cong., "Legislative History of the Fishery Conservation and Management Act of 1976."

73. U.S. Cong., "Territorial Seas," pp. 101, 230, 122; U.S. Cong., "Fisheries Jurisdiction," p. 240.

74. Bill Mustard and Lucy Sloan, "Two Views on Possibilities of 200-Mile Limit: It's a Sure Thing Say 2 Observers," *National Fisherman* 55, no. 4 (Aug. 1974): 5A.

75. U.S. Cong., "Territorial Seas," pp. 24–25, 45–48.

76. U.S. Cong., "Fisheries Jurisdiction," p. 245.

77. The Truman Proclamation of Sept. 28, 1945, declared that the United States could establish conservation zones to protect its coastal fisheries from overfishing; that in order to protect fisheries the U.S. could act unilaterally where only American fishermen were concerned and in conjunction with other nations where they shared the resource; and that the U.S. recognized the right of other nations to take similar steps to protect their coastal fisheries. "Proclamation by President Harry S. Truman . . ." in U.S. Cong., "Twelve-Mile Fishery Zone," p. 33.

78. U.S. Cong., "Fisheries Jurisdiction," pp. 174–175.

79. Stevenson and Oxman, "Third United Nations Conference on the Law of the Sea, 1975," pp. 778–779.

80. Numerous articles in *National Fisherman*, 1972–1975; among these are: Burton T. Coffey, "Regional Lobster Managing Plan Progresses But Faces Rough Seas," *National Fisherman* 53, no. 8 (Dec. 1972): 3A; "New Fisheries May Ease Pressure on Lobster: Me. Fisheries Commissioner Weighs Management Ideas," *National Fisherman* 53, no. 10 (Feb. 1973): 4A; John Enos, "Steps Taken to Control Shrimping," *National Fisherman* 53, no. 11 (March 1973): 20A; William B. Walker, "Me., N.H., Mass. Act to Preserve Shrimp Fishery," *National Fisherman* 54, no. 5 (Sept. 1973): 4A; Tom V. Binmore, "Regional Management Seen As Cure for Ailing New England Shellfisheries," *National*

Fisherman 42, no. 6 (Oct. 1961): 4; Burton T. Coffey, "Apollonio Hopes for Direct Management Control," *National Fisherman* 53, no. 11 (March 1973): 8C.

81. Coffey, "Lobsters Top List in Move Toward Regional Management," p. 3A; Burton T. Coffey, "New Lobster Management Plan Imperiled by Federal Decision," *National Fisherman* 53, no. 11 (March 1973): 3A; Comptroller General of the United States, "Action Is Needed Now to Protect Our Fishery Resources" (Washington, D.C.: GAO, Feb. 18, 1976), pp. 9–15.

82. U.S. Cong., "Fishery Jurisdiction," pp. 61, 105–106.

83. U.S. Cong., "Fishery Jurisdiction," p. 109; U.S. Cong., "Emergency Marine Fisheries Protection Act of 1975," pp. 170–175; Edward Wenk, Jr., *The Politics of the Ocean* (Seattle, Wash.: University of Washington Press, 1972); Francis T. Christy, Jr., and Anthony Scott, *The Common Wealth in Ocean Fisheries* (Baltimore, Md.: Johns Hopkins University Press, 1972); Francis T. Christy, Jr., "Alternative Arrangements for Marine Fisheries: An Overview," RFF Program of International Studies of Fishery Arrangements, Paper no. 1, Resources for the Future, Washington, D.C., May 1973; James A. Crutchfield and Giulio Pontecorvo, *The Pacific Salmon Fisheries: A Study of Irrational Conservation* (Baltimore, Md.: Johns Hopkins University Press, 1969).

84. "Marine Fisheries Conservation Act of 1975," report of Committee on Merchant Marine and Fisheries, House of Representatives, Aug. 20, 1975, in U.S. Cong., "Legislative History of the Fishery Conservation and Management Act of 1976," p. 1081; Christopher H. Foreman, Jr., Harvard University Ph.D. candidate, Washington, D.C., personal communication, Aug. 1980.

85. U.S. Cong., "Fisheries Jurisdiction," pp. 235, 238.

86. U.S. Cong., "Fisheries Jurisdiction," p. 235.

87. P.L. 94-265, sec. 302.

88. P.L. 94-265, sec. 303, sec 3(18).

89. P.L. 94-265, sec. 301.

90. In addition to sources noted below, conclusions in this section are based on statements at early meetings of the New England Fishery Management Council and on Mary Lord's and Meta Cushing's interviews with fishermen about their work histories and their impressions of fishery management, 1978–79.

91. Hennemuth, personal communication; Bradford Brown, chief, resource assessment division, Northeast Fisheries Center, National Marine Fisheries Service, Woods Hole, Mass., personal communication, May 1978.

92. U.S. Cong., "Fisheries Jurisdiction," pp. 235, 250, 252.

Chapter 6   *Implementing Fishery Management*

1. Jerry Murphy, "Gloucester's Brancaleones, New Dragger Owners, Are Veterans of Rugged Industry," *National Fisherman* 45, no. 5 (Sept. 1964): 22; Gloucester fisherman, statement at meeting of New England Fishery Management Council; Meta Cushing, interview with Gloucester fisherman, 1979. The

Brancaleones decided against buying the new boat as problems with fishery management became clear later, but other fishing families followed through with their purchase of new vessels.

2. Peter K. Prybot, "Former Capital City Lawyer Finds Fishing in Gloucester a Challenge," *National Fisherman* 59, no. 1 (May 1978): 45, 53. Leber's boat sank in 1980.

3. Prybot, "Former Capital City Lawyer," p. 45; Cushing, interviews, 1978–1979; Paul Langner, "200-Mile Limit Buoys N.E. Fishermen," *Boston Globe*, April 27, 1977, p. 1; Burton T. Coffey, "Effects of 200-Mile Limit Will Be Slow in Coming," *National Fisherman* 56, no. 13 (April 30, 1976): 6; Henry S. Galus, "NMFS Official Says Future Rests on Fisherman Attitude," *National Fisherman* 56, no. 11 (March 1976): 15A; Ed Francis, "Fishing Boat Demand Exceeds Supply," *Boston Herald American*, June 26, 1977, p. 20; Roger Farquhar, "N.E. Fish Catch Is Up, Experts Not Sure Why," *Boston Globe*, June 12, 1977, p. 1.

4. Statements at meeting of New England Fisheries Steering Committee, July 1977, New Bedford, Mass.; Ken O. Botwright, "Has Limit Improved Fish Catch?" *Boston Globe*, April 3, 1977, p. 30; Stanley R. Tupper and George H. Taylor, "Five Years May See Big Revival of Long-Hurting Northeast Industry," *National Fisherman* 57, no. 7 (Nov. 1976): 14A.

5. Brooks Townes, "Regional Council Members Named by Elliot Richardson," *National Fisherman* 57, no. 6 (Oct. 1976): 25A; "Background and Reactions to the Regional Council Selections," *Maine Commercial Fisheries* 4, no. 1 (Sept. 1976): 14; Ed Bradley, "Feds Attempt to Regulate Regional Council," *Maine Commercial Fisheries* 4, no. 6 (Jan. 1977): 9.

6. Timothy Dwyer, "Soviet Vessel off Cape Cited But Not Seized," *Boston Globe*, April 3, 1977, p. 1; Paul Langner, "Fishermen Angry at Handling of Limit," *Boston Globe*, April 10, 1977, p. 21; Brooks Townes, "Who's In Charge? Is the Question Still Unanswered in 200-Mile Limit," *National Fisherman* 58, no. 2 (June 1977): 3A.

7. "Trawler Incident Irks Kennedy, Studds," *Boston Globe*, April 3, 1977, p. 30; "Seizure—Who's to Know?" *Maine Commercial Fisheries* 4, no. 10 (May 1977): 9; Townes, "Who's in Charge?"; Paul Feeney and Jerome Sullivan, "Soviet Fish Seized on Mother Ship; Trawler Impounded," *Boston Globe*, April 11, 1977, p. 5.

8. Stephen F. Crimmin and Timothy Dwyer, "Coast Guard Seizes Russian Trawler," *Boston Globe*, April 10, 1977, p. 1; Feeney and Sullivan, "Soviet Fish Seized on Mother Ship; Trawler Impounded," p. 1; Mary Thornton, "Diplomats Key to Court Fate of Soviet Ships," *Boston Globe*, April 13, 1977, p. 1; "244,093 Pounds Is a Lot of Fish," *Boston Globe*, April 13, 1977, p. 10; Paul Langner, "Russian Ship Sails But Faces a Fine; Trawler Still Here," *Boston Globe*, April 15, 1977, p. 3; Paul Langner, "Illegal Fish Found Ship Unloaders Say," *Boston Globe*, April 14, 1977, p. 5; William F. Doherty, "Captain of Russian Trawler Told He May Face Prison Term and Fine," *Boston Globe*, April 16, 1977, p. 1; Paul Langner, "Were the Herring Illegal?" *Boston Globe*, April 16, 1977, p. 5;

Jerome Sullivan and Paul Feeney, "Soviet Trawler Skipper Charged—Fish Reloaded," *Boston Globe*, April 29, 1977, p. 1.

9. New England Fishery Management Council to Cyrus R. Vance, Sept. 23, 1977; "Polish Trawler Seizure Blocked by State Department," *Maine Commercial Fisheries* 5, no. 4 (Nov. 1977): 24; "Interference of State Dept. Irks Council," *National Fisherman* 58, no. 8 (Dec. 1977): 27A.

10. Langner, "Russian Ship Sails But Faces a Fine"; Coast Guard monthly reports on foreign fishing off the East Coast, *Maine Commercial Fisheries*, 1977.

11. "Fishery Conservation and Management Act of 1976," P.L. 94-265, 94th Cong., 2d sess., Title 2.

12. Comments at meetings of the New England Fishery Management Council, fall 1977.

13. "Stock Assessment Questions Highlight Herring Hearing," *Maine Commercial Fisheries* 4, no. 10 (May 1977): 2; Tim Sullivan, "N.E. Council Asks Second Look at Herring Quota," *National Fisherman* 58, no. 2 (June 1977): 34A; Robin Alden Peters, "Where? When? How Old? Council Raises Herring Questions," *Maine Commercial Fisheries* 4, no. 12 (July 1977): 12; "Court Action Sought on Herring Quota," *Maine Commercial Fisheries* 4, no. 8 (March 1977): 1; "Herring Suit Appealed," *Maine Commercial Fisheries* 5, no. 1 (Aug. 1977): 1; "Foreigners Retain Herring Quota," *Maine Commercial Fisheries* 5, no. 2 (Sept. 1977): p. 1; Ed Bradley, "Foreign Affairs and Fisheries," *Maine Commercial Fisheries* 5, no. 3 (Oct. 1977): 7.

14. New England Fishery Management Council meetings, Sept.–Nov. 1977; Melody Barlow, "Council Grapples with Administrative Problems," *Maine Commercial Fisheries* 5, no. 4 (Nov. 1977): 15.

15. Information in the following sections comes from meetings of the New England Fishery Management Council, 1977–1979, and from documents, press releases, and other written material from the Council and from the National Marine Fisheries Service (hereafter NMFS). Also particularly useful for the study of the Council's work were Tim Sullivan's reporting in *Gloucester Daily Times*, Melody Barlow's reports of meetings in *Maine Commercial Fisheries*, and Robin Peters's analyses of issues facing the Council in *Maine Commercial Fisheries*. Additional sources are noted.

16. Lars Vidaeus and Joseph Mueller, "Management of the Commercial Groundfish Fishery Off the U.S. Northeast Coast," Discussion Paper, New England Fishery Management Council, Nov. 1978, p. 37; Steve Saft, "First Quotas on N. England Fish Issued," *National Fisherman* 58, no. 1 (May 1977): 2A.

17. P.L. 94-265, sec. 303; "Final Environmental Impact Statement for the Implementation of a Fishery Management Plan for Atlantic Groundfish—Haddock, Cod, Yellowtail Flounder," prepared by New England Regional Fisheries Management Council in consultation with Mid-Atlantic Regional Fisheries Management Council, April 1977 (hereafter "Groundfish Plan").

18. "Groundfish Plan," pp. 132–134; P.L. 94-265, secs. 2, 3, 301; Robin

Peters, "Where the Quotas Come From," *Maine Commercial Fisheries* 5, no. 1 (Aug. 1977): 17.

19. Discussions with biologists at New England Fishery Management Council meetings; presentation on stock assessment issues, Northeast Fisheries Center, Woods Hole, Mass., Oct. 1977; David E. Pierce and Patricia E. Hughes, "Insight into the Methodology and Logic behind National Marine Fisheries Service Fish Stock Assessments or How Did You Guys Come up with Those Numbers Anyway?" Commonwealth of Massachusetts, Executive Office of Environmental Affairs, Boston, Mass., Jan. 1979.

20. Comments in following pages are based on "Groundfish Plan," pp. 134–143, 155–157.

21. For members' names and affiliations, see "New England Regional Fishery Management Council," brochure with list of names (New England Fishery Management Council, Peabody, Mass., 1978).

22. Tim Sullivan, "Fishermen Find Flaws in Cod, Haddock Rules," *Gloucester Daily Times*, Nov. 11, 1977, p. 1. Aside from these problems, NMFS depended on the dealers' good will to obtain data on landings, the most important component in NMFS's economic and biological data on which the Council and NMFS had to base fishery management decisions. NMFS agents were reluctant to involve the dealers in any enforcement issues.

23. Robert S. Ryder, essay, Chatham, Mass., Sept. 15, 1977.

24. Tim Sullivan, "Unrestricted Fishing Approved over Protest," *Gloucester Daily Times*, Dec. 8, 1977, p. 1.

25. Sullivan, "Fishermen Find Flaws in Cod, Haddock Rules," p. 9.

26. Tim Sullivan, "Fishermen Unwilling to Unite over Quota Fines," *Gloucester Daily Times*, Dec. 22, 1977, p. 9.

27. Newsletter, Massachusetts Inshore Draggermen's Association, Jan. 1978, p. 1.

28. Dan Arnold and Jay Lanzillo, Massachusetts Inshore Draggermen's Association—Cape Cod Commercial Fishermen's Coalition Plan, Jan. 1978, p. 1.

29. Ryder, essay; Cushing, interviews.

30. Newsletter, Massachusetts Inshore Draggermen's Association, March 1978, p. 1.

31. This is not to say that appointees went unopposed; any candidate was usually opposed by groups pushing for someone else for the same position.

32. Tim Sullivan, "Plans Drafted for Fish Quota," *Gloucester Daily Times*, March 24, 1978, p. 9.

33. In some states industry opinion was more important than in others. For example, "Apollonio Gets Solid Industry Approval," *Maine Commercial Fisheries* 6, no. 7 (Mar. 1979): 20–21.

34. No consumer representative ever came to a meeting.

35. Comments at meeting of New England Fisheries Steering Committee, Boston, Mass., Aug. 1977.

36. Tim Sullivan, "Unrestricted Fishing Approved Over Protest," *Gloucester*

Daily Times, Dec. 8, 1977, p. 9; M. Estellie Smith, "The 'Public Face' of the New England Regional Fishery Council: Year 1," Technical Report 78-36, Woods Hole Oceanographic Institution, Woods Hole, Mass., April 1978.

37. Tim Sullivan, "Eight-Day Halt to All Fishing," *Gloucester Daily Times*, Dec. 22, 1977, p. 9.

38. Tim Sullivan, "Eight-Day Halt to All Fishing"; Tim Sullivan, "Doubts about Fishing Closure—Some Boats May Defy Ban," *Gloucester Daily Times*, Dec. 22, 1977, p. 1; Tim Sullivan, "75 Fishermen Join in Brawl on Waterfront," *Gloucester Daily Times*, Dec. 28, 1977, p. 1.

39. Tim Sullivan, "Fishery Council Suggests Old Rules, Lower Quotas," *Gloucester Daily Times*, Feb. 16, 1978, p. 9.

40. Tim Sullivan, "Fishery Shake-Up—Action Delayed on Haddock Ban," *Gloucester Daily Times*, Feb. 24, 1978, p. 1; Tim Sullivan, "Fish Council Asks Haddock-Limit Cut," *Gloucester Daily Times*, March 3, 1978, p. 1; Tim Sullivan, "Group Goes to Washington to Avert Haddock Closure," *Gloucester Daily Times*, March 6, 1978, p. 1; Tim Sullivan, "Haddock Decision Postponed," *Gloucester Daily Times*, March 7, 1978; Tim Sullivan, "Fishing Cut Asked to Avert Closure," *Gloucester Daily Times*, March 10, 1978, p. 1.

41. The NMFS data were not necessarily a good indication of increasing fishing effort. Many boats could have taken out permits and not actually fished for groundfish. Further, the requirement that boats in groundfisheries have permits may have been observed more strictly at some times than at others.

42. Richard G. Seamans, Jr., "Summary of Minutes of New England Regional Fishery Management Council Meeting—May 17–18, 1978," NMFS, May 22, 1978, p. 2.

43. Tim Sullivan, "Fleet Stunned by Quota Cuts," *Gloucester Daily Times*, June 23, 1978, p. 1.

44. The Council had to ask the permission of the Secretary of Commerce because they were implementing rules under emergency regulations and trying to avoid lengthy public hearings and formal approval procedures.

45. Scientific and Statistical Committee, memo on groundfish to the New England Fishery Management Council, June 27, 1978, p. 1.

46. "Draft Fishery Management Plan for the Atlantic Groundfish Fishery," "Part I: Statement of the Problem," prepared by New England Fishery Management Council Staff, April 1979, pp. 66–69.

47. *Ibid.*

48. Newsletter, Massachusetts Inshore Draggermen's Association, May 1979, pp. 1–2.

49. Other options existed, but they probably would not have helped the Council out of its difficulties and were not under Council or industry consideration. See Frederick W. Bell, *Food from the Sea: the Economics and Politics of Ocean Fisheries* (Boulder, Colo.: Westview Press, 1978), ch. 4; Lee G. Anderson, *The Economics of Fisheries Management* (Baltimore, Md.: Johns Hopkins University Press, 1977), ch. 5.

50. Bell, *Food from the Sea*, pp. 148–150.

51. Newsletter, Massachusetts Inshore Draggermen's Association, Feb. 1979, p. 2.

52. Jay Sperling, "Me. Fisheries Chief Questions Quota Approach," *National Fisherman* 60, no. 2 (June 1979): 38.

53. For example, Vidaeus and Mueller, "Management of the Commercial Groundfish Fishery." Limited entry is neoclassical economists' solution to problems in the use of a common property resource such as fish. Though they used the same term, "limited entry," the Council was not concerned about the same issues. Economists argue that because of technological externalities, fishermen produce on a backward-bending industry average cost curve where marginal cost exceeds marginal revenue in the long run. This means that free entry into fishing leads to misallocation of labor and capital in the economy and, if demand is high enough, to overfishing. Fewer boats and fishermen can produce more fish, and those who move to other industries will add more to production in the economy than they do by fishing. A limit on entry could make the industry produce on the marginal cost curve and correct the allocation of labor and capital. Concerns about allocation of labor and capital in the economy did not enter the Council's considerations. See Bell, *Food from the Sea*, ch. 3, 4; Anderson *The Economics of Fisheries Management*; Colin W. Clark, *Mathematical Bioeconomics: The Optimal Management of Renewable Resources* (New York: John Wiley and Sons, 1976).

54. Sperling, "Me. Fisheries Chief Questions Quota Approach," p. 38; Leah J. Smith, "Case Studies on Economic Effects of Limiting Entry to the Fisheries," paper prepared for Workshop and Conference on Limitation of Entry into Fisheries, June 1978; C. H. B. Newton, "Experience with Limited Entry in Fisheries: British Columbia," paper prepared for Workshop on Limitation of Entry into Fisheries, May 1978; Allan Adasiak, "Experience with Limited Entry: Alaska," prepared for National Conference to Consider Limited Entry as a Tool in Fisheries Management, July 1978.

55. Cushing, interviews, 1978–1979.

56. Mary Lord, interview with Chatham, Mass., fisherman, 1979.

57. Generalizations on limited entry are based on Cushing and Lord, interviews with Gloucester and Chatham fishermen; New England Fisheries Management Council meetings; "Limited Entry—Questions," editorial, *Maine Commercial Fisheries* 6, no. 8 (April 1979): 6; "Limited Entry–Doubts," *Maine Commercial Fisheries* 6, no. 8 (April 1979): 1; Tim Sullivan, "Limited Entry Debate Begins," *Gloucester Daily Times*, March 7, 1978, p. 1; Tim Sullivan, "Limited Entry Suggested," *Gloucester Daily Times*, April 21, 1978, p. 1; Christi Duerr, "Fishing Forum Centers on Politics, Canadian Imports," *National Fisherman* 59, no. 1 (May 1978): 17; Bruce J. Cole, "Limited Entry—Is It Something Whose Time Has Arrived?" *National Fisherman* 59, no. 4 (Aug. 1978): 14; Economic Resources Center, Gloucester Fisheries Association, "Limited Entry Discussion," Aug. 14, 1978.

58. Newsletter, Massachusetts Inshore Draggermen's Association, Dec. 1978 (pp. 2–3), March 1979 (p. 4).

59. Michael Knight, "Plummeting Prices End New England's Fishing Boom,"

New York Times, July 6, 1980, p. 1; Bruce A. Mohl, "At Port, Supply vs. Demand," *Boston Globe*, June 24, 1980, p. 25; Bruce A. Mohl, "An 'Us-First' Fishing Bill Given Boost," *Boston Globe*, Sept. 10, 1980, p. 33.

Chapter 7   The Failure of Government Efforts

1. Nick Mencher, "Fish Prices Sag as Fuel, Mortgage Payments Soar," *Gloucester Daily Times*, May 20, 1980, p. 1; Nick Mencher, "Fishing Industry Problems Abound, But Solutions Scarce: Prices Will Stay Low, Fishermen Predict," *Gloucester Daily Times*, June 5, 1980, p. 1; Nick Mencher, "Soaring Fuel Costs Sap Slim Profits from Low-Priced Fish," *Gloucester Daily Times*, June 6, 1980, p. 13; Bernie O'Donnell, "Sliding Prices Alarm Fishermen," *Gloucester Daily Times*, May 14, 1981, p. 1.

2. Nick Mencher, "Boatowner Sends SOS for Fleet," *Gloucester Daily Times*, June 3, 1980, pp. 1, 13; Mencher, "Fishing Industry Problems Abound," p. 13; Mencher, "Soaring Fuel Costs," p. 13; Nick Mencher, "Glut Forces Fish Prices Down," *Gloucester Daily Times*, May 13, 1980, p. 11.

3. Mencher, "Fishing Industry Problems Abound," p. 13; Anne L. Millett, "Watered-Down Fisheries Bill Passes," *Gloucester Daily Times*, Dec. 5, 1980, p. 1.

4. Except where otherwise noted, information in this chapter has been documented in earlier chapters.

5. Vinok K. Aggarwal with Stephen Haggard, "The Politics of Protection in the U.S. Textile and Apparel Industries," in John Zysman and Laura Tyson, eds., "American Industry in International Competition" (unpublished manuscript); Gerald R. Jantscher, *Bread Upon the Waters* (Washington, D.C.: Brookings Institution, 1975); for example, "New Plan to Aid S&Ls Is Adopted by Bank Board," *Wall Street Journal*, Sept. 8, 1981, p. 10.

6. Joel S. Hirschhorn, "Troubles and Opportunities in the United States Steel Industry," in Margaret E. Dewar, ed., *Industry Vitalization: Toward a National Industrial Policy* (New York: Pergamon Press, 1982); Robert W. Crandall, *The U.S. Steel Industry in Recurrent Crisis: Policy Options in a Competitive World* (Washington, D.C.: Brookings Institution, 1981).

7. Gerald R. Jantscher, "Lessons from the Maritime Aid Program," in Dewar, *Industry Vitalization*.

8. David B. Yoffie, "Orderly Marketing Agreements as an Industrial Policy: The Case of the Footwear Industry," *Public Policy* 29, no. 1 (winter 1981): pp. 93–119.

9. Comptroller General of the United States, "Slow Productivity Growth in the U.S. Footwear Industry—Can the Federal Government Help?" no. FGMSD-80-3 (Washington, D.C.: GAO, Feb. 25, 1980), pp. 43 ff.; James E. McCarthy, "Trade Adjustment Assistance: A Case Study of the Shoe Industry in Massachusetts," Research Report no. 58, Federal Reserve Bank, Boston, Mass., June 1975.

Glossary

ad valorem— duties levied in proportion to invoiced value.

bag— the cod end of an otter trawl, the area at the end of the net where the catch accumulates as an otter trawl net is towed over the sea floor.

bycatch— fish caught unintentionally during fishing for other species.

crew share— the income paid to a crewman at the end of a fishing trip; over a year, the payment to a crew site, not the year's earnings of a crewman unless the crewman worked whenever the boat did.

directed fishery— the species which the industry seeks to catch.

dragger— an otter trawler, usually a smaller one which works inshore.

ex-vessel price— price paid for fish at the dock to the fishermen and boat owners.

fillet— boneless sides of fish cut lengthwise along the backbone, without head or tail.

fishery— the industry involved in fishing including fishermen, boat owners, and dealers; a species or group of related species in their natural environment.

gross stock— the total proceeds of the catch from a vessel's trip.

gross tons— the permanently enclosed capacity of a vessel; a gross ton is 100 cubic feet.

groundfish— fish which live near the ocean bottom; cod, cusk, hake, haddock, pollock, and redfish (ocean perch).

highliner— a boat or captain with the highest or consistently among the highest earnings in a port.

incidental catch— bycatch.

239

inshore—   fishing areas near enough to the coast for fishermen to work during one day's absence from port; the industry made up of fishermen who work near shore on smaller vessels (generally under 60 gross tons) and the dealers who buy from them.

landings—   quantities of fish and shellfish brought ashore and sold.

lay—   the system for distributing the proceeds of the catch of a vessel between crew and vessel owners.

longlining— fishing by using longlines or line trawls; use of a long line with many baited hooks laid out on the ocean floor or at some level above it.

Loran—   acronym for long range aid to navigation, a system that allows a fisherman to pinpoint his exact location on the ocean based on signals from points on shore.

midwater trawling— fishing by towing a net in the "midwater" area some distance from the bottom, a method not possible with traditional otter trawl gear.

net stock—   the proceeds of the catch from a vessel's trip after certain expenses are subtracted, to be divided between the vessel owners and the crew.

offshore—   fishing areas distant from the coast, normally not accessible except in trips that last several days or more; the industry made up of fishermen who work far from shore on large vessels (generally over 60 gross tons), vessel owners, and dealers who buy fish from them.

optimum yield— according to the Fishery Conservation and Management Act of 1976, "the amount of fish— (A) which will provide the greatest overall benefit to the Nation, with particular reference to food production and recreational opportunities; and (B) which is prescribed as such on the basis of the maximum sustainable yield from such fishery, as modified by any relevant economic, social, or ecological factor."

otter trawl— a funnel-shaped net towed over the sea floor behind a fishing vessel.

pulse fishing— direction of intense fishing efforts toward one stock of fish until the stock is badly depleted.

recruitment— the number of young produced from a given stock each year, or the addition to a stock of new fish large enough to be caught as a result of migration or growth of smaller fish.

round fish—   fish without entrails but with head and tail, as unloaded from vessels at the dock.

site—   any job on a fishing boat other than captain.

side trawler—   a trawler that hauls in its otter trawl net over the side.

stern trawler—   a trawler that hauls in its otter trawl net over the stern.

trawler—   a fishing vessel that uses an otter trawl.

weigh out—   weighing in port of the catch from a vessel to determine the amount of each species to be sold.

year class—   fish of the same species spawned in the same year.

Index

25, 70, 107–9, 111. *See also* Foreign
fleets
Spain, 108, 119, 128
Sport fishing, 79, 136, 150, 157, 202; on
partyboats and charters, 116, 136
Standing Committee on Research and
Statistics, 119. *See also* International
Commission for the Northwest Atlantic
Fisheries
State, Department of, 112, 115, 120, 127,
143, 150, 165, 227; in controlling for-
eign fishing, 133, 135, 145–46, 151–53;
and position on fishery jurisdiction,
129–32, 134, 138–40, 187; Secretary of,
126, 132, 152; on tariffs, 47, 51
State-Federal Fisheries Management
Programs, 140
Steel industry, 8, 185, 194–95
Stevens, Herbert N., 48
Stevenson, John, 129–31
Stinson Canning Company, 60
Stinson, C. L., 60
Strike by fishermen, 54, 86, 99. *See also*
Atlantic Fishermen's Union
Studds, Gerry, 138, 151
Subsidies, 8, 79, 182, 184–85, 192, 195.
See also Vessel construction subsidies

"Taras Shevchenko," 151
Tariff Commission, 42, 74, 102, 188;
groundfish ruling of, 1952, 47–48;
groundfish ruling of, 1954, 48–52;
groundfish ruling of, 1956, 52–53, 62,
66, 102. *See also* International Trade
Commission
Tariffs, 8, 12, 57, 59, 184–85, 188, 210;
campaigns for, on groundfish, 46–54,
58, 76, 189; effects of, on industry, 82,
102–4, 223; on fish sticks, 50–51
Technology, 54, 82, 181; for fish handling
and processing, 11, 13, 54, 65, 70; for
fish sticks, 49–50; of foreign vessels,
108–9, 111; for freezing fish at sea, 11,
65, 70–71, 96; of instruments for vessels, 18, 26, 202; for irradiation of fish,
53, 212; of "Seafreeze Atlantic," 70; of
vessels, 13, 65, 66, 96, 114, 147
Territorial sea, 127–30, 132–33, 136
Textiles industry, 8, 57–58, 73, 78, 185
Thurmond, Strom, 78
Tocco, Rosemarie, 183
Tollefson, Thor, 44, 78
Trade Act of 1974, 195
Trade adjustment assistance, 195–96
Trade Agreements Act of 1934, 46, 51

Trade Agreements Extension Act of
1951, 47
Trade restrictions, 8, 46–54, 57, 78, 195;
escape clause, 47–53; peril point, 47;
quotas, 46–54, 102, 188. *See also* Tariff
Commission; Tariffs
Training programs, 64–65, 78, 102;
reasons for results of, 92–93, 186
Truman, Harry S., 46, 52, 139, 231
Truman Proclamation 139 (Sept. 25,
1945), 231
Tuna, 60, 130–31
Tupper, Stanley, 78
200-mile limit, 3–4, 7, 112, 118, 123, 126–
27, 130–31, 133–36. *See also* Fishery
Conservation and Management Act of
1976; Fishery jurisdiction
Tyndale, Elmont S., 3

Unions of fishermen. *See* Atlantic Fishermen's Union; New Bedford Fisher-
men's Union
United Nations Conference on the Law
of the Sea, 118, 123; failure of, to resolve fishery jurisdiction, 126, 129–32,
136, 140, 189; first conference of, 127;
second conference of, 127–29, 138;
third conference of, 129–32
University of Rhode Island, 141
University of Washington, 141

Vessel construction subsidies, 79; reasons
for, 60; reasons for results of, 89–91,
94–97, 191, 193; results of, 68–73, 78,
82, 101, 104–5, 190, 222
Vessel costs and earnings, 102, 112;
adjustment to change in, 38–41; during
Depression, 12–13; determination of,
28–29; in inshore fishery, 23–24; in
offshore fishery in postwar period, 26,
33, 37, 43–46, 81, 97–101, 186; related
to insurance, 64; related to vessel construction, 76, 90–91, 104–5; trends in,
during 1970s and 1980s, 114–15, 177,
182–83
Vessels, factory, *See* "Fair Try"; "Seafreeze Atlantic"; "Seafreeze Pacific"
Vessels, numbers of: after extension of
the fishery jurisdiction, 147, 170, 177,
182, 186, 194, 236; postwar trends in,
4–5, 11, 24–25, 32–33, 37, 81, 114, 118,
202, 224; and vessel owner-dealers,
101; during World War II, 13, 16
Veterans Administration, 62
Volpe, John, 55, 70